acid

John Simon

test

Introduction by Dwight Macdonald

Stein and Day / Publishers / New York

809

To my Parents *for their patient support*

And to Lisl   *for more kinds of help*
than a mere dedication can enumerate

10764

Acknowledgment

The pieces in this book originally appeared, sometimes in
slightly altered form, in the following publications, whose
permission to reprint them is gratefully acknowledged:

Arts,	*The Hudson Review,*	*The Reporter,*
Audience,	*The Mid-Century,*	*Show,*
Audit,	*The New Leader,*	*Time,*
Horizon,	*The New Republic,*	*The New York Times*

Designed by Joan Stoliar
Printed in the United States of America

Contents

■

■

critics

■

Introduction

When John Simon asked me to write an introduction to his book, I agreed because I think he is a good critic and also the kind of critic we need in this country today. An avalanche of Culture, fed since 1945 by increasingly heavy college enrollments, is now roaring down on us. Even the TV programs are becoming aware that we are in the midst of what they call a Culture Boom. It is an amorphous, protean, contradictory affair. Who can object to the huge sales of quality paperbacks or the increase in amateur musicians from 19 million in 1950 to 34 million today? And who can forget the chilling glimpse one had into the Cultural underworld when Mona Lisa visited us lately: the orgiastic rites at the National Museum in Washington, with M. Malraux sounding not very different from Mr. Kennedy, the six-block lines outside the Metropolitan Museum in New York waiting patiently to shuffle (quickstep—fifteen seconds was allotted for contemplation) past a picture their press had told them was Great. Like *Ben Hur*.

In this situation, when the good, the bad and the indifferent—especially the last, that *faux bon* or midcult that has become our age's trademark—are proliferating and interbreeding as never before, we need critics (fr. Gr. *krites,* judge) or native guides to lead us through the jungle. In his Foreword Mr. Simon describes the terrain:

> Culture has become so widespread as to have, for most practical purposes, attenuated itself out of existence. The fault is not only the public's or the educators': there is also too much around us today that needs, or seems to need, keeping up with. . . . A half-educated public (I may underestimate it) and the semiliterate artist (I may overestimate him), bristling with answers and solutions, aggressively confront the critic at the very moment when, out of humility or condescension, he divests himself of learnedness and trenchancy in an attempt to please. . . . As for the notion that ours is an Age of Criticism, it is merely a desperate euphemism for a period in

which the arts are in decline—but the cause of this decline is less likely to be the prevalence of criticism than its scarcity.

Humility has never been Mr. Simon's problem, nor has he eschewed either trenchancy or learnedness. He is acerb and cold-eyed, as unmoved by avant-gardists' pleas to be judged indulgently because they represent Art and The Future as by the commercial entrepreneur's grumbling about his Property. But he is also a fair-minded judge (krites) who has all the precedents to hand and can bring them to bear on contemporary work. In a period of confusion, this combination of knowledge and uncompromising sharpness is just what is needed.

The Oxford English Dictionary distinguishes two uses of CRITICISM: "1. passing judgement, esp. unfavorable. . . . fault finding, censure" and "2. the art of estimating the qualities and the character of a literary or artistic work." It is interesting that (1.), which is of course not exclusive of (2.), is the older usage. The first citation is from Dekker (1607): "Therefore, reader, doe I stand at the mark of criticisme (and of thy bolt) to bee shot at." The first (2.) citation is Dryden (1674): "Criticism, as it was first instituted by Aristotle, was meant a standard of judging well, the chiefest part of which was to observe those excellencies which should delight a reasonable reader."

So with CRITIC. The two earliest citations are in the (1.) sense, from Shakespeare (1588) and from Florio's Italian Dictionary (1598): "To Readers, those notable pirates in this our paper sea, those sea-dogs or lande-criticks, monsters of men." Something there is that does not love a CRITICK. The first (2.) or neutral use is years later, in Bacon's Advancement of Learning (1605). And the very next year we have Dekker again—as a professional writer he may have been particularly sensitive— warning in his News from·Hell: "Take heed of criticks, they bite like fish at anything, especially at bookes." And so through the centuries. "How strangely some words have lost their primitive meaning!" exclaims the author of The English Theophrastus (1702). "By a critick was originally understood a good judge; with us nowadays it signifies no more than a fault-finder." His linguistic history was wrong but his heart was in the right, or at least the usual, place. As somebody observed in 1766: "We are never safe in the company of a critic."

True. A critic is unsafe by definition and by profession. He will betray you at the drop of an adverb. His loyalty is not to friends, ideologies, or movements but only to the quality of the specific work he is considering. And he complains loudly if this is not up to the standards his taste and experience have developed.

Mr. Simon is a good complainer. "There is a simple law governing the dramatization of novels. If it is worth doing, it can't be done; if it can be done, it isn't worth doing." There may be exceptions but offhand I can think of none. Nor can I quarrel with a lapidary sentence like: "Thornton Wilder's plays have an inverse-Antaean quality: the closer down to earth they get, the weaker they are." For him as CRITIC (1.), the role in which he is best known, see his pricking of Billy Wilder's reputation, "Something for Everybody"; "Sleight of Foot," in which he analyzes the vacuity of certain schools of contemporary poetry ("Mr. Allen's anthology divides all gall into five parts"); and " 'Me, Too!' in Arcadia," which gives the movie, *Phaedra*, as brutal a review as it deserved. (I tried in *Esquire* but must confess myself invectively outgunned.) The last two pieces demonstrate some of Mr. Simon's special virtues. He is erudite about both past and present: the title of the *Phaedra* review is a witty switch and he has read Panofsky's classic essay, "Et Ego in Arcadia"; he has also done his homework on the *oeuvre* of Jules Dassin, probably the most overrated director of our time, and he is able to specify just which earlier movies Mr. Dassin borrowed his effects from. Another virtue is—unexpectedly, considering his polemical élan— a sense of moderation and fairness; thus, after showing in detail the defects of beat poetry, he adds: "Nevertheless, there are two things at which these poets can be good: rhetoric and humor." Right on target—cf. Kerouac's commentary for *Pull My Daisy* or many passages in *Naked Lunch*.

What is not so well known is that Mr. Simon is also very good as CRITIC (2.)—"a disinterested endeavor to learn and propagate the best that is known or thought in the world" (Matthew Arnold, 1865). Here I would call your attention to "From Waste to Wonderland," the most scholarly and informed criticism I know of David Jones's remarkable anti-epical epic of the first world war, *In Parenthesis*; to "Boredom in the Theatre"; and to his reviews of the Metropolitan's exhibition of 17th century French art and of the Museum of Modern Art's retrospective show of Redon, Moreau, and Bresdin. His description of the latter's etchings and lithographs seems to me exactly right:

> What we see in his works is mostly bleak rock struc-
> tures, fleecy little clouds, distant cities, an occa-
> sional solitary human being, a goodly number of

beckoning or threatening skeletons, and, most of all, vegetation grown megalomaniac: trees and bushes displaying unheard-of anfractuosities, opacities, writhings, intertwining—and where a little space is left, there, to be disentangled by the eye, are little beasts: gamboling, grimacing, or gobbling up one another. Bresdin worshiped Rembrandt and, apparently, revered Dürer, and their influence on him is unmistakable; one may also be reminded of Altdorfer . . .

Mr. Simon has a baroque style and an amplitude of references. Sometimes the style is a bit too rich, the references ample to the point of plethora, or showing off. His weakness is for stylistic bravura, and especially for puns: "Nabokov, who in his private life is somewhat of a lepidopterologist ("lepidopterist" would have been enough but the longer word is undeniably more baroque) approaches his characters more with a pin than a pen." This is really not true: Nabokov is a great stylist (his pen is mightier than his pin) but the play on words was irresistible—it had the added attraction of displaying a knowledge of Mr. Nabokov's private hobby—and it hurried Mr. Simon into error. The form imposes the meaning, the chance of turning a phrase (or, often, of turning it inside out) seduces the critic into statements he would otherwise not have made. I know because I have the same weakness. This is a defect of talented young writers—Mr. Simon is thirty-seven, which to me seems young. This may be corrected with advancing age. In any case, it is a defect of virtue: it exists precisely because the writer has a sense of style and form.

In many ways Mr. Simon reminds me of Mencken and Nathan in their great days, the period of *Smart Set* and later of *The American Mercury*. They too were baroque stylists, they too were implacable enemies of the pompous, the second-rate, the philistine, the *idée reçue*; and there was in them a joy of battle, a berserker rage which I find in this book and which I think is most useful for our present state of cultural confusion. I also see here a quality which they didn't have: a sensitivity to a wide variety of modes of art and thought and a judiciousness in evaluating them, as in the section on criticism in which Mr. Simon is actually appreciative of other critics—James Agee is the most striking example—who are quite different from him. A critic who is tolerant of and even generous to other critics is, at the very least, original.

Dwight Macdonald

Foreword

It would be pleasant to be able to equate the role of the critic with that of the forthright child in Andersen's tale who simply had to say "The emperor has no clothes." But the critic as wise child—however much he knows his spiritual fathers, and however militantly candid he may be—is no longer conceivable: in a world in which everyone is naked, even a child cannot cast the first aspersion. It is not cricket to criticize skins.

By this general nudity, I mean, of course, the sparseness of culture in our society. True, with only a little juggling and rigging, one can make out an attractive case for a greater spread of culture today than ever before. But that is just it: culture has become so widespread as to have, for most practical purposes, attenuated itself out of existence. The fault is not only the public's or the educators': there is also too much around us today that needs, or seems to need, keeping up with. The essential is then denatured to the point of dissolution: culture thins out into invisibility, and we stand there, at best, in the underwear of our preconceptions. For though it is undeniable that the Few, in their time, did a handsome bit of debasing, it is obvious that the Many are far better equipped for the task. A woman stranded on a desert island with three men can hardly be expected to scale such heights of promiscuity as are afforded her by a heaped-up metropolis.

To describe the critic in his present state, the metaphor must be shifted a little. In most cases, he is rather like that lecturer at a nudist camp who, wishing to do as the Romans do, appears on the rostrum naked, only to be faced with an audience dressed to the teeth for the occasion. A half-educated public (I may underestimate it) and the semiliterate artist (I may overestimate him), bristling with answers and solutions, aggressively confront the critic at the very moment when, out of humility or condescension, he divests himself of learnedness and trenchancy in an attempt to please. Beat poet, action painter, new-wave filmmaker—whoever they all are—each is encouraged to produce elaborate credos and statements of intention, while the public, told that we live in an Age of Criticism, merrily criticizes away, i.e., likes and dislikes vociferously. As for the notion that ours is an Age of Criticism, it is merely a desperate euphemism for a period in which the arts are in decline—but the cause of this decline is less likely to be the prevalence of criticism than its scarcity.

What is the critic to do in this dark night of the soul of criticism—for the shell of criticism, as I said, is very much with us, but the essence is missing. He has been deprived of his criteria: Aristotle is no more, done in by his enemies, such as Brecht; pretty soon Brecht will be no more, done in by his friends. The various Academies are no more—as least, no more than in name only; even the Dictionary is no more, thanks to structural linguistics. In such an anomic state in which authorities are over-thrown (or, what is worse, obsolete) before new ones can be developed, the critic cannot judge by existing tenets, but must himself evolve the standards by which to do his evaluating. How-ever good this may be in making him more creative, it is extremely arduous: to obtain a panorama, the critic must not only laboriously scale a mountain, but also, out of the critical flatlands, make his own mountain as he climbs.

This is why no criticism today can belong to any particular school: no school can keep pace with the speed of experimentation and innovation, good or bad, as the case may be. And that is why the essays in this book are perfectly willing to be what they seem to be: reviews of plays, books, movies, and art shows, superficially unconnected. But the observant reader will perceive in them the effort to arrive at a standard by allowing those two constants, the critic's taste and his aspirations, to mould and be moulded by the work of the artists under examination. If some repetition and overlapping is present, it was left in deliber-ately, to act as a leitmotif or thread which reveals the continuity in this book. If some sign of the journalistic origins of the pieces is allowed to remain, it remains in emulation of those sculptors who permit a bit of unhewn stone to subsist at the base or head of the statue, to remind us of its origin in the materials, the things of this world. Which is not to say that I conceive of these studies toward a critical outlook as being sculptured out of pure and perennial Parian marble. But I do hope that they convey some-thing more abiding than newsprint.

part one : film

■

To Live in Pieces

■

An increasingly popular topic with movie makers is the sickeningly sweet life of the amoral, jaded, murderously bored upper classes. The first film which came seriously to grips with this problem was Jean Renoir's masterpiece, *The Rules of the Game* (1939), but the censorship it provoked and the war it so closely preceded squelched any immediate influence it might have had. Recently the theme has been picked up again in such French films as Louis Malle's *The Lovers*, Marcel Carné's *The Cheaters*, Claude Chabrol's *The Cousins*, and Roger Vadim's *Les Liaisons Dangereuses*. Some American films have also addressed themselves to the topic, but in timid or sanctimonious terms; the only one worth mentioning, perhaps, is *Butterfield 8*. Now two very important Italian films have come along that face the problem of the decadent upper—or, at least, idler—classes with unremitting honesty. They are Federico Fellini's *La Dolce Vita* and Michelangelo Antonioni's *L'Avventura*.

It would be tempting to distinguish between these somewhat similar movies by saying that Fellini's comes mainly from the heart, whereas Antonioni's comes chiefly from the head. But this would be a lamentable oversimplification. Very briefly, *La Dolce Vita* is the story of Marcello, a Roman newspaperman, who writes yellow journalism and talks about his serious book; who lives with a devoted, silly, possessive mistress, and yearns for *the* woman to love. He gets more or less involved with a variety of women, from a wistful, nymphomaniac millionairess to a dizzy but pitiful Hollywood star, whose brain recedes as strenuously as her bust protrudes.

In other episodes of the film he covers an alleged appearance of the Virgin to a couple of lying children, which turns into a tragic stampede of the gullible; has a bitter fight with his mistress (who previously tried to commit suicide); entertains unsuccessfully his businessman father on a brief visit to Rome; and attends various parties. These consist of an "intellectual" one at the house of Steiner, a man of taste and culture (who subsequently kills his two winsome children and himself because of a deep mistrust of the world); an absurd and effetely lecherous one among the aristocracy; and finally, a gross, wearily orgiastic one among the *nouveaux riches* and their hangers-on. In the end Marcello, in flashy dress and flabby face, has become a press agent without illusions of being either a writer or a man. We leave him and his fellow debauchees on a beach at dawn where a huge, dead manta ray stares at them reproachfully. "A monster!" they cry; but it is they who are the true freaks.

What makes these seemingly disjointed scenes snap together with alarming neatness is, to begin with, a number of connecting visual refrains. One of them is the writhing Via Veneto; another, the vicious breed of free-lance photographers, whose flash bulbs sting the eye, shutters whirr, and Vespas buzz— ghastly, overgrown insects pursuing their preposterous but pitiable prey. A more important device is the threefold irony which provides, aside from flavor, cohesiveness.

The basic irony simply comments on the action: so, in a scene of *La Dolce Vita*, an ostensibly respectable paterfamilias, mildly amused by the heartbreaking antics of a clown in a night club, is unaware that the gallivanting old clown is his own pathetic alter ego, enacting a playlet that would catch the conscience of any king who still had a conscience left.

There is secondly the connective, transitional irony, which ties together scenes or parts of scenes. Thus, in the prologue (based, like several subsequent episodes, on actual happenings reported in the newspapers), a helicopter carries a large, foolishly dangling gilt figure of Christ toward St. Peter's. A quick cut, and we are in a night club and stare into the gilt masks of Siamese dancers. Their resemblance to the statue of Christ is further emphasized by their rhythmic swaying. Two of the main themes of *La Dolce Vita* are herewith established: that the more things change, the more they are alike; and that nothing is sacred because of its intolerable similarity to, or imitation by, something profane or downright vulgar.

Thirdly, and most frequently, there are echo-ironies which hark back from one episode to another. At the intellectual gathering, a young British gigolo seems moved enough, as he plays back on a tape recorder some sounds Steiner recorded from nature, to recite a verse from his national poet, Shakespeare: "Sounds and sweet airs, that give delight, and hurt not." Lovely, but these words in *The Tempest* are spoken by Caliban, the monster. In a later scene, Marcello's father visits a Roman night club with his son; they meet a chorus girl who is a friend of Marcello's, and the old man decides to seduce her. Showily, he quotes from *his* national poet, Dante: "Disperato dolor che il cor mi preme." But this line about the desperate grief that clutches at his heart is spoken in the *Inferno* by Count Ugolino, the father who, to assuage his hunger, ate his son. It emerges that Marcello was utterly neglected by his father.

Gradually, ineluctably, *La Dolce Vita* establishes its most important point: there is no cure for human insufficiency and unhappiness. Too much money destroys as surely as too little; the loving woman is as much of a bore as the intelligent one is a whore; the intellectual life and the life of the senses are only different façades erected before the identical void. "One would have to live detached," says Steiner, and immediately adds, "Let us rejoin our company."

Antonioni's *L'Avventura* concerns a group of socialites on a pleasure cruise off Sicily. All of them are profoundly addicted to, and excruciated by, their respective partners in sex or sexlessness. Anna, a rich, neurotic girl, is exasperated by her lover, the prosperous society architect Sandro; suddenly, during a stay on a small deserted island, she vanishes. Her best friend, Claudia, the only vaguely moral member of the group, joins Sandro in the search across Sicily for Anna. They never find her, but Claudia succumbs to Sandro, fights off her guilt feelings, and happily plans for their future. Sandro promises to become a self-respecting architect again. But that night Claudia discovers him in the arms of a fancy American floozie. Deeply shaken, Claudia nevertheless manages to forgive the remorseful Sandro. But will things ever be any better? Earlier, when Claudia complains that having an affair with her missing girl friend's fiancé is totally absurd, Sandro replies, "Good! If it's absurd, it means we can't do anything about it." And when at one point the uneasy Claudia refuses to make love again to someone who still seems to her a stranger, Sandro retorts, "You should be glad—it's a new adventure then." And, indeed, it is that same night that Sandro seeks out the only possible new *avventura* remaining to him.

To emphasize the vacuity of these lives, Antonioni makes his images and sounds so beautiful that by contrast the happenings become even more drab. Every frame of his film is a work of art: Bonnard and Matisse would have envied him his sense of composition. The way two heads in a close-up fill or do not fill the rectangle of the screen becomes a matter for breathless wonderment. People walk in and out of the field of vision in the most elegantly choreographed ballet. Crickets, birds, distant trains or cars, thunder or sharp intakes of breath, an occasional footnote's worth of astringent music: what soundtrack was ever more poetic? Buildings and landscapes are either sumptuous or, at least, rich in texture. Antonioni never runs out of cake, never lets us eat bread. But enveloped by such beauty, things remain negative: museums are not open when they should be; a brand new town is mysteriously uninhabited; after three months, a marriage is already a gladiatorial fight; if a wife is faithful, she is so out of indolence; a teen-age painter paints only to be able to sleep with his models; and so on and on. The plot itself is a giant shaggy-dog story: Anna, the beautiful, disheveled bitch, disappears; and in the end, instead of being told what happened, we are made not even to care.

If Fellini is not all emotion, neither is Antonioni all intellect. Consider the highly-charged use of black and white in *L'Avventura*. Now this is not the chiaroscuro, the gradual intermingling of light and dark, that seventeenth-century painters were so fond of; this is a juxtaposition of the sharpest whites and blacks that, for all their jostling each other, remain achingly distinct. Antonioni, who is also a Sunday painter, gives us a pictorial Manichaeanism: good and evil, white and black, are pitted against each other. Significantly, Claudia is so light a blonde that her hair photographs close to white; all the others in the film have darker hair, and that of Sandro, the hero, is black. Shortly before Claudia yields to Sandro, she is playfully trying on wigs and covers her luminous hair with a black one, to emerge for an instant as a glossily sinister dressmaker's dummy. The climax of the picture is the moment of forgiveness, when Claudia, discovering her lover's intransigent unfaithfulness, brings herself to lay her hand on the sobbing Sandro's head: the whiteness of that hand blessing the black hair is both stunning and meaningful. Similarly, when Sandro, the architect who has sold out to crass commercialism, chances on a younger man's architectural drawing, he deliberately knocks over a bottle of India ink standing on it: the miniature black lava spreads malevolently across the innocent whiteness of the paper. The next moment, a group of priests ushers out of a church a phalanx of little seminarians in black garb, and an identically spreading black mass spills across the screen. (This seems to me a much stronger anticlerical touch than anything Fellini is supposed to have perpetrated.) Such a black-and-white view of the world is as childlike and emotional as is the charmingly naïve explanation which Antonioni gives for Claudia's innocence: an impecunious childhood.

Under the surface calm of *L'Avventura* the hostilities and ennui are all the more rampant. In *La Dolce Vita,* Fellini makes his point by whirling us around from bright color to bright color at such a speed that everything resolves itself into a pathetic grey; Antonioni shows us such inertia, pettiness, insignificance in people's lives that they become submerged in boredom and move awkwardly as if under water, as if at the bottom of their own heavy discontent.

Ultimately, both Fellini and Antonioni overshoot the mark. Antonioni's picture conveys boredom so minutely that it becomes boring itself. Fellini surrounds what he hoped would be images of hope with so much gloom that they, too, become suspect: Steiner's intellectual crowd seems phoney and pretentious; Paola, a little girl who beckons Marcello away from his degenerate companions, looks like an Umbrian angel but suggests a Roman nymphet. Yet both of these movies are works of art. (Neither would, like *Butterfield 8,* end in a cowardly about-face, and prove the slut's heart pure gold under her pilfered mink, and the playboy so purified by adultery as to be actually willing to do some honest work.) Fellini's is the more successful one, especially in such superb scenes as those between Marcello and his mistress, and Marcello and his father. Both films, however, imply, with equally unforgettable images, the impossibility of loving. "Love, as it exists in society," wrote the eighteenth-century French moralist Chamfort, "is only the exchange of two fantasies and the contact of two outermost layers of skin." Not so in these movies. Even the fantasies have atrophied; only the epidermis remains.

■

Something for Everybody

■

When the American mastermind of Billy Wilder's new film, *One, Two, Three,* wants to squelch an East Berlin Communist with the superiority of the non-Communist cause, he cracks: "Look at it this way, kid: any world that can produce the Taj Mahal, William Shakespeare, and striped tooth paste, can't be all bad." Does this, as the witticisms in a good farce should, make sense? If it is meant as a defense of Western culture, what is the Taj Mahal doing there? If it is meant as a defense of democratic culture, again, why the Taj Mahal? If it is intended as a defense of American culture and its striped tooth paste, what are the Taj and Shakespeare doing there? If it is ridicule rather than a vindication of America, what is the whole thing doing in that context? Neither does the "epigram" tell us anything about the character who utters it, since it is delivered absolutely dead-pan. But, of course, it is not meant to make any sense or reveal any character. It is merely supposed to make us laugh at the crazy juxtaposition and, at the same time, flatter the snobbishness of even the lowest middlebrow in the audience who has once seen a picture of the Taj Mahal and read *Romeo and Juliet* in high school. There is, however, something more contemptible at work here besides: a shallow, gratuitous cynicism, which, somewhere in the back of Mr. Wilder's mind, seems to say, "I laugh at the whole damned world—whether it's Shakespeare, striped tooth paste, or you." Now, it is all right to laugh at striped tooth paste, or us, or even Shakespeare, provided there is somewhere, at least by implication, something that one does not laugh at. And provided that that something is something other than Billy Wilder.

One, Two, Three, and the *bon mot* just quoted, are, I suppose, typical of what is alleged to be Billy Wilder's marvelous double-barreled quality of being able to please intellectuals and just plain folks alike. As a press release sent out by his secretary states, "There is nothing phony or affected about Billy Wilder, but [notice that "but"!] he is an intellectual in the true sense of the word. He is as familiar with baseball as with art—being expert in both these areas and many others." Let us see now how this expertise both in baseball (and similar demotic endeavors) and in the "area" of intellectuality "in the true sense of the word" is manifested in Billy Wilder.

There is a small-town newspaper editor in *Ace in the Hole* who wears both belt and suspenders; he is promptly taunted by the villain-hero for being such a cautious fellow. By the end of the film, the moral values of the belt-and-suspenders man are seemingly affirmed, even though in the beginning they were made to appear laughable. So, too, Billy Wilder's films are belt-and-suspenders films: they combine the jaunty, *sportif* appearance of the belt-wearer with the comfortable, homespun look of the suspenders-wearer. I wish I could report that the results are foolproof and unimpeachable. Actually, they fall between two wears.

Billy Wilder had achieved a considerable reputation in Germany even before coming to this country, where he worked first as a writer for, among others, Ernst Lubitsch. With Charles Brackett, he formed a highly successful writing team (*Bluebeard's Eighth Wife, Ninotchka*); soon they branched out into producing and directing as well. (Though he split up with Brackett after 1950, Wilder always uses collaborators on his screenplays.) There came first the engaging if preposterous *The Major and the Minor* (1942), to be followed by such noteworthy—or, at least, notorious —films as *Five Graves to Cairo* (1943), *Double Indemnity* (1944), *The Lost Weekend* (1945 Oscar-winner), *The Emperor Waltz* and *A Foreign Affair* (1948), *Sunset Boulevard* (1950 Oscar-winner), *Ace in the Hole* (1951), *Stalag 17* (1953), *Sabrina* (1954), *The Seven Year Itch* (1955), *Love in the Afternoon* (1957), *Some Like It Hot* (1959), and *The Apartment* (1960 Oscar-winner). The titles of several other films of his I shall charitably pass over in silence. His fame as writer-producer-director is at its height; he has won numerous major and minor awards here and abroad, and no one in Hollywood enjoys more respect from reviewers, film people, and audiences alike. We are assured on all sides that he is the most daring, inventive, and, beneath the façade of sophistication, profound Hollywood movie-maker. Mr. Wilder's public utterances indicate that this is a judgment he heartily seconds. Yet it is time to realize that, though Wilder has made some extremely skillful, effective, and, in part, even penetrating films, he has never done anything first-rate. One reason for this is, probably, insufficient artistic imagination; another, certainly, is excessive caution.

Wilder has repeatedly declared that prize-winning

is all very well—he is, as he modestly puts it, an old hand at it—
but that the real achievement is packing audiences into movie
theatres. Thus in an interview with Colin Young (*Film Quarterly*,
Fall 1959), he remarked: "It is an absolute cinch to make a film
so that it will win a prize at some festival in Zagreb. It is much
more difficult to make a film which has world-wide popularity. I
have no interest in making arty films to appeal to a group of
critics full of false aesthetics." Actually, Wilder's formula is films
that are vulgar enough to appeal to the typical movie audience,
yet spiked with just enough cynicism, naughtiness, tough wise-
cracking, and *double-entendres* to make the avant-garde moviegoer detect "meanings within meanings," an action that takes
place "on several levels," and a Wilder who is really "laughing
at the whole thing"—or whatever phrases are currently fashionable among avant-garde viewers. In other words, Wilder's films
combine solid suspenders with sophisticated belts.

In *A Foreign Affair,* for example, we are in the
post-war Berlin of 1946; the hero is an American denazification
officer consorting with the former mistress of a high-ranking Nazi
while pretending to court a visiting congresswoman from his native
Iowa so as to divert her from unmasking his girl friend. (He also
has a quasi-fiancée back home in Iowa who sends him a chocolate birthday cake which he promptly trades on the black market
for a mattress for his *Fräulein*—thus making charity both begin
and end at home.) In a scene showing this stout denazifier in
action, an unctuously servile, minor ex-Nazi stands with his son
before the officer: the little boy, a scowling monster, is accused
of chalking swastikas everywhere. The officer comments sardonic-
ally that last year papa must have been kowtowing just like this
to the other team; as papa bows and blithers he notices that
junior has chalked a swastika onto the officer's desk. While papa
wipes off the offending artwork with his sleeve and gives the artist
whatfor, the officer declares: "Some baseball and a little less
heel-clicking—that's what he needs," and directs papa to take
the young reprobate to one of the new American kiddie camps
where the spirit of Abner Doubleday will exorcise that of Adolf
Hitler. Papa mutters obsequious thanks, and as he and junior turn
to go, father's black-garbed back reveals another freshly-chalked
swastika, and Billy Wilder chalks up another belly laugh.

It is, I suppose, a truism to say that a serious, indeed tragic, problem is here reduced to slapstick. But the particular meretriciousness lies in the glib purveying of something
to everybody. The unthinking spectator sees (a) a funny little

German and his even funnier little son being neatly put in their places by a clever captain from Iowa, and (b) a hilarious mess on pompous papa's back, perpetrated while he was busily cleaning up another one. The "sophisticated" viewer, on the other hand, sees a worthless opportunist (American) sitting in judgment over worthless opportunists (German), and prescribing a cure about which he himself must be secretly snickering with his ex-Nazi concubine. Superficially, Wilder has pleased everybody: he has been realistic—for such piddling nostrums were doubtless all that was available to the denazifiers; he has been "brilliantly" cynical—for he has, if you are shrewd enough to spot it, sneered at everyone and everything; and he has been popular—for the scene has enough laughs on the banana-peel level to "recover," in Wilder's words, "the lost audience."

The reprehensible thing, moreover, is the moral equivocation, here as almost everywhere else, in Wilder's work. The forces of ostensible right and demonstrable wrong are shown to be equally out for the main chance, though the former, to be sure, outwit the latter. The ultimate winner is right, first, because he outsmarts someone else; secondly, because, like the captain from Iowa at the end of the movie, he performs one stagily gallant action (after heaven knows how many infamous ones); and, lastly, because, after all, he is one of *us*, not one of *them*. If Mr. Wilder were honest, he would have to take one of three positions: he could commit himself to dissatisfaction with one way of life and approval of another, and be a moralist; he could come out against humanity in general with a curse on all our houses, and be a satirist; or he could stay away from enormous, shattering problems, and be an entertainer and escapist. Instead, he wants to be jolly, informative, and misanthropic all at once: he is offering us a product that is to be simultaneously a sneezing powder, an encyclopedia, and an atom bomb. It is a proof of Mr. Wilder's adroitness that, at his best, he can produce enough outrageous sneezing to make us overlook that the encyclopedia contains insufficient and incorrect information, and that the atom bomb is a dud. I realize that for saying this I shall become in Mr. Wilder's eyes a critic with "false aesthetics." In my eyes, he is something worse: a film-maker with false or no morality.

This kind of moral double-entry bookkeeping appears repeatedly in Wilder's work. The hero of *The Lost Weekend*, as we can surmise from the flimsy but not quite so glossily dishonest novel on which the film is based, has homosexual problems which drive him into alcoholism. The hero of Wilder's film is a suave and virile Ray Milland, whose drinking is a purely adventitious quirk, slickly and factitiously treated from the outside. The heroine of *Love in the Afternoon* is a teen-age playmate to a middle-aged roué; in the novel by Claude Anet, which is trashy enough, the girl is at least cursorily examined—with some attempt at psychological insight—as a curious sexual phenomenon. In the film, the whole relationship may in fact be Platonic, so that the main point becomes a salacious "Did they, or didn't they?" In *Some Like It Hot,* the two chief humorous motifs are wholesale gangland killings and cute transvestitism, with the peculiar implication that the difference between life and death, as between one kind of sexuality and another, is trivial indeed. In *The Apartment,* the lovable hero is a special variety of pimp who lets his office superiors conduct their extramarital affairs in his apartment in exchange for maintaining, or perhaps advancing, his position with the firm. The heroine is a ludicrous girl who allows a callow adulterer to lead her by the nose, until, when he tosses a hundred-dollar bill at her, she attempts suicide. But neither being treated like a prostitute, nor being ignored after near-death, wholly awakens her perception or even just her pride. (The attempted suicide, by the way, is viewed by Wilder as a huge joke.) Yet this spineless hero and brainless heroine are presented as the charming little people who shall, deservedly, inherit the earth; we are to participate warmly in their tribulations, and draw hope for ourselves from their ultimately triumphant doltishness.

Perhaps the best example of Wilder's moral and intellectual confusion is *Sabrina*. The play on which it is based, Samuel Taylor's *Sabrina Fair,* drew the following comments from Eric Bentley: "Mr. Taylor [is] adept at having-it-both-ways . . . which enables him to claim and disclaim as he pleases. . . . Isn't drama for the audience? Well then, let them have illusion and reality as they want them; which is to say, let them chiefly have illusion, but let us keep them from knowing it by administering small doses of reality. In the fun-fair of the mind let there be a booth marked Reality Inc." The heroine, a millionaire chauffeur's daughter, falls in love with the employer's younger son, a playboy, just by watching him, over the years, manipulate women and sports cars, his only visible aptitudes. When the older brother, a ruthless business genius who has scheduled his brother to marry another tycoon's daughter, discovers that Sabrina threatens his scheme, he begins to take her out in order to break up the relationship, and ends by marrying her himself. The ease with which Sabrina switches her affection to another millionaire, this one's chief charm being his ability to live by schedule and make a million every hour on the hour, is, in Wilder's film, appalling. So, too, is the graciousness with which the feckless younger brother abdicates his rights to Sabrina, plays Cupid to the elder brother, and calmly marries the vapid and simpering thing assigned to him, so that both Sabrina and the additional millions can happily come into the family. Wilder adds his particular cynicism in various details—as when the playboy parks his sports car smack at a "No Parking" sign, only to be deferentially saluted by a mounted policeman; or when he casts in the roles of the lovers a Humphrey Bogart looking like an ill-preserved veteran of the Civil War, and an Audrey Hepburn with the appearance of a child dubiously dipping its toes into the cold waters of puberty. And the jokes have a double bottom—thus: "*Younger brother:* I hope you remember what to do with a girl.—*Elder brother:* It'll come back to me. It's like riding a bicycle." The punch line, while capitalizing on the absurd, contains, in a hidden compartment, the scabrous.

Because this equivocal vision enters even into the language of his films, Wilder's most successful works are those in which the equivocation fits in with the personalities portrayed. In *Sunset Boulevard,* the principal characters are all movie people —writers, actresses, directors—who naturally speak that flamboyant and stilted Hollywoodese, consisting mostly of machine-made repartee and gimcrack similes which are the stock in trade of scenarists, Mr. Wilder no exception. That is why it is most apt for the second-rate script-writer turned into an ex-movie queen's gigolo to answer the question "Where have you been keeping yourself lately?" with a prompt "I haven't been keeping myself at all, lately." That, too, is why it is appropriate for him to tell the ingénue, who modestly attributed to her shampoo his compliment that she smells good, "That's no shampoo! It's more like freshly laundered linen handkerchiefs or a brand new automobile." The images are facile and gratuitous (one catches an echo, moreover, of Pépé le Moko's famous "Tu sens le métro!"), but, for a typical Hollywood scenarist, wholly apposite. Again, in *Double Indemnity,* where the hero and heroine are a slick, sleazy insurance salesman and a vicious, sex-oozing murderess, a flashily streamlined cockiness in the dialogue is entirely to the point—"We're both rotten, only you're a little more rotten," says the hero to the heroine as each plots to kill the other. Or, in *Ace in the Hole,* it is perfectly right for the hero—a brash, ruthless big-city reporter fallen upon a sixty-dollar job on an Albuquerque paper—to complain: "When the history of this sun-baked Siberia will be written, these words will live in shame forever: 'No chopped chicken livers!' '' And, again, ''What do you use for noise around here?'' The style is half-way between the clever and the cheap, the incisive and the merely showy; yet the moviegoer recognizes in this precarious balance the ambivalence of those who use such a language. The best light Wilder's dialogue can shed is of the shoddy, neon species; put into the mouths of slippery, smart-aleck characters, however, it fits in with, and even creates, the characterization. Thus Wilder makes a virtue out of necessity—if not, indeed, out of vice.

For Wilder's provinces are plot and dialogue; charac-terization, other than the skimpiest surface variety, is beyond him. He does not, as James Agee rightly noted, get inside a character; still less can he make real the feelings of one character for another, except by using a conventional notation closer to stenography than to depth psychology. And so we find, even in Wilder's best films, characters depending on the whims of the plot, dictated, in turn, by what the public demands, or by what Wilder thinks it demands. In *Ace in the Hole*, the protagonist, a heel with no sense of social or moral responsibility to check the elephantiasis of his ego, is so shattered by a death he inadvertently causes that he becomes a model of selflessness who immolates himself in the service of truth and humanity. In *Sunset Boulevard*, the ''hero,'' while being kept by a pathetic yet imperious faded film diva, manages to get involved with his only friend's fiancée and have little compunc-tion about it; in the end, for no convincing reason, he summons the girl to his Babylonian love nest, wises her up, sends her back to her fiancé, and attempts to leave his decaying enchantress and the riches she lavishes on him, only to be shot in the back by her. In *Double Indemnity*, the unscrupulous, peroxided Cleo-patra, who has used the corrupt hero as she has used or killed all men, has a sudden change—or birth—of heart, drops the gun with which she has already wounded him, and is herself killed by him. As Agee said of this film, ''the expertness [is] as sharply controlled by what is dead sure at the box office as by what is right.''

Is this fatal inconsistency of character merely an obeisance to the box office, or something more than that? Partly, doubtless, just that. Thus Dwight Macdonald writes of ''Mr. Wilder's remarkable ability to have it both ways. An opportunistic ambiva-lence is the hallmark of his films.'' Now, one reason for these belt-and-suspender tactics is that Wilder has set up an incorrect choice: either films that win prizes at some phoney festival, or films that bring the crowd back into the movie houses. That is a specious alternative. The real one is: films that tell the truth—tragically or comically, simply or elaborately, but the truth—and films that do not tell it.

Yet there is more to it: Mr. Wilder is also a cynic. At the end of *Stalag 17,* an honest but stupid tough guy says admiringly of the opportunist turned hero: "What do you know? The crud did it!" In Wilder's films the cruds almost invariably end up doing the grand thing. "Although Mr. Wilder is considered a very cynical fellow," observes Dwight Macdonald, "he seems to me not cynical enough; he uses bitter chocolate for his icing, but underneath is the stale old cake." But it seems to me very cynical indeed to make us swallow the stale old cake as though it were a rare treat, simply because of the icing. Put it this way. Mr. Wilder tells us we are all fools and rogues. That is cynical. He sugarcoats this with laughs and miraculous conversions in which he himself does not believe. That is more cynical yet. But we happily swallow his insults, which makes us fools; and he cashes in on them, which makes him a successful rogue. All fools and rogues: Q. E. D. But whereas cynicism undisguised is a bitter pill that has curative value, cynicism cynically sugarcoated, and so thickly as to nullify the medication, has no therapeutic, moral, or artistic validity. So that the point, ultimately, isn't how much cynicism Mr. Wilder brings to his artistry, but how little art he brings to his cynicism.

■

Ingmar the Image-Maker

■

Several years ago I saw my first Bergman film. It had been called in Sweden *The Clown's Evening,* but the imagination of the American distributors went to work on the title, and the movie was released here as *The Naked Night.* The theatre entrance was bedecked with large posters revealing the meatiness of the star and the meagerness of the quoted reviewers' comprehension. I went in expecting either something like Arne Mattson's *One Summer of Happiness,* all ponderousness and naked bosoms, or like Alf Sjö-berg's *Miss Julie,* all pretentious artiness and refined suggestions of bosoms. Well, there was a partially bared bosom and even a naked bathing scene of sorts, but what really stood unveiled in all its sensitivity and starkness was the genius of Ingmar Bergman.

This genius was evident from the bathing sequence in the first reel. Alma, the aging wife of the clown Frost, is trying to prove to herself that she is still alluring by flirting with a whole regiment on maneuvers by the sea. Her own maneuver is to accept to go in bathing in the nude with the gayer blades among the men, while the others, titillated, watch from the shore. Meanwhile her husband is informed, mischievously, of what is going on. In a mag-nificent portrayal of panic controlled with great dignity, the gangly, equine-faced Frost strips off his tinseled garb, enters the water, clutches the wilting Venus Anadyomene to his chest, and, shielding her nakedness as best he can, carries her home. As he stumbles up a craggy path, wounding his feet, almost dropping his burden, he is followed by the belly-laughs of the soldiery and by a prancing, grinning retinue of his own circus folk. The expression on Alma's face has turned to anguished repentance, and, sadder yet, the whole face has become cowering, old. As for Frost's expression, it has become that of Christ on a baroque crucifix. Supreme stroke of genius: the story is told by a coachman in flashback; we hear no dialogue, only the voice of the crude narrator rattling indiffer-ently on, with, for additional sound, the thump of heavy artillery, and the rowdy guffawing of the troops. The photography has the deliberate harshness and glare of overexposure, contrasting spec-tacularly with the oppressive dark of the film's opening scene, in which another murky relationship, that of the semibrutish circus director and the bareback-rider of this traveling show, is uneasily hinted at. In the bathing sequence, we are given long shots of the frolicking bathers alternating with close-ups of the military's rictus, and, at last, a medium tracking shot of the unhappy couple's cal-vary. For the shuddering march home, during which Alma forgets her own humiliating exposure in a heartbreaking effort to aid her stumbling and bloodied husband, is an experience half golgotha, half journey through hell. Yet there is also a glimmering pinpoint of hope: the ability to endure.

The reason I have dwelled with such prolonged af-fection on this scene is that I was trying, however inadequately, to convey how technical expertise and profound artistic and intellectual integrity make the films of Ingmar Bergman (who else, with the one exception of Fellini, could have made this scene?) works of art. Film, called the Seventh Lively Art, all too often usurps its title after the fashion of the Holy Roman Empire: it is generally not in the least bit lively, not seventh but seventh-rate, and decidedly not art. But in Ingmar Bergman's films, scenes like the one I have described are not the exception but the rule. They do not appear as discrete bravura passages, connected only like croutons by a surrounding mass of pea soup. On the contrary, these sequences flow into one another with entire naturalness and ease, and whatever might be called connecting matter is, in its own way, no less beautiful than what it holds together.

In no other man's films is imagery as important as in Bergman's. Let the characters of one of his movies go into the woods, and Bergman manipulates the forest into a metaphor. It can be the forest full of morning mists and noonday chiaroscuro, bringing back the hopes and loves of youth as in *Wild Strawberries, Summer Interlude,* or *Summer with Monika,* or the lowering forest where man is stalked by death as in *The Magician* or *The Seventh Seal,* or a forest more deceptively ambiguous as in *Three Strange Loves* and *The Virgin Spring.* It can be even a good-natured afternoon forest, suited to middle-aged dalliance, as in *A Lesson in Love.* And in between all these things it can be imperturbable and mysterious, for which Ludwig Tieck, the German romantic, coined the beautiful word *Waldeinsamkeit*—the loneliness, solitariness of the woods.

Or consider another recurrent image: mirrors. Mirror images, of course, are a device that few directors have passed up; but when Bergman uses a looking glass, it is to enter, like Alice, into a world of revelations. In *Smiles of a Summer Night,* Anne, the pretty little wife-in-name-only, looks at herself in a mirror; the glass is photographed as creamy, sensuous, inscrutable. "Who am I?" she appears to be asking, "What are my chances of really loving and being loved?" And the glossy yet somehow veiled surface of the mirror seems to promise infinite possibilities. How different is that bathroom mirror in *Three Strange Loves* (whose decent Swedish title is *Thirst*), which shows the severely neurotic but delightful young wife, played with absolute authority by Eva Henning, brushing her teeth. The picture of someone giving himself a workout with a toothbrush or straight razor is always slightly ludicrous (was it Apollinaire who compared the latter's facial contortions to those of a mute, inglorious Caruso?), but here it becomes even more so: the mirror has a beveled edge, and in the slanting surface a marginal image appears—an absurd distortion, almost hideous, of the woman's face—the objectification of a split personality. In *Secrets of Women* (properly, *Women Waiting*), a husband and wife who have been deceiving each other are locked up together when their elevator gets stuck. The walls of their prison are lined with mirrors: small wonder if, being forced at last to see each other in the round, they penetrate beyond each other's façades to a rounded view of the truth. In *Dreams* (actually *Women's Dreams*), a woman is mirrored, this time in a train window. Her unhappy face is almost impassive, but the rain beating down on her reflection is her own true tears. She contemplates hurling herself out through this windowed door. But as her resolution solidifies, she—and the spectator with her—notices that there is a light in the window, a stationary light. The train has pulled into the city of her destination; she realizes that she must make a go of living. In *The Naked Night* all of the stages in the seduction of Anne by the effeminate actor (and what a great actor, Hasse Ekman, portrays this actor!) are viewed in a mirror: it is as if some vainer, less real, less responsible self lived in mirrors. It takes over, acts for you, and can be blamed for whatever happens. Consequently, when Anne's shamed common-law husband, the circus-owner Henrik, attempts to blow his brains out, he ends by shooting his reflection in a mirror: the scapegrace self that gets you entangled becomes the scapegoat self that dies to set you free.

If I were to name now Bergman's five main themes: youth, love, marriage, old age, and the meaning of life and death, you could already see how some of the images I have spoken of stand for and develop these themes. Yet it might seem either naïve or arrogant for a mere movie-maker to address himself to these fundamental subjects with the magnitude of which not even the ever-widening screen can be presumed to catch up. It may seem all the more foolhardy because Bergman does not give the subjects glancing blows, as we see in those ordinary films that deal, say, with a death. No, he attacks, in *The Seventh Seal,* the heart of that overwhelming question: "What is death?" But his very integrity gives him the right to presume. This might begin to sound as though the writer in Bergman preponderated. Not so; he is neither a Jean Cocteau in whom the author outdistances the director, nor an Orson Welles who overdirects his writing. In Bergman, the writer and movie-maker are, as German can put it, *kongenial,* which means "collaborators coequal in genius," and they are also, in the English cognate of that word, congenial. Thus we are free to read *Four Screenplays of Ingmar Bergman** as literature. True, Bergman has written: "I find it humiliating for my work to be judged as a book when it is a film." Very well, I shall not *judge* it, only assimilate it. And what am I to make of a man who, unlike other screenwriters, does not write *for* the screen but *with* the screen? It is as though that famous camera of Bergman's—old, beat-up, noisy—were a trusty fountain pen pouring directly onto celluloid its ink of light. This is Bergman's "écriture de lumière" of which Jean Béranger has spoken, and the imagery it projects onto the screen makes its creator if not (to defer to his wishes) a writer, certainly a dramatic poet.

Bergman, indeed, seems to me the Shakespeare of our moving picture theatre. *Smiles of a Summer Night* is plainly Bergman's version of *A Midsummer Night's Dream,* and one could, I think, draw useful parallels between *The Seventh Seal* and *Hamlet. The Magician* deals with the problem of the artist, which, happily, did not yet exist in Shakespeare's time; the film's literary analogue is to be found in the tales of E.T.A. Hoffmann. But, again, *Wild Strawberries* is a modernized and mellowed *King Lear.* And it seems to me that the reason for *reading* these screenplays is the same one that makes us *read* Shakespeare: some things emerge clearer in the study than on stage or screen. With Shakespeare, moreover, there is the difficulty of his diction; with Bergman, there is the language barrier. The English translation of the book is far more accurate and elegant than that of the subtitles, and, above all, it is complete.

Those who have not seen Bergman's films can enjoy the screenplays as excellent dramas or novellas in their own right; and when these readers get around to seeing the films, their understanding of them will be heightened, and their pleasure keener. And for those who have seen the films, not only will meanings emerge more fully, but it will also be possible to recreate before the mind's eye the magical processes by which the word becomes film. As Jacques Siclier wrote: "Bergman succeeds in soldering together his ethics and his aesthetics, in expressing one by means of the other."

And there is one little extra attraction that I can promise even the most time-hardened Bergman fan—over and above the occasional interesting deviations of the finished films

* Four Screenplays of Ingmar Bergman, New York, 1960.

from the scenarios. In *Smiles of a Summer Night* there is a succulent little scene between Ulla Jacobsson and Harriet Andersson—the young mistress and her saucy maid. I remember that at the first performance of the film in New York—which I devoutly attended —I had to burst out laughing. Our worthy censors decided to eat this juicy morsel all by themselves, and for some three minutes the two girls chattered away, tumbling all over a bed, with nary a subtitle in sight. The effect was even more ludicrous than infuriating. Well, the charming scene—along with its prelude involving the old cook—whose unriddling has been my *beau souci*, my precious bune, is now at last available to us. You will be able to recognize the true Bergmanite by the fact that he will begin reading his copy of the *Four Screenplays* at the bottom of page fifty-one.

■

"Me, Too!" in Arcadia

■

Jules Dassin's *Phaedra* is a curious love story, indeed. There is the love of a man for a man, made even more fetching by the fact that they are father and son, which expresses itself in chastely male kisses and pawings, and those symbols of healthy masculinity, affectionate little punches in the biceps. There is the love of a woman for a woman, made ever so heart-warming by the fact that they are mistress and servant, which manifests itself in frenetic embraces, glowing caresses, and sleeping together in a narrow bed.

There is also the high and pure love of a boy for his automobile, made exquisitely colorful by the fact that the automobile is a red Aston Martin and the boy is a pallid Anthony Perkins; and the nuzzling, fondling, kissing, and rubbing up against are made, if anything, more poignant by the fact that they are, of necessity, one-sided. There is Jules Dassin's love for his great and good friend, Melina Mercouri, whom he shows off ardently in such various aspects as her bosom and her French pronunciation: if she is a little too long on the one, she makes up for it by being somewhat short on the other. There is, lastly, that tenderest of all emotions, Dassin's love for himself, or, more precisely, for his genius—a gesture of sweeping munificence when you consider how gallantly in excess it is of mere rational appropriateness. Under these conditions of abundance, it may seem a trifle ungrateful of me to call attention to the absence in *Phaedra* of a shred of love for Euripides, Racine, good sense, or good taste.

Before considering more closely Dassin's perfectly awful film, let us examine on what his widespread international reputation as a leading film-maker is founded. It cannot be his American films, like *Brute Force* or *Naked City,* since they represent nothing more than what Howard Hawks or Otto Preminger have turned out time and again, and no one outside the *Cahiers du cinéma* and in his right mind would consider these men artists. It could not be *Rififi* either, for what avails all that proficiency and suspense when the film is—in general outlook, main incidents, and even a number of details—plagiarized from John Huston's *The Asphalt Jungle.*

It could begin to be *He Who Must Die,* which, were it not such a sentimentalizing and tendentious rendering of the harder and more complex novel, could be reckoned a good movie. But it could certainly not be *Never on Sunday,* which owes its few good things (including two of its three principals) to Michael Cacoyannis's fine Greek film, *Stella,* and its multitudinous bad things to Dassin's rabid anti-intellectualism, pretentiousness, and lack of integrity. The anti-intellectualism is particularly offensive coming from someone whose notions of intellect, as evidenced by the movie, are listening to some Bach records, displaying a few Picasso reproductions, and mouthing a platitude or two about Greek culture.

To make matters worse, the palpable chief purpose of *Never on Sunday* is to demonstrate that Miss Mercouri is truly the most gorgeous creature to cast her shadow on the Parthenon since Phryne and Laïs. Nowhere else (except perhaps in Roger Vadim's unsavory pictures with his then wife, Brigitte Bardot) has the camera indulged in such unbridled concubinage with the heroine as in *Never on Sunday.* In fact, not since Popeye put that famous corncob to Temple Drake was there such a publicly celebrated deflowering as that of Miss Mercouri by Dassin's lens.

She who in Cacoyannis's hands had been an artist of perhaps limited range, but passionate persuasiveness, was now degraded to a hunk of raw carnality pruriently anatomized by a camera from whose vocabulary the word "candid" is egregiously missing. And this boastful dangling of Miss Mercouri in front of the audience is, again, one of *Phaedra's* many shortcomings.

Dassin is either obtuse enough to suppose that by preserving a semblance of the Euripidean and Racinian outlines, drained of all the mythic urgency and poetic splendor, one still has a work of merit; or crass enough to assume that by superimposing the mythic framework (though rather bent out of shape) on a lurid tale and banal dialogue, one could obtain a work of interest. In any case, he is quite unsure about how to carry off his transposition.

A shipping magnate gives a harbor cocktail party to celebrate the launching of his newest vessel. It is a high-fashion whirl with music and fireworks and mundane chitchat. Suddenly, a static image: peasant women in black in a *recherché* grouping, entoning a pseudo-archaic chorus: "They are powerful. They speak many languages. And they celebrate with fire in the sky." Then back to the small talk and the to-and-fro of the party. The chorus is now forgotten until nearly the very end of the picture, to return there as a bunch of keening banshees lamenting their drowned husbands. What connection here between the old and the new? What are those drowned seamen to Euripides? What are these moaning Hecubas to us?

The screenplay by Dassin and Margarita Liberaki sets up a triangle involving an Onassis-like shipping millionaire, his sensual wife, and her artsy-craftsy stepson to whom, feeling neglected, she turns for consolation. Phaedra and Hippolytus start out passionately happy, but must presently, with hazy motivation, torment and betray each other. To prevent Hippolytus's marriage to another, Phaedra confesses. Theseus beats up his son and kicks him out. Phaedra is now eager to go off with the youth, but he rejects her, and they go to their separate suicides.

The dialogue provides soul-searching *non sequiturs* like Phaedra-Mercouri saying, after the first fulfillment, "I'm a little cold" (repeated twice, for extra pathos). To this Hippolytus-Perkins replies, "You're my first love," thus betraying the Aston Martin model DB 4 about which, shortly before, he had rhapsodized, "There's my girl; I haven't kissed her today!" and proceeded to do so with more passion than he ever musters for Miss Mercouri, a somewhat older model, to be sure. More often, however, the dialogue goes in for what in its simple-mindedness it mistakes for classic simplicity, such as Tony-Hippolytus, in his wrath, "You're ugly!"

or, in his despair before death, "I want you to die. I am 24 years old—that's all. Just 24!"

Repetition, too, is a device that the writers must have thought of as mightily Euripidean. For we have a long sequence in which Miss Mercouri says nothing but a reiterated "I'm tired," while several other characters ominously mumble, "She looks tired." And there is the scene in which Perkins, after having made boyishly impetuous love to his stepmother (a not inconsiderable departure from the Greek prototype), lies on his back, smirking. In response to her friendly teasing, he repeats, "Yes . . . yes . . . yes . . . ," an idea Dassin got from the end of *Ulysses,* but through which Perkins does not quite succeed in conveying Molly Bloom's rich femininity.

Of Jacques Natteau's photography, I need say only that it is the last word in fashion-magazine artiness. Never before on film have there been so many shots of highly illuminated hair while the face is in total eclipse. Nor, I think, have there been so many lacrimose close-ups in which glycerine and mascara indulge in a running battle.

As for Dassin's direction, it is an album of plagiarism from all over: an arrival by plane on a photographer-infested airfield that is straight *La Dolce Vita* (as are also one or two other scenes); bored lounging around on a luxury yacht that is straight—or, rather, diluted—*L'Avventura;* a seduction scene between pouring rain on the windows and flamboyant firelight in the hearth that is right out of *Devil in the Flesh* (the uncut version, not shown here), with those naked, squirming bodies from *Hiroshima, Mon Amour* added for good measure. There are also pointless montages, like the lengthy superimposition of the inside of the British Museum on a London street scene; and there is top-heavy symbolism, as when the grief-stricken Theseus collapses on a door showing the map of the world.

Melina Mercouri's performance verges on sheer exhibitionism, though she has an occasional quietly effective moment when, apparently, Dassin was not making her say "Cheese." (But he did make her dub her part in English afterwards, with less than felicitous results.) Tony Perkins moves as if some power from within were picking at his nerves, one by one: his face twitches and scowls and occasionally contorts itself into a kind of double-jointed smile; his words creep down his jaw like nasty little maggots. Perkins deprives his character of even the slightest suspicion of heterosexuality, but then, I suppose, the tragic actor must take his *hamartia* where he finds it. Raf Vallone invests the millionaire Theseus-figure with genuine charm and virility, but he should be discouraged from acting in English: someday he might be in a movie in which the dialogue matters.

Perhaps the most characteristic episode of the picture, and the one most revealing of Dassin's mind, is the one in which Perkins is racing into suicide with his sports car. He turns on the radio, which is playing a Bach toccata, and lunges into a final soliloquy that so froze the blood in my fingers that I could get down only a few fragments of it: "A little banishment music, maestro, please. . . . Aha, nothing but the best for us, good old John Sebastian . . ." And he continues to address "John Sebastian, old boy" with Dassin's characteristic condescension to that of which he is incapable—art.

Yet, even if it means making mincemeat of the classics, Dassin must elbow his way into Hellas. *Et in Arcadia ego*: the words, as Erwin Panofsky has shown, are not spoken by the artist or shepherds, but by the grinning death's-head. Dassin's deadly pretentious way of aspiring to culture is to derogate to it. If a more sleazily arrogant film than *Phaedra* is ever made, it will have to be made by Jules Dassin.

part two : books

■

Before Lolita, What?

■

If there is one law in literature we think we have long since broken, it is the one that insists on "poetic justice": that the good end happily, and the wicked unhappily. That, as Wilde put it, is the meaning of fiction. But as you sit there, hard-boiled reader, name a few novels, plays, stories in which evil unabashedly triumphs. Indeed, name one. True, the virtuous may suffer and die, but somewhere there is retribution for the villains. The name in which these are brought low may vary: it used to be God or conscience, now it can be anything from natural law to dramatic necessity. But whether in the name of Christianity or the Production Code, the villain, rest assured, gets his due: that is the law of something more sacred, alas, than literature: wish fulfillment. It is, therefore, against you and me and—more dreadful yet—against himself that Vladimir Nabokov has dared to go in *Laughter in the Dark,* whose off-white but still whitish hero, Mr. Albinus, meets a terrible end, while his girl and the other man, a pair of billing buzzards, fly off rich and victorious.

    Laughter in the Dark, first published in 1938 and thus preceding *Lolita* by some 17 years (which is more than a nymphet's life expectancy), is none the less *Lolita's* logical antecedent. Before the *femme fatale* could be a child of 13, and her victim still in his nubile thirties, the less extreme and better known fiasco of the married man in his forties and the temptress in her late teens had to be explored. If *Lolita* shows us, certain allegations to the contrary notwithstanding, the normality of perversion, the earlier work reveals to us the perversion of normality. The hero is a harmless enough man who makes only one mistake (though that turns out to be a whopper); the girl is quite insignificant in every respect except her profound, spectacular amorality; and the other man is just a little more cynical, a little more depraved, than any other other man. The sensationalism of *Lolita* is absent. But make no mistake: *Laughter in the Dark* is a far more daring, or, if you prefer, a far more wicked book than *Lolita*.

Laughter in the Dark is the story of Albert Albinus, a Berlin art expert and critic, decent, cultivated, and prosperous. He is the possessor—as far as her frigidity will allow it—of a well-meaning but pallid wife, and of a quite ordinary eight-year-old daughter who shows no promise of ever becoming his concubine. But one day, in a second-rate movie theatre, he comes upon an eighteen-year-old usherette whose rate is rather higher: Albinus's possessions, happiness, and very existence. It is a case of what the Germans call *sexuelle Hörigkeit* and is but feebly rendered by our "sexual slavery." Margot Peters, as the bittersweet young thing is called, makes Albinus abandon wife, child, friends, and the better part of his respectability for the sake of a love affair all love on his part, and all affairs on hers. When a famous young movie cartoonist, Axel Rex, arrives on the scene, there ensues one of the saddest, cruelest, funniest silly symphonies ever recorded; while Axel and Margot make beautiful music together, Albinus's silliness and blindness reach monumental proportions. *Le coeur rend bête,* said the poet Pierre Reverdy: "The heart makes stupid. The more heart one has, the greater the need for strength and intelligence to sustain it." And poor Albinus's intellectual and moral fortitude is pitiably wanting. Besides, he is getting bald.

The stupidity of Albinus, the cupidity of Margot, and Rex's debonair diabolism bring about a triangle which, for sheer viciousness, leaves any circle far behind. That in telling of a *ménage à trois* so savage, ending in such disaster, Nabokov could maintain a tone of objectivity and even humor—without falling into the excesses of Evelyn Waugh—is the triumph of careful literary construction.

For under the apparent realism of this rousing tale of passion and suspense there hides a control, a manipulation of the material that is sheer contrivance—but contrivance in the sense a sonnet or sestina is contrived: with a design, and, in this case, an ironic purpose in mind. Take the names of the three principals; though the locale is Berlin, none of these names is patently German. Albert, to be sure, is Teutonic, and means "bright with nobility"; Albinus is derived, of course, from the Latin for "white." But our hero is merely a sedulous auxiliary of the arts, a well-to-do supernumerary of the intellect, whose *embourgeoisement* is mitigated by a genteel sensitivity rather than any brightness, or whiteness, or illustriousness. Even in his intense yearning for a passionate love affair and the indulgence of his enflamed heart, which up to a point is touching, there is more naïve expansiveness than nobility. As for Margot, it is the Villonesque diminutive of Marguerite, which means "pearl." But if dear Margot is any kind of pearl at all, she is a black pearl, and a fake one at that. And the Peters seems to allude to that other rock-like creature who likewise betrayed his master in the wee hours before the cock crows. Axel is, of course, the "axle" around which passions spin the plot; the name comes from the Swedish for "a supporter," but our Axel is, in fact, supported *by* Margot on Albinus's money. And in this absurd and deeply indecent world the kept man is king: Rex. As you can see, the substructure of Nabokov's realism is a carefully constructed irony.

This irony, as bitter as it is subtle, underlies every superficially realistic aspect of the novel—for instance, the unusual handling of coincidence. Lesser artists will use coincidence merely to produce a sensational effect which, after all, is consistent with the existential situation (as lesser artists now refer to life) and, at the same time, conveniently furthers the action. Not so with Nabokov. Before our garish love triangle came into being, each participant had a prehistory involving each of the others. Rex and Albinus were corresponding about a chimerical movie venture; Albinus had been consulted about somebody's charcoal sketches and had preferred among them a bearded cripple to a fetching little nude who was none other than Margot; Margot and Rex had been lovers. Rex, who had treated Margot like a common prostitute, gave her an alias, "Miller," and soon left her and disappeared. Albinus also tries, at first, to palm off an alias on Margot: "Schiffermiller," a quaint, fortuitous variation on Rex's. When, at the end of the book, Albinus is summoned to his doom, Margot's unwitting tool is a janitor who happens to be called—Schiffermiller. Clearly it is not the plot which requires these recurrent names. Nabokov's point, discreetly understated,

is that the writer's ironic game is the replica of the great, horrible game in which we all are involved: life, whose circumstances
mock us cruelly in the darkness through which we are groping.

This cosmic irony manifests itself also in a grizzly
foreshadowing that runs through the book. Albinus meets Margot in the *darkness* of a movie theatre. The trashy film that is
nearing its end accurately prefigures the tragic conclusion of
the book. So, too, does a foolish exercise in acting, with which
Margot, posturing before her mirror, hopes to achieve a movie
career. At the first meeting of the three, "Albinus handed over
his lady to Rex"; she is to be led in to dinner and Albinus down
the garden path. And when he finally discovers the obvious,
Albinus exclaims "I was blind," little realizing that what he takes
to be a metaphor about his past is the literal truth about his
future. In the final phase of his humiliation, Albinus, doubly be-
nighted, must play a tragic game of blindman's buff. And Margot, the evil little Antigone who leads the sugar-daddy she
blinded, leads him not by the hand but by the nose.

Regrettably, however, what could have been a
great novel, turns out to be only a good one. Edmund Wilson
is right when, in speaking of Nabokov's book on Gogol, he
tempers his otherwise considerable admiration by pointing to the
author's self-indulgence in poses, perversities, and vanities. With
reference to *Laughter in the Dark,* one might add that it lacks
the rich local color of Berlin between the wars that writers as
diverse as Alfred Döblin and Christopher Isherwood have made
memorable. Nor do Nabokov's characters have the marvelous
rightness of tone that, for example, Evelyn Waugh's have, whose
conversation carries their whole existence on its back. Nabokov,
who in private life is somewhat of a lepidopterologist, approaches
his characters more with a pin than a pen. But this gives the book
its very own kind of cruel brilliance.

At the beginning of *Laughter in the Dark* Nabokov
speaks of "a phrase in Conrad (not the famous Pole, but Udo
Conrad . . .)," a minor novelist who is one of the characters in
the story. But when we read Mr. Nabokov's fiction, we are reminded precisely of the famous Pole—not so much because of
yet another Slavic writer's dazzling mastery of the English language, as because of a similarly corrosive evocation of a respectable man's deterioration and downfall. The novel could
worthily bear the Conradian title of *Albinus's Folly.* But *Laughter
in the Dark* is more appropriate: not only literally, on account of
the enormously brutal and baleful final section, but also sym-

bolically. If there were any gods, Nabokov seems to be saying, what would be heard in the universe—except, of course, that it wouldn't be heard, because of the distance from gods to man— is their ghastly laughter in the dark.

■

Solo for Violin and Organ

■

Like any other religion, art needs martyrs. One remembers the exhibition into which a practical joker sneaked a glass case containing a garish wax counterfeit: presently no one was looking at the pictures, and people were elbowing one another for a glimpse of the "exhibit" labeled VAN GOGH'S EAR. I do not doubt that to many the brightest color in Van Gogh's glowing palette is still the red of a bleeding ear.

With the possible exception of Rimbaud, no one in our age qualifies more aptly for the martyr of art than Vincent van Gogh. Everything was denied him: parental sympathy, comfort, a wife, children, a decent mistress, a lasting friendship, recognition by more than one or two people, good looks, ease in conversation, money. He sold nothing in his entire lifetime, even though he charged almost nothing. He lived wretchedly off a younger brother's charity, which, I imagine, must be even more painful than that of an older brother; often, moreover, he had reason to believe that this devoted brother, Theo, did not understand or appreciate him. But, unlike Rimbaud, Van Gogh never reneged; instead of hurling himself into a shady business, he plunged into the shadows of madness and suicide. Dying at the age of 37, he felt ineffably old. Even the most bloodthirsty fan of tabloids and martyrologies could scarcely ask for more.

This, however, is the very thing that might put the discriminating reader off Van Gogh's letters. The legend of Vincent has been so much with us that such a reader would approach these letters, not with the vulgar fear that the man might not live up to his legend, but with the refined apprehension that he *did* live up to it: that his letters are nothing but its gaudy, tautological confirmation. Such is hardly the case. To begin with, Van Gogh never thought of himself as a great man; on the contrary, he had, along with an underlying faith in himself, the most tragic delusions of pettiness. Thus he was wholly free from the great man's epistolary sin of addressing himself, if not directly to the aspect of eternity, certainly to the gaze of more than one reader. Furthermore, Vincent was a man—despite his various fanaticisms and ultimate madness—of great good sense, and his comments on any subject, from painting to cab horses, from literature to prostitutes, are piercingly sane; witty or poetic at times, they are always imbued with the grace of unpremeditated originality. The tone may become, especially toward the end, profoundly sad—but never maudlin; more often, however, there is manly resilience and irrefrangible hope. One can see that writing, very nearly like painting, had therapeutic value for him: when he was tired from painting or drawing, he could say in a letter "writing rests and distracts me." The Van Gogh of the letters is not only an admirable, admirably plain human being, but also one who almost unprecedentedly combines in his correspondence the virtues of a writer with those of a non-writer.

It is for this reason that New York Graphic Society, publishers of the three-volume *Complete Letters of Vincent van Gogh*—a luxury item retailing at $50—decided that for the less special reader, for whom not only time but also money is money, a one-volume abridgment was called for. (There have been other such selections before, but none based on the one and only *Complete Letters*.) W. H. Auden, who had shown himself a most sympathetic and canny critic of the three-volume edition, was, therefore, requested to make an, as it were, definitive selection from it, and the result is *Van Gogh: A Self-Portrait*.

In making his choice, Mr. Auden says that he was guided by the fact that Van Gogh was above all a painter. Therefore, though Auden found all the letters interesting, he picked only those which deal principally with painting, or throw light on Vincent's life as a painter. Fortunately for us, however (though not always for him), Van Gogh did not separate life from art, so that those letters which contain the most painterly matter have in them also the greatest amount of living. Besides, Mr. Auden is too much of a humanist and Van Gogh-sympathizer not to be better than his somewhat austere word; I don't think I found a single one of my favorite pieces in the *Complete Letters* missing from *A Self-Portrait*. I deliberately say "pieces" in order to include the various letters by others than Vincent, as well as recollections and miscellaneous documents, which fill in gaps, and which, too, Mr. Auden has preserved for his one-volume edition. More than that, he has arranged all this material in chronological order, whereas the *Complete Letters* tended to group letters together by addressee, so that in one respect, at any rate, *A Self-Portrait* improves upon its parent book.

"Some artists," wrote Van Gogh, "have a nervous hand at drawing, which gives their technique something of the sound peculiar to a violin . . . others . . . remind one more of piano playing . . . Millet is perhaps a stately organ." I find in this the key to Vincent the artist and Vincent the man. For in him, as in his work, the nervous and the stately, the jaggedly harassed and the unfalteringly noble, manage to coexist. Not peacefully, to be sure; but coexist, none the less. Baudelaire, whom Vincent disparaged, once said of Delacroix, whom Vincent worshiped, "C'est l'infini dans le fini." This applies even more to Vincent van Gogh. For it is he who managed to make a symbol both of his painting and of his life—and what is a symbol other than the infinite reflected in the finite, than the nervous scrape of the violin becoming simultaneously the massive sweep of the organ. Thus Van Gogh is the man who could write "it is *absolutely certain* that I shall never do important things" in his perennial nervous dissatisfaction with himself; yet he could tell a friend to whom he gave a sketch that he did not sign: "Actually it isn't necessary; they will surely recognize my work later on, and write about me when I'm dead and gone. I shall take care of that, if I can keep alive for some little time." So, too, Van Gogh may paint a mere rough-hewn peasant chair, but suggest in it—if not exactly Gauguin's absent presence, as he intended to—the strong, uncompromising quality of men who make and sit in chairs like that. The tempestuous brush strokes and frenzied application of curious colors ("Color expresses something in itself . . .") spell out the image, ultimately, of an unshakable, peace-bringing strength.

Let me give two examples from *A Self-Portrait* of this very beautiful ambivalence. Vincent is trying to persuade his young colleague and friend, Emile Bernard, of the greatness of Dutch painting, which Bernard underestimates. Van Gogh begins by admitting that "those Dutchmen have hardly any imagination or fantasy," but proceeds to characterize Rembrandt as follows:

> He paints a self-portrait, old, toothless, wrinkled, wearing a cotton cap, a picture from nature, in a

mirror. He is dreaming, dreaming, and his brush resumes his self-portrait, but only the head, whose expression becomes more tragically sad, more tragically saddening. He is dreaming, still dreaming, and I don't know why or how, but just as Socrates and Mohammed had their familiar spirits, Rembrandt paints behind this old man, who resembles himself, a supernatural angel with a da Vinci smile.

I am showing you a painter who dreams and paints from imagination, and I began by contending that the character of the Dutch painters is such that they do not invent anything, that they have neither imagination nor fantasy.

Am I illogical? No.

Rembrandt did not invent anything, that angel, that strange Christ, the fact is that he knew them; he felt them there.

Now consider the following passage from a letter to Theo, also dated 1888, two years before Vincent's death. "Perhaps death," Vincent writes, "is not the hardest thing in a painter's life." And he continues:

> For my own part, I declare I know nothing whatever about it, but looking at the stars always makes me dream, as simply as I dream over the black dots representing towns and villages on a map. Why, I ask myself, shouldn't the shining dots of the sky be as accessible as the black dots on the map of France? Just as we take the train to get to Tarascon or Rouen, we take death to reach a star. One thing undoubtedly true in this reasoning is that we *cannot* get to a star while we are *alive,* any more than we can take the train when we are dead.
>
> So to me it seems possible that cholera, gravel, tuberculosis and cancer are the celestial means of locomotion, just as steamboats, buses and railways are the terrestrial means. To die quietly of old age would be to go there on foot.

In both these passages, as in everything that Vincent lived, painted, or wrote, the disturbed, grieving, and earthly slowly passes into the eternal and serene.

The most obvious conclusion to be drawn from reading these letters concerns the meaninglessness of obscurity and fame. Here is a man living on a perpetual dole. The picture he paints of his physician and gratefully gives to him becomes an improvised window pane to keep the draft out of the latter's attic. When Vincent dies, his family refuses to take in a trunkful of his paintings and sketches because worms have got at them and might infect the house; instead, the pictures are abandoned, scattered, many of them lost. Most heartbreaking of all, Vincent himself writes Theo about a masterpiece, *The Bedroom,* which has become damaged by moisture: "That, I *imagine,* ought to be repaired for 5 francs; if it is more, then don't have it done." Today, on the other hand, enormous prices are fetched by these very pictures; Van Gogh is recognized as one of the three men who made painting what it is today; and cheap reproductions of his work hang in almost every American apartment or mind—where, however, the name of Morris Graves, for instance, may never penetrate. But Vincent himself, in the midst of his awful struggle, was well aware of this. To be ignored or reviled is nothing: "I most decidedly expect that, as I gain in . . . expressive force, people will not say *less* frequently, but on the contrary *even more* frequently, that I have *no* technique." And approval and fame are nothing either: "Success is almost the worst thing that can happen," he writes; and we read that "when a so-called picture lover . . . told him that he thought a thing of his was beautiful . . . he knew for certain . . . that it was bad, and as a rule such studies were destroyed or repainted." Small wonder that these letters became a favorite reading and important source of inspiration to such diverse writers as, for example, D. H. Lawrence, the German expressionist Carl Sternheim, and the mysterious Antonin Artaud.

In *Le Jardin d'Epicure,* Anatole France expressed the wish that man could live his life backwards; that, like the butterfly, he could go from a wizened larva to youthful loveliness; that he should end not only wise, but also at the height of his power and splendor. To a large extent this is true of Van Gogh's life. His letters, except those of his illness, are progressively braver, wiser, and more cheerful. From the early humorlessness and religious and existential confusion, Van Gogh moves to directness, forcefulness, luminosity—often even fun. "When I was younger," he writes, "I looked like one who was intellectually overwrought, and now I look like a bargeman or an ironworker." But even if in his life he could not quite achieve France's ideal, in his work he did: from somber, naturalistic Dutch genre painting, he grew into that invincible freedom of shape and color which is the very genius of childhood.

Twenty-four years after Van Gogh's death, that remarkable painter August Macke defined the aims of modern art: "Diese raumbildenden Energien der Farbe zu finden, statt sich mit einem toten Helldunkel zufrieden zu geben . . ." To find the space-creating energies of color, instead of contenting oneself with a dead chiaroscuro—how Vincent would have approved these words. For his paintings, and his letters likewise, did nothing if not explore and extend our existing space—both outward and inward.

As we read *Van Gogh: A Self-Portrait,* we find ourselves looking into the margins as much as into the text; for there, in the white spaces, we see the brilliant canvases of Van Gogh's final period. Out of the cocoon of drunkenness and debauchery, misery and madness, come pictures and words that are—I say it unflinchingly—sublime. Vincent's contemporaries objected to his *modus operandi:* he would actually smear colors on with his thumbs! ("Even with my heels, if necessary," he would answer.) But that is what Vincent's art is: all thumbs and genius.

■

Philosopher's Fables

■

How refreshing it is in this age of "anti-novels" to turn to Voltaire's supremely intelligent and ardently committed fiction, ably translated by Donald M. Frame in a volume called *Candide, Zadig and Selected Stories.* Professor Frame has chosen three short novels and thirteen stories and parables: a generous selection from the work of the man who was, along with Juvenal and Swift, one of the three greatest satirists the world has seen.

Good satire is very possibly the most difficult of all literary genres. The writer must, first of all, perceive the intellectual and ethical failures and self-deceptions of his age, unmask them, and, at least by implication, suggest sounder values. This is a dialectical problem. But there remains the artistic task of making such criticism and moralizing attractive to the reader who, like any self-respecting person, abhors mere didacticism. The satirist has the awesome duty to be both wolf in sheep's clothing—having murder in his heart but wit and jollity in his words—and sheep in wolf's clothing—writing out of his basic love of the good the most cutting and crushing things conceivable.

But that is not all. The writing must be so entertaining, so cogent, so flawless, that those whom it attacks cannot get back at it either with replies that point out holes in it or with a dignified silence that overwhelms petty attackers. And if such good satire is to be also great, it cannot have for its butt merely this or that particular fool, fraud, or foe, but must address itself to the universal failings that you and I are guilty of: our withers must be wrung. And it is over this mighty coalition of you and me that the great satirist must triumph, even though we have centuries of added wisdom for our allies. But Voltaire beats us, and all we can do is to kiss the rod.

For it is you, reader, and I who tell Candide that the world he lives in is, barring perhaps the Congo and taxes, the best imaginable (would you want to return to the Crusades? would I want to be at the mercy of the Borgias?); it is you and I who, in an endless series of wickeder and wickeder disguises, exploit and torment the admirable Zadig; you and I who force the lovely Mlle. de Saint-Yves into our beds in exchange for letting her ingenuous beloved out of the Bastille; you and I who, like the Jesuit Berthier, kill our fellow man with our contumely, unless, of course, we have already bored him to death. It is we who are arrogant ingrates like Jeannot, the nouveau-riche marquis, or charlatans like the tutor who makes him what he is. And who, like Chaplain Goudman, forgets the wisdom adversity has taught him, when by shady means he becomes an overdog? You, reader, and I. And what can we do to get back at this Voltaire who hits us where it hurts and ridicules us in all eyes, including our own? The only way to get the better of him is to make ourselves better—and there! he has won again!.

Furthermore, these are stories that are not afraid of being stories. Everywhere, despite the incisiveness of thought and stylishness of writing, there is action such as the general reader in a scientific age demands. Ingenuous, for example, is a novella which, though rather more complex even than Mr. Frame suggests in his excellent introduction, holds us in that state of unmitigated suspense we associate with slick thrillers. And the translation, though a little unaristocratic and colloquial in places, may be justified even in that. The imperturbable elegance that characterized the 18th-century writer, whether he extolled, like Diderot, the noble savage, or, like Sade, ignoble savagery, is not our literary currency: Mr. Frame's angularities and occasional simplifications may be Voltaire's exact 20th-century equivalent. Thus in the original of *Zadig*, the Queen feels humiliated when she is treated as a *demoiselle suivante*, a lady in waiting. But Mr. Frame translates this as *maidservant*, assuming that it takes more to offend even a queen nowadays.

The one objection that has been made to these novels and tales is that the characters in them are skeletal: that Voltaire reduces them to the bare bones of their essential humanity or inhumanity. Maybe so. But what these superbly animated skeletons perform for us is no medieval Dance of Death: it is, observed with x-ray eyes, the Dance of Life. If these stories are fables, they are, in their author's words, "the fables of philosophers . . . emblematic of the truth."

■

Robbed of Immortal Things

■

The story of a young girl and an old man has two archetypal forms in English literature; one occurs where the college survey course begins, and the other where it ends. I am referring to Chaucer's May and January, and to "that lust and rage" that "danced attention on the old age" of William Butler Yeats. The one is comic, indeed burlesque, yet not without serious overtones; the other, heart-rending, almost tragic, yet not devoid of a ludicrous element. The story of Bernard Shaw and Molly Tompkins, as it emerges from *To a Young Actress*, adds a third archetype: one that is in equal measure comic and tragic, delightful and pathetic; as gay, sad, and absurd as life itself. For it is possible to read this book as the story of a fascinating relationship, frothy and poignant; or as letters from Shaw to his last temptation, letters witty and wise and, at times, almost unbearably touching. But it is best to read this book as a marvelous metaphor for the splendor and misery of human existence.

To a Young Actress is made up of Shaw's letters of 28 years to Molly Tompkins; her letters to him were destroyed or lost. The result is rather like Strindberg's The Stronger: a play for two persons of whom only one speaks; but the drama stems not only from the speeches of the one but also from the silences of the other.

Mary Arthur was an extremely alluring and vivacious girl, descended not inappropriately from the author of Ten Nights in a Bar Room: like her great-grandfather, she had a flair for the theatre but no great talent. She was brought up in Georgia, had a walk-on part in Ziegfeld's Follies, and married an aspiring sculptor, Laurence Tompkins. The young couple and their infant son went to London in 1921: Laurence was to design and build a new theatre dedicated to their hero, the savior of humanity, Bernard Shaw; Molly (as Shaw persuaded her to call herself), aged 24, was to become a great Shavian actress, the interpreter of the new Messianism. What two-year-old Peter was to do was not yet clear —not until 1960, that is, when he edited Shaw's letters to his mother and so became the only Tompkins to erect a lasting memorial to GBS.

The character of "Mollytompkins," as Shaw nicknamed her, appears in the first sentence he wrote to her (December 27, 1921): "What a shocking little fraud you are, pretending to have read all my books when you haven't read one of them." Molly, we gather, was clever, had an intuitive understanding of people, and was possessed of a small, haphazard talent which successively tried, and failed, to realize itself in acting, writing, and painting. The failure wasn't total in any of these fields, which made it all the more tantalizing. She seems to have been unstable in every sense of the word; uneducated and, despite the ability to pick up snatches of this and that, uneducable because of insufficient perseverance. At the age of 29, for example, she was irritating Shaw with such spellings as Polotics, tackless (for "tactless"), and bear trees; and exasperating her husband by dallying with Italian noblemen, themselves married. She was scatterbrained, impetuous, neurotic, and bewitching.

Shaw was in most respects her exact opposite and, besides, her senior by 41 years. He was, above all, the world's greatest ungreat playwright: a man of enormous intelligence, huge wit, and a Dickensian ability to create character and dialogue.

Moreover, he was a great businessman, his own brilliant impresario, a social and political thinker of remarkable, if eclectic, ideas, a critic, an epigrammatist, a stylist of utmost distinction. But he was not a poet, which is perhaps why he was not a lover, or the other way around.

His letters to Molly make the matter of a Shavian play: Molly partakes of all those foolish, wilful, irresistible, idiot-savant young girls in Shaw's plays; and Shaw himself begins as a kind of Henry Higgins and ends as one of those dignified but pathetic figures in Shaw's later work, like Lord Summerhays and Captain Shotover, old gentlemen drawn to and repelled by the young girls they fascinate—figures in which Shaw comes much nearer to poetry than in his Marchbankses and Saint Joans.

Of course, the question everybody asks is what really did happen between this married man of 65 and this young mother of 24? When Peter Tompkins was asked about it recently (for a front-page story in *The New York Times*), he answered, "Who knows? And who cares?" But this was spoken, I suspect, more like a son than like an editor. It would be truly interesting— more than that, reassuring—to hear again that Shaw was capable of loving, or even just making love to, something other than an abstraction. Something indeed seems to have happened in the gardens at Godalming, at the Cerro passage at noon, and, most often alluded to, on the Baveno road at night; these were things, as Shaw wrote Molly, to "steal into your sleep at night." But as he again wrote her much later, "Have you not yet discovered that the only roads that remain beautiful are those that never led any-where? For you never come to the end of them." It has always seemed likely to me that the Baveno road never led anywhere, that Shaw never consummated an amatory relationship (whatever the records say), and that this is part of that "small, obstinate margin" by which, as one critic has remarked, his plays fall short of the first rank. But, in another way, this does not exclude mo-ments of strange, bittersweet happiness, tête-à-têtes fraught with the thrill of the illicit, even if they chiefly fed Molly's ego and Shaw's penchant for the avuncular. How they must have felt (or imagined that they felt), in Meredith's words, that

> Love that has robbed us of immortal things,
> This little moment mercifully gave . . .

The deciphering of this curious relationship which elicited so much vexation, good advice, and gruff tenderness from GBS is not the least hold the book has on us. But the fascination lies as much in what is patently there. For *To a Young Actress* is not merely unlike other volumes of correspondence between Shaw and actresses like Ellen Terry and Mrs. Pat Campbell; it is truly a book *sui generis,* unlike any volume of letters I have ever seen, and an absolute success. For here, as in no other book, we are the seemingly direct recipients of a great man's immensely charming and perceptive letters. There are no missives from Molly. But on beautiful, laid paper, in quarto format, here is an almost uninterrupted flow of exact photolithographic reproductions of letters and postcards—both the text and the picture sides—from Shaw, in his hand or typewriting, or whimsical combinations of both. Here is that ever-changing handwriting, sometimes elegant, sometimes spindly, and, at the last, pitifully distorted by age; here are the dirty typewriter keys and worn-out ribbons just as they would have been foisted on us had we been the lucky and unlucky correspondents. Here, too, are the quixotic postscripts squeezed in in odd places, the careful corrections and rare misspellings (I was rather amused by "lappel"—how wonderful to catch the champion of simplified, phonetic spelling making matters *more* complicated!), until, in the last letters, we are grieved to see the control weakening. And here are the odd choices of picture postcards, many of them, with splendid megalomania, photographs of GBS, and others ranging from Italian landscapes to Rubens nudes with schoolboyishly mischievous captions scribbled on them. These reproductions are surrounded by the minimum of explanatory notes at the bottom of the page, and the maximum of lovely, white margin, encouraging our meditation and reverie. And to cap it all, the book has such a tasteful and aristocratic binding, jacket, typography, and lettering, that I would loudly extol its designer, Christopher Simon, were it not that this to me unknown gentleman is my namesake, and I thus apt to incur the suspicion of family pride. Instead I shall congratulate the imaginative and enterprising publisher, Clarkson N. Potter, because not even the closest scrutiny of my family tree will yield a single Potter.

Shaw is at his perceptive, spirited, amusing, and grandly condescending best in this correspondence. In the opening paragraph of the first letter, from which I have already quoted, he speaks of his youthful distress at "not living up to the precept 'Be ye perfect, even as your father in heaven is perfect.' " Shaw continues: "Nowadays I perceive that even HE is not perfect." And the categorical tone, somehow delectable rather than annoying, goes on unabated: the stage pronunciation of "wh" as "hw" is all right because "*I* use it." For Molly to go to class at the Royal

56

Academy of Dramatic Arts without wearing make-up (at Shaw's suggestion) is a "magnificent swank . . . I am impressed." For the longest time Shaw does not even bother to learn Mr. Tompkins's name; at one point he is referred to as Horatio. Eventually intimacy sets in, and he becomes "Lawrence"; it is not till fourteen years later that the spelling becomes, correctly, Laurence, only to revert almost immediately to the "w." And, of course, Molly is often reminded by her correspondent of his genius: "It is the anniversary of Mozart's birth in 1756 (I followed in 1856)."

Mostly, however, there are sound insights into art and life. About a bad performance of *Don Giovanni:* "You don't get masterpieces quite so cheap as you expect when you are young. Mozart can afford to wait." On acting ("method" actors, please note!): "An actor stands in much the same relation to an author as a carpenter or mason to an architect: he need not understand the entire design in the least; and he would not do his own part of the job any better for such understanding." Or: "I rather doubt whether the stage is really your job: you are neither a very ignorant egotist nor a superficially lively and fundamentally brainless person." On O'Neill (or is it sleeping cars?): "As I passed last night in a sleeping car, mostly reading O'Neill's plays, I am good for nothing today." To Molly in Italy: "Remember also that homicide is much commoner in Italy than in England, and much more privileged when it is a reaction of sexual infatuation. So when you go husband stealing don't forget your gun." On romance: "There are moments, of course, when you want to consummate it. But they pass; and the romance remains. You get tired of waiting; but suppose there were no longer anything to wait for?" On Henry James: "James felt buried in America; but he came here only to be embalmed."

Shaw offers advice and illumination on any number of subjects such as calligraphy, stage diction, postage rates in England, fresco painting, and how to coax good pictures of himself out of photographers for the least money. Even on these humdrum subjects he manages to sound perfectly entertaining, but his best humor is often not so lapidary as to lend itself to excerpting. A longer comic passage must, however, be quoted as a sample:

> Before learning to write beautifully, acquire the art of saying no in a convincing manner. It is the most useful accomplishment in the world; and your life will be a long misery unless you can bring it out swiftly and unanswerably without the slightest re-

gard to the feelings or the importance of the peti-
tioner or autocrat or whoever it is who asks or orders
you to do something you don't want to do. Will you
have a drink? NO. Will you lend me two pounds
until Saturday night when I will— NO. Will you sign
a contract to dress yourself on £5 a week? NO. Will
you accept this little rope of pearls, and come with
me in my Rolls Royce from Sunday morning to Monday afternoon? NO. . . . Will you give me an introduction to Bernard Shaw as I think he might give me
a part in his next play? NO. Do you call yourself a
lady? NO: get out.

The last part of the correspondence, however, is far
from lighthearted. Shaw, who all along felt he was playing Tithonus
to Molly's Aurora, is little aware that she herself can no longer be
the dazzling Mollytompkins. He feels more and more humiliated by
his age. In 1937: "We are now very old (over 80) . . . You mustn't
come near us." In 1942: "The man you knew is dead." But then
comes the letter of 1944, announcing the death of Mrs. Shaw. "I
have had some offers of marriage since, as I am rather a catch
now, having only a few years at most to live (quite probably a
few days). . . ." And then the tremendously moving: "We can write
more freely now that Charlotte can never read our letters. I could
never bring myself to write a line that could hurt her; but now I
can write *anything*." And, almost heartbreaking, the conclusion:
"Goodnight. I can now go to bed as late as I please." But in the
end a kind of humor returns; thus in 1949: "You must cast me off
like a laddered stocking"; and the old autocracy: "You must make
Lawrence remarry you. . . . Let me have no more nonsense about
it; but do as I tell you, both of you."

In this latter part of the correspondence, Peter Tompkins is particularly chary of notes. This leaving a little too much
unsaid is perhaps the one flaw of an otherwise unexceptionable
book. But such a defect can be turned into a virtue: it gives our
imagination leave to fill in the later chapters in the life of that
charming hanger-on of the arts, Molly Tompkins, according to its
predilection.

I know of only one other volume of twentieth-century
letters that compares with *To a Young Actress*: Rilke's *Letters to a
Young Poet*. In both of them the would-be artist is only guessed
at, not heard. The anonymity of Alfred Kapus and Molly Tompkins
serves two great purposes: it makes Rilke and Shaw stand out

more clearly, and it makes them seem to address themselves not to one specific person, but to all of us—to that little bit of the artist that, like Faustus his hell, we all carry with us. But the Shaw volume alone, thanks to its beauty of presentation and faithfulness of reproduction, does justice to its contents.

■

A Little Feverish Joy

■

Belle de Zuylen, who sometimes called herself Zélide, was both an eighteenth- and a twentieth-century heroine.

One of the basic givens of the animal *homo* is that, for all its sapience, it is not rational. Twice in history man has, more or less officially, proclaimed his reason supreme: in classical Greece, the so-called Age of Pericles, and in neo-classical Europe, the even more so-called Age of Reason. Both ages produced their symbolic heroes: Socrates who thought that the syllogism is mightier than the hemlock, and Voltaire who thought that Shakespeare was a babbling savage. To treat one's fellow men as philosopers is as dangerous as to treat poets as barbarians. But one or the other quixotic error will be committed by figureheads of rationalistic eras. Though neither Socrates nor Voltaire tilted with windmills, one was ground exceeding small by the mills of godlessness and the other blown away by the winds of romantic inspiration. There is, in fact, something irrational about putting all one's trust either in dialectic or in diatribe.

No one has shown better than Jacques Barzun in his *Romanticism and the Modern Ego* how irrational in many ways the Age of Reason was. It tightened the belt in one place, and proceeded to bulge in another—the head. And fine swellheads they were who, pretending that common sense is intellect, tried to juggle into an Age of Reason what was at best an age of reasonableness paid for with manifold eccentricities. But delusions are fascinating—even rational delusions. If Sancho had mounted

Rosinante and ridden it in the opposite direction from the Don, but with equal conviction, the result might have been scarcely less absorbing.

Zélide—or Belle de Zuylen, or Isabella van Serooskerken van Tuyll—was a member of a distinguishedly stuffy aristocratic family of Holland. Against the propriety, pompousness, and common sense of her family, country, and age, she was spirited and brilliant enough to react, but to react, unfortunately, in two divergent, indeed opposite, directions. She had to be at once more passionate and more logical than all of them. Now where reason is brought to bear on the passions, it can simply curb them. This is safe, but seldom admirable. Or it can enlist the passions in a grand fight on behalf of reason (or what passes for reason to such an assemblage of passions and sound sense). This is always admirable, and inevitably spells grief if not disaster. Belle de Zuylen's reason attempted to subsume her passions: she became a person of great taste, wit, charm, courage; fearlessly she talked and wrote, in her wonderfully lucid style, about her independent ideas; and was, as a woman, a profound failure.

She was, as I said, a truly eighteenth-century heroine. Having decided, rationally, that marriage was a way to emancipation, she proceeded, none the less, to spurn any number of eligible suitors. With irrational suddenness she fell in love with Constant d'Hermenches, a typical *charmeur,* but alas, a married one. The passionate thing would have been to have an affair with him; the sensible, to forget him. Zélide (the name she assumes in a character sketch of herself) chose neither. She embarked on a long analytical and amorous correspondence with him (passion cautiously and common-sensically deployed) and then started sedulously plotting with him her marriage to his good friend, the mediocre, elderly Marquis de Bellegarde (passion at the service of ostensible common sense). In target shooting, this would have been perfectly logical: if you can't hit the bull's-eye, try for the circle nearest to it.

The earlier part of Geoffrey Scott's *Portrait of Zélide* concentrates on this unsuccessful maneuver, punctuated by passing dalliance with the idea of other potential husbands, among them James Boswell. After four years of heroic and comic intriguing (Zélide actually wrote a letter with which Hermenches, as a well-meaning neutral, was to win over her staunchly Protestant father to a Catholic son-in-law—a letter in which Zélide indulged in some judicious praise of herself) against an unyielding father and an overawed, only faintly interested Marquis, the campaign failed abjectly with the Marquis's polite bowing out. Boswell had been spurned because he was too narrow in his ideas of human and, more particularly, wifely behavior; others were rejected for other reasons, and some did not make a firm proposal. But it was the seductive and scintillating Hermenches whom she had really wanted, and the failure to get his stand-in, Bellegarde, was a terrible blow. The reasonable—or was it the passionate?—thing to do then was to turn about and find a decent, solid, and unexciting man. Such a one was found in M. de Charrière, who was so sensible that he not only tutored Zélide's brothers in mathematics, but was also Swiss. Zélide herself had a passion for algebra, and by some quaint substitution of x for y, the passion was extended from mathematics to the mathematician. But then, as Yeats would have it, how can we tell the dancer from the dance?

Once again neither family nor timid suitor could easily be won over, but her threat of either becoming a nun or marrying a ruthless and shady Scottish lord if thwarted in her designs, finally convinced the Van Tuylls and M. de Charrière. Another suitor of the same period, a M. de Wittgenstein (a name which to twentieth-century eyes epitomizes logic), though eminently suitable and willing, was rejected: Belle felt that, soured by the loss of what she really wanted—or of its shadow—she could only make such an excellent person unhappy. Which did not mean, I should think, that marrying a lesser person would make anyone happier. Still, to commit actions of singular illogic in the name of reason was a distinguishing feature of that age which, with Belle as its eponymous heroine, might well have been called the Age of Zélide.

But I have spoken of Zélide as a twentieth-century heroine as well. Consider this passage from Goeffrey Scott's *Portrait*, which in limpid words appears to describe a situation as eighteenth-century as can be:

> She was twenty-eight: an age which, in the eighteenth century, might well fill a maiden heart with dismay. Her last hopes of the Marquis had vanished; what was to take their place? A marriage of reason, or of inclination? She had thought about it so much that, in her own phrase, she no longer knew what a good marriage meant. She was weary and disillusioned, the prey of conflicting moods; and the morbid activity of her mind entangled each mood in a chain of arguments. She had at different

times reasoned herself into love with Bellegarde and out of love with Hermenches; she could reason herself in or out of anything or anybody. What process should she adopt toward Monsieur de Charrière? The dull routine of the great house at Zuylen gave her the vapours. She relinquished algebra and mechanics and applied herself listlessly to painting. But nothing availed to lighten her neurasthenia.

Here, behind such old-fashioned words as *neurasthenia* and *vapours,* and a classical simplicity of expression, hides a contemporary problem. It is that of the modern woman with intellectual and artistic gifts, who is independent and bright enough to make high matrimonial demands, but who with her very intellect and unconventionality scares away some men, contemns others, and in the resultant neurotic state rejects the possible right man in order to hurl herself at the tragically wrong one. M. de Charrière himself warned Zélide: "You mistake for love what is only a transitory fever of your imagination." In her mind, this should have attached itself to words Boswell had once written her: "If you resign yourself to fancy, you will have now and then a little feverish joy, but no permanent satisfaction." Both men were blaming Belle's imagination; what neither they nor she knew was that this imagination was at fault only in that it tried to serve an inappropriate rationale. And this rationale of yesterday is today's rationalization. Be that as it may, when Belle de Zuylen, at the age of thirty, became Mme. de Charrière, there was an ominous wedding night: the bride was racked by a toothache and the groom was sick from the punch.

And so Zélide, whose graces and matrimonial campaigns had been the delight of princes and despair of proper Dutchmen, who had once fed David Hume beef and plum pudding and been regaled by his ideas, who, if she had steered closer to plum pudding and farther from ideas, might have become Mistress Boswell, ended up as the mistress of a small Swiss country house, Colombier, and lived among an uninteresting husband, his two duller sisters, and their provincial circle.

She had chosen the simple life, and she set herself to live it in all good will. Since Mademoiselle Henriette ruled the saucepans and Mademoiselle Louise was the mistress of the cabbages, gay Madame de Charrière, the admired of princes, the "favourite of Nature" and the ornament of art, betook herself to washing clothes at the fountain in the court. Was it not healthier, she asked, than to talk—and to listen to talk—all day long? . . . And in the evening they played at "Comet," an excellent game, but not the best for Mademoiselle Henriette's temper; or Madame de Charrière would cut silhouettes out of black paper; and Monsieur Chaillet, the interesting young pastor, would drop in and read his sermon on "Spring."

However much Voltaire may have approved of Mme. de Charrière's thus cultivating her garden, or, at any rate, her laundry, this intellectualized enthusiasm could not last. And yet, for a decade and a half there were to be only two diversions.

One was a violent but, as it turned out, wholly wasteful passion for a young man in Geneva whose name, like the details of the episode, remains unknown. But this fiasco was extremely painful to Zélide, and provided people around Colombier, who disapproved of her liberal ideas, with no end of malicious gossip. Not that she cared; any more than she did when she began to write her novels which (though weak in inventive imagination and, consequently, plot) were full of sound judgments and all too penetrating descriptions of real people, and so turned an even greater public against her. The novels scandalized also by their frankly autobiographical aspect, yet what could be more touching than the de profundis of one of these heroines in a letter to her husband: "I am not a rational woman, and we have both discovered it too late." The pathetic irony of it is that in real life, if Mme. de Charrière ever fully made this discovery, she preferred to suppress it.

Still, at the age of forty-seven, Zélide was to get her chance when she met the twenty-year-old, awkward, unstable Benjamin Constant, who made up for those deficiencies by being equally brilliant in psychological analyses, humorous insights, and, ultimately, style. Immediately they fell in love, or, rather, into conversation: "Madame de Charrière seldom went to bed before six in the morning. By day she slept and Benjamin got into mischief. At night they talked about it. To talk! the joy of it. Benjamin's talk is unforeseen, swift like the summer lightning. Before a word is well said he has understood you and answered you out of some new quarter of the sky." They were, apparently, never lovers in the physical sense, but to two such acutely analytical, prolific, and hearty verbalizers, love of talk, or love through talk, was the profoundest kind of love-making.

Disparate as they were in age, they were perfect for each other. Constant's mistresses always had to be older than he; plagued by a father both despotic and absurd, he was clearly in search of that mother who died soon after his birth. And Mme. de Charrière seemed the opposite of his father: rational and yet indulgent. As for Zélide, for her this was an *embarras de richesses*. Benjamin was the nephew of that Constant d'Hermenches, the great love of her youth, and he was young enough to be her child. The Italian humorist Massimo Bontempelli once wrote of a princess who was so ethereal that she had to enter a room twice in order to be in it. So, more seriously, Zélide needed a man to come to her doubly, as son and as lover, to penetrate all her defenses. Against the spontaneity of the youth, coupled with the nascent genius of a great writer, thinker, orator, and statesman, no irrationally rational temporization could prevail.

Into the story of their eight years of *amitié amoureuse* I will not go: it is related so well by Geoffrey Scott that to tell it in any other way seems to me, if not exactly sacrilege, at least *lèse-majesté*. The bare outlines, of course, may be rehearsed here —they are as moving in their naked irony as the bare branches of a winter tree against a sky reminiscent of summer: how Constant was forced by his father to live far away from Zélide; how she, fearing to lose him because of the two great distances, chronological and geographic, proceeded to harden her heart and write drier and drier letters; how it was she who urged Constant to look up Germaine de Staël who admired her, but whom they had both scoffed at; and how, when Constant fell under the spell of Mme. de Staël's vulgar but undeniable attractions, Zélide's pride and fastidiousness forbade her to recoup a love she so desperately needed, easily reclaimable as it might have been.

Scott is fully aware of both the psychological reasons and the cultural implications of what happened. Psychologically, Zélide was a rationalist, a spectator who "forgot that life is a theatre built without an auditorium"; whereas Constant, for all his destructive self-analysis, learned, as Scott quotes him, that "in standing aside and seeing nothing but the absurdity of things one touches no depths." Culturally speaking, in Mme. de Staël, Constant embraced—both figuratively and literally—the rising power of the romantic movement, which was beginning to make a clean sweep of that rationalism Mme. de Charrière embodied. But the supremacy of Constant's masterpiece *Adolphe* lies in combining with the breast-baring and intense self-involvement of the nineteenth-century romantic, the lapidary lucidity of an eighteenth-century aphorist. And reading *The Portrait of Zélide*, one realizes how in those endless nocturnal *tête-à-têtes*, when Constant sat talking with Mme. de Charrière on the crimson-covered bed in which she lay, his restless genius was truly born, in a rutilant ambience similar to that in which the Byzantine emperor-to-be, the *porphyrogenetos*, was born to an empress in a chamber of porphyry.

But it is not of Constant's greatness, nor of Zélide's wistful decline among a motley assortment of human nonentities (for whom she cared most humanely, though a bit autocratically) that I want to talk now. I want to conclude with some words about Geoffrey Scott, who in a book of barely more than 200 pages has written one of the few classic biographies. He may owe his success to his having been a poet and architect as well as a prose writer, and having thus discovered that solid structure and succinctness, buttressed by style, can produce a masterpiece of prose. It is a clear, cerebral, fluent prose, whose character perfectly matches that of the eighteenth century, even in its occasionally somewhat fantastical metaphors. Just as there are sins of omission, there are virtues of omission: in Scott's book there are very few dates, minimal backgrounds, almost nothing is said about antecedents (none of that favorite biographer's game of reporting in detail how the grandfather's second cousin by marriage had once . . . etc. etc.), nothing about famous contemporaries except when strictly necessary to the matter at hand, and about the events of the time, even if they happened to be the French Revolution, only what is pertinent to Zélide. Lionel Trilling has reminded us cogently of Scott's debt as a biographer to Lytton Strachey; I would merely like to add that Scott too seems to have fathered a school of biographers of "quiet lives" like David Cecil and Marchette Chute.

There are in *The Portrait of Zélide* a few minor flaws, such as the mock-epic device by which the author invokes "the gods" or evokes "the spirits of irony" reflecting on human actions. Such devices are outmoded, as are certain images like "a tragic harlequin" or that of time passing "on silver wheels, while the light of dawn dimmed the guttering candles." I could also do without the stagey curtain lines with which some chapters are made to end—but all this is insignificant compared to the gems of quotation and description, tied together by tersely elegant narrative and comment, that are the substance of this work.

I cannot refrain from quoting two immaculate vignettes. This of M. de Charrière:

> Monsieur de Charrière was in truth a very monument to the indissolubility of marriage. Year in, year out, he displayed, like a good Swiss clock, the same meticulous correctness, the same unchanging regularity. On the even dial of his face no emotion could be discerned. He spoke, in order to control his stammer, with an inhuman, a clock-like distinctness. There he sat between his two sisters, always accurate, always courteous, always reasonable, always there. To Madame de Charrière he may have seemed like some relentless, impassive mechanism, timing, registering, and remorselessly exhausting the counted hours of her life.

And this paraphrase from Constant:

> Benjamin, aware with customary self-knowledge of every working of his mind, makes the penetrating reflection that dramatic and sudden actions are no index of decision of character: on the contrary, the absence of any capacity for decision, and the corresponding sensation that nothing you do is really done, lands you neatly in the decisive fact on which at no moment can you be said to have decided. . . .

Yes, Mme. de Charrière was a supreme rationalist. To the doomed royal couple of France she could send little fables advocating "an almost passionate commonsense and a kind of scornful moderation." And this "passionate commonsense" led Mme. de Charrière to the two symbolic fallacies with which I began my essay: treating men as philosophers, and poets as barbarians. Zélide could spend hours daily teaching her maid Latin and the works of John Locke; it drove the girl no less quickly into the arms of a valet (named, by a coincidence nothing less than symbolic, Racine) and, when she became an illegitimate mother, into government-decreed exile. And when Zélide came, in the writings of Mme. de Staël, upon the poetic oxymoron "contemporary posterity," she considered it a vile catachresis and shut the book with a shudder. These, surely, are flaws, but as a French adage has it, we love a woman for her virtues, but adore her for her faults. In Mme. de Charrière at least, the failings of rational-

66

ism were adorable. So much so that her most scholarly biographer, Professor Godet, neglected his wife for the sake of this long-dead lady to whom he dedicated years of passionate research and writing. I do not know if Geoffrey Scott neglected anyone for the sake of *The Portrait of Zélide;* he certainly remembered all the needs of his readers.

■

Nowhere Is Washing So Well Done

■

Since the poetic frontier between Britain and America runs smack through T. S. Eliot and W. H. Auden, I can, happily for my argument, consign them to a temporary no man's land while I assert that Robert Graves is the greatest living English poet. But Graves is also a prose writer of imposing stature and variety. Let me begin with the variety, as the more immediately demonstrable. His numerous writings include novels whose subjects range from history through utopian fantasy to mystery, short stories, drama, literary criticism, miscellaneous essays, biography and autobiography, travel notes, sociology, mythology, religion, translations, and, appropriately enough, an excellent handbook for writers of English prose.

The admirable thing about Graves the poet and Graves the prose writer is that there is no fence between them. Graves is a complete human being (which, in our world, is hardly a commonplace), full of enthusiasms, crotchets, odd loyalties and crackling prejudices, vast learning of the most unlikely sort, and an overarching sense of humor. All this, indivisibly—though, of course, in varying degree—manifests itself in everything he writes. Unlike Eliot, whose earlier poems bear no family likeness to his later *machines* (as the French call overblown and synthetic compositions), anything Graves wrote after his juvenilia is kissing kin with any other work of his, in prose or verse. To the prerequisite for all knowledge, a prodigious memory, he adds the essential poetic faculty, to perceive parallels, and the essential critical faculty, to perceive contrasts and differences. Because Graves's mind works like a tremendous photomontage, he is able to grasp the interrelationships of ideas and perceptions; he can see the connection between, say, an ancient Irish rune and a modern Italian custom, between a snatch of contemporary poetry and a passage in Macrobius or the Talmud. To reconcile the eternal and the diurnal, as he said in writing about Cummings, is the function of the true poet. This decompartmentalized way of seeing leads Graves to daring deductions and theories which, whether or not one wholly agrees with them, have a fructifying effect on the mind.

Why, then, is Graves not generally recognized as the literary giant he is? First, because despite a delightful and largely conversational style, he can be difficult to read. The lazy or uneducated reader may be put off by references to Welsh bards, Aztec customs, Alexandrian poets, medieval scholiasts, Greek inscriptions, a mistake in the translation of the Vulgate, and the like, all within one essay. The more erudite reader, who can follow the argument with ease but is not himself a polymath, may resent being spellbound by something he has not sufficient knowledge to agree or disagree with. The scholar himself—infuriated by the fact that though in his own special field he may know as much or more, he none the less lacks this author's breadth and imaginative penetration—will latch on to some trivial error or unprovable conjecture of Graves's and try to dismiss him altogether. This is what happened when the anonymous reviewer (doubtless some Oxford or Cambridge theologian) of *The Nazarene Gospel Restored* and the co-authors Graves and Joshua Podro clashed in perhaps the longest and most fascinating exchange of letters in *The Times Literary Supplement*. T. S. Eliot knew better when, confronted with Graves's *The White Goddess*, he said that only a man of Mr. Graves's learning could evaluate the book, and, on that basis, he knew of none other than Mr. Graves himself who could qualify.

Again, there is a body of literary snobs, or *petits-maîtres*, who think that anyone who writes as much as Graves cannot possibly be a good writer. The prescribed output for a major poet, nowadays, is a sizable volume of collected poems, a companion volume of collected literary criticism, and, scattered about, some uncollected pieces, soon to be, nevertheless, triumphantly collected. It is therefore inconceivable that someone whose writings cover everything from *Homer's Daughter* to the

Wife to Mr. Milton, from mythology to mycology, from a hilarious essay on *The Future of Swearing* to an iconographic retrospect called *Adam's Rib,* from Byzantium to the War of Independence, could be a serious writer. Yet it must be stressed: Graves is a polyglot and a polyhistor, but not a polygrapher. Being a writer by both vocation and avocation, he has simply more time to write than such major poets who are or were also bankers, publishers, professors, or insurance men.

But perhaps the most widely disconcerting feature of Graves is his individualism. His ideas cannot be pigeonholed, his personality resists being categorized. He is equally apt to tear holes in Christianity as in atheism, he will exonerate marihuana and poke fun at mescalene, and he will deride the academically accepted idols of English poetry: Milton, Wordsworth, and Yeats. There is no form of iconoclasm that he cannot be accused of—except that of breaking windows from the outside (to use his own metaphor); he breaks them only from the inside to chase out the stifling staleness. Thus Graves is neither a member of a literary coterie, nor the mentor of an ideological clique. It follows that he cannot cash in on either of today's great formulas for success: the mutual admiration society or stellarization by fan mail.

Graves's weapons tend to be satire and irony, neither of which is understood or tolerated by middlebrow culture. The quality Aristotle called *eutrapelia* was once redefined as "the justifiable arrogance of the superior" by Oscar Wilde, who promptly arrogated it. Graves too has his *eutrapelia* which, in his case, is an intolerance of humbug or stupidity, and insouciance about public opinion. Observe this statement from "The Cult of Tolerance" (1936): "The remarkable result of some sixty years of popular education has been that practically no illiterates are left, and that practically no literates are left either; nearly everyone is semiliterate, as the suburb has superseded the town and the country." The Coriolanian position is even more pronounced in his foreword to *Poems 1938-1945,* surely the shortest and very possibly the most brilliant preface ever written, and one that Dylan Thomas was fond of reading aloud during poetry readings, as though it were itself a poem. Here it is entire:

> Since poems should be self-explanatory I refrain
> from more foreword than this: that I write poems
> for poets, and satires or grotesques for wits. For
> people in general I write prose, and am content

that they should be unaware that I do anything else. To write poems for other than poets is wasteful. The moral of the Scilly Islanders who earned a precarious livelihood by taking in one another's washing is that they never upset their carefully balanced island economy by trying to horn into the laundry trade of the mainland; and that nowhere in the Western Hemisphere was washing so well done.

The trouble is that too many "people in general" treat even Graves's prose as though it were written in hexameters.

This brings us to the pleasant purpose which *Food for Centaurs* serves. It is a collection of Graves's more recent stories, talks, critical studies, and poems. *Food for Centaurs*, then, is a group of parerga, a sort of by-product of his more heroic labors—but precisely therein lies its great usefulness: it is the perfect introduction to the work of Robert Graves. Almost every piece in this book is not only a delectable miniature, to be recommended to all readers, whether intimate with Graves or not, but also a valuable introduction to one or another of his larger works. The book thus affords not only its intrinsic pleasure but also the convenience of a sample case of Gravesiana, permitting one to decide there and then from which direction one would prefer to approach so many-sided a genius. You may, for instance, be especially attracted by such pieces as "What Was That War Like, Sir?" or "The Butcher and the Cur," and from these proceed to that great autobiography and shattering account of World War I, *Good-bye to All That*. The excitement of unscrambling the truth about the Emperor Claudius's demise in "New Light on an Old Murder" will lead to those superb novels *I, Claudius* and *Claudius the God*. From an enthusiasm for items like "To Be a Goy" or "Legends of the Bible," one will be drawn into Graves's Biblical reinterpretations: *King Jesus, Jesus in Rome*, and *The Nazarene Gospel Restored*. From such dazzling essays as "The Making and Marketing of Poetry," "Preface to a Reading of Poems," and "Pulling a Poem Apart," one will be propelled to those two important volumes of literary criticism, *The Common Asphodel* and, bitterer and more heretical, *The Crowning Privilege*. If one is particularly captivated by pieces like "Centaur's Food," "The Fifth Column at Troy," or "Sweeney Among the Blackbirds," one will hasten to that central book, *The White Goddess*, or to *The Greek Myths* and *The Anger of Achilles*,

and to such astounding novels as *Hercules, My Shipmate* and
Watch the North Wind Rise. And so on. But what about *Food for
Centaurs* by and for itself?

The book begins with a handful of short stories,
most of them taking place in Majorca, where Graves lives. The
author usually appears as a minor character or silent observer,
and whereas the stories as stories may be a little forced and
improbable, the descriptions of peculiar local types are pungent
and often murderously funny. Take, for instance, the eccentric
Majorcan aristocrat who defines "the enemy" as follows:

> Those who smoke blond tobacco; those who
> strew our quiet Majorcan beaches with pink, peeling
> human flesh; those who roar round the island in for-
> eign cars ten metres long; those who prefer alumi-
> num to earthenware, and plastics to glass; those
> who demolish the old quarters of Palma and erect
> travel agencies, souvenir shops, and tall, barrack-
> like hotels on the ruins; those who keep their radios
> bawling incessantly along the street at siesta time;
> those who swill Caca-Loco and bottled beer!

Perhaps the only unreal character in this gathering of Spanish
grandees and peasants, and Anglo-American expatriates, is Ava
Gardner, who makes a brief appearance. But, then, she is probably non-existent—a mere Hollywood symbol of the White
Goddess.

We come next to some talks on poetry which might
be the best place for anyone to start reading this book. Graves's
eminently sane view of poetry appears here ("to me, poetry is
truth-telling," he wrote in *Occupation: Writer*), along with much
else that is of lively interest. Consider an observation on modern
cities which runs in part:

> Old-fashioned, hand-constructed cities are safer
> to work in and to make love in; since they suffer
> less from rectangularity, rectolinearity, and the mer-
> cilessly perfect circle. One day, perhaps, architects
> will realize with a startled 'Oh!' that a major func-
> tion of functionally-designed houses and offices is
> to preserve the mental health of the inhabitants;
> whereupon they will try to counteract the monotony
> of the rectangle and the straight line by inventing
> machines capable of building houses and offices
> with a slight curve or a wobble. However, the hu-

man eye will not be deceived; only man's fallible hand can pleasurably serve it with lines and curves that convey a *living* waywardness. One great fault of modern building-technique is that hard timber has fallen into disuse. Steel is exploited, the cruellest of metals; lifeless concrete; frivolous plastics. But hardly any timber; few stones even. And no love at all.

There follows a group entitled "Studies in History" for which the label, as any label for anything Graves does, proves inadequate. Even though these were occasional pieces on a multiplicity of subjects, the marvelous thing about them, besides their wit and acuity, is the healthy consistency of the spirit that informs them. Whether he is writing about *poltergeists* in "Praise Me and I Will Whistle to You!" or about "Was Benedict Arnold a Traitor?" Graves is always providing the cure for the ailment he diagnosed in *The Greek Myths:* "What seems to be lacking today is centripetal, rather than centrifugal, scholarship." No other writer of our time can make the greatest possible diversity become so wholly of one piece.

Then comes "Critiques of New Books" in which the ever-amazing Graves writes with original insight on subjects like dope addiction (in "Maenads, Junkies and Others") and incompetent attempts at historical fiction by men like Rex Warner; there is also an amused and amusing assessment of Bertrand Russell's and Julian Huxley's freethinking, and a warning about the hero worship of Carl Jung, "The Archetypal Wise Old Man," whom (like that other greybeard, Nestor, lampooned in a poem of this volume) he takes down a few notches. The book ends with some recent poems which, as Graves wittily says, fall short of his past masterpieces. And yet, *Trudge, Body* (a revision of an earlier poem), *Heroes in Their Prime,* and *Old World Dialogue* are by no means inconsiderable.

Graves has his faults also. There is his occasional inaccuracy, his jumping to conclusions—usually where he is not particularly interested in his topic. Thus he will misidentify Sweeney's female companion in Eliot's "Sweeney Erect" as the protagonist's wife—when among "the ladies of the corridor," as also in heaven, no marriage is. Or, because he wants to force it into a large-scale argument, he comes up with an unconvincing interpretation of the "little foxes" passage from *The Song of Songs.* There is also his intolerance for most rival contemporary poets, which, in this book, is illustrated by the unappreciative obituary on Roy Campbell. Whereas Graves is brilliantly and convincingly able to extenuate the guilt of a Benedict Arnold, indeed of Judas himself, for fellow-poets like Campbell and Pound he has no mercy.

But such flaws, serious as they can become, are minimized by the fact that Graves is the only poet of our time whose work in verse and prose consistently contributes to a new, or newly rediscovered, philosophy of art, world view, and religion—in the cult of the White Goddess, a *Weltanschauung* that, for me, surpasses Blake's and Yeats's attempts at a poetic working model of the universe. It may be that, if one is devilishly learned, one can find a number of mere conjectures, of half-truths in Graves's argument. But on subjects of such existential and eschatological importance, to learn things that are even 50 per cent true—just think, not 10, 20, or 30, as is usual, but fully 50!—this is not to be sneezed at. "M'illumino/ d'immenso," goes a gnomic poem by the contemporary Italian poet Ungaretti: "I light up with immensity." Even the mere possibility of the Gravesian conception being right should illumine our inner horizons with the persistence of a midnight sun.

What this Gravesian world view is, I cannot even begin to explain here. Readers of *Food for Centaurs* will get some introductory awareness of it. But what shines from almost every page of this book is the singularly potent blend of Intellect and Imagination. Take this paragraph:

> 'No, ma'am,' said the ticket-inspector, 'no ma'am! Cats is dogs, and rabbits is dogs, and dogs is dogs, and squirrels in cages is parrots; but this here turkle is a hinsect. We won't charge you nothing, ma'am!' For me, dogs is dogs, cats is cats—who would think of exhibiting a pedigree Siamese at a dog show?—prose is prose, and experimental writing is experimental writing. But poetry is poetry. It makes certain minimum requirements on the poet.

It is really too bad that even today Graves is a fine and private place, for more than a few of us could there embrace revelations of stunning refulgence.

■

Unlucky Pierres

■

Today's most revolutionary fiction is the *alittérature* (non-literature) written by the so-called "antinovelists" of France. Man is no longer viewed as an actor on the stage of life, but as a plant, microorganism, or atom gravitating according to obscure formulas of physics and biochemistry. Leaders of this movement are Nathalie Sarraute, Alain Robbe-Grillet, Marguerite Duras, and Michel Butor whose new book, *Degrees,* is perhaps the most complex antinovel to date. For, paradoxically, by some mysterious, aliterary law, the more schematic and mechanistic an author's view of life, the more complicated and device-ridden his style.

A page of *Degrees* may look like a page of the Bible with long run-on verses, or a surrealist prose poem, or highly idiosyncratic free verse, or a laundry list. Sometimes it may even look like a page in a novel. In this story within a story a paragraph will begin "Now (actually months ago)"; and there are parentheses within parentheses, so that a question asked on page 126 is answered on page 148. One sentence may refer to three different times, skip backward and forward to three or four unrelated events, be spoken or written down (one does not know which) by either of two characters impersonating another. A New York FM station features a program called "Music Not to Read By"; Butor's book is "Prose Not to Read By."

The novel deals with a Paris high-school teacher, Pierre Vernier, who keeps a minute-by-minute log of all that happens in his eleventh-grade geography class in which his nephew Pierre Eller, is a student. Vernier is obsessed by the need to record the *total* experience: this drives him to include, first, accounts of other students and teachers, then of their families and friends, then of their past and future lives. Next, the compulsive Vernier must procure the manuals and textbooks for all the courses these students are taking, to bone up on them, and to include parts of them in his chronicle. Hence at least half of *Degrees* is taken up with quotations from textbooks, classroom recitation, synopses of lectures, transcripts of homework including mathematical problems complete with errors and corrections, and bits of such surreptitious reading as science fiction.

In order to record out-of-school events, even secret thoughts and dreams, as well as concealed classroom activities and whispered exchanges, Vernier must gather information from his colleagues, occasionally invent things, and, reluctantly, enroll his nephew, Pierre, as a spy. In the first part of *Degrees*, Vernier writes from his own point of view: he is "I" and Pierre is "you." In the second part, it gradually emerges that things have been reversed: Vernier is "you" and Pierre is "I." But it is not Pierre writing—it is Vernier writing for and as Pierre. In the third part, the real identity of the writer, or writers, cannot be determined. Throughout, incidents from curiously arid, sexless lives are interlarded with quotations from the stultifying curriculum, and all this repeated over and over again, with tiny variations, as many as half a dozen times or more. It is obvious that, to achieve this, Butor—like Vernier—must have used diagrams, filing cabinets, extensive research into high-school studies, and a private system of advanced algebra:

> During the evening, you began writing the text that I am continuing, or more precisely that *you* are continuing by using *me*, for actually, it's not I who is writing but you, you are speaking *through* me, trying to see things from my point of view, to imagine what I could know that you don't know, furnishing me the information which you possess and which would be out of my reach.

When the three pages worth of story finally end on page 351, even violence and tragedy come as relief.

Butor's novel, in its attempt to encapsule forever a chunk of reality, is as unreal as a fly enclosed in a glass globe. The fly becomes magnified beyond its importance, and the revolving globe presents the insect from angles irrelevant to human experience. Moreover, the whirling glass dizzies and loses the audience, and, worst of all, the fly is dead. Like Pierre Vernier, Butor is hopelessly obsessed with the need to live out within himself a whole group of related lives that seem to multiply by geometric progression. The result is that instead of the author writing the book, the book writes the author. And that is chaos.

Some of the antinovelists seem to be motivated by nothing more than a craving for the new and different; others, unable to deal with genuine human feelings, escape into atomizing and itemizing; still others think that a "scientific" approach is nowadays a guarantee of high seriousness. In Butor's method there is, at least, genuine madness. But not even the most maniacal scrutiny of cell after cell will permit anyone to see the tree—to say nothing of the forest.

Almost as a Prophet

We read *The Journal of Christopher Columbus* with something more than mere interest: we read it with curiosity. For who would not thrill at the sudden discovery in his attic of ancestral diaries belonging to that forefather to whom one's lineage can be traced? Whatever discord may jaundice one's view of immediate forebears, the distant retrospect at the founder of one's line can produce nothing but shudders of delicious anticipation—or whatever the antonym of "anticipation" might be. It matters little if Columbus was the father of us all not by blood but by resourcefulness, daring, and luck—by geography rather than by genealogy—the fact remains that it is thanks to him that the bottom fell *into* our world. Even if in some respects he had no leg to stand on, we, without him, would have no ground on which to stand. It is therefore of little importance that the Journal is somewhat sketchier and drier than we might wish it, for it stimulates our imagination as strongly and felicitously as some of the finest works of fiction.

The sketchiness, or, more exactly, the foreshortening, is caused by the fact that this is to a large extent only a précis of the Journal, made by the Dominican historian Bartolomé de las Casas in the middle of the sixteenth century. (I think we can discount the allegations that Las Casas indulged in any falsifying or tampering.) What Las Casas did was to summarize wherever summary seemed indicated, and to transcribe wherever Columbus's remarks seemed to warrant full quotation. It would be idle to debate the Dominican's judgment in this matter; his abstract is all that remains today of the Journal, and something, in this case, is vastly better than nothing. The presentation has at least a certain dramatic value, reminiscent of some radio plays: the impersonal voice of the historian-narrator is superseded, suddenly and dramatically, by the personal, impassioned voice of the Admiral.

The Journal, or ship's log, as it comes down to us, becomes, first of all, a portrait of Columbus. We see his sentimental side when he repeatedly refers to the journey into the unknown as perfect: warm weather, smooth sailing—nothing lacking except the song of the nightingale! It is with similarly endearing naïveté that he keeps insisting that he has not praised some newly discovered land to the hundredth part of its value, or that a thousand tongues would not suffice for the telling of its beauties and wonders. At the height of this simple lyricism he will exclaim that "all is as green . . . as . . . Andalusia in April. The singing of little birds is such that it seems that a man could never wish to leave this place; the flocks of parrots darken the sun. . . " We see him as a shrewd strategist, too: keeping twofold reckoning of the distance covered sailing westward—one truthful, and one considerably reduced for the benefit of the men's morale. Or, again, interpreting a ground swell as a miracle of the Lord, comparable to the parting of the Red Sea for Moses; this also to boost the crew's sagging spirits. He is an optimist, and can turn anything into a positive omen: if he finds a lump of wax in an Indian hut, he immediately declares that where there is wax, there must be a thousand other good things; from the tiniest bit of gold leaf in an Indian's nose he deduces the nearness of large quantities of the precious metal.

But there is also a frightening ambivalence in the Admiral's attitude. On the one hand, he admires the virtuousness of the Indians. They are "a people so full of love and without greed . . . that I believe that there is no better race or better land in the whole world. They love their neighbors as themselves, and they have the softest and gentlest voices in the world, and they are always smiling." Some of the young women are very beautiful and "as white as any that could be found in Spain," and all of them could, if taught to wear clothes and thus to avoid suntans, be as white as any *hidalgo*. The land is an "earthly paradise" whose inhabitants give "with a great readiness to give." Therefore, Ferdinand and Isabella "may believe that in all the world there cannot be a people better or more gentle. Your Highnesses should feel great joy, because they will presently become Christians and will be educated in the good customs of your realms. . . ." And they are to become servants or, as he plainly says in one place, slaves of Spain.

What are we to make of this Admiral who had just seen the Jews driven out of Spain because they could not be converted, whose crew had mutinied, who could barely restrain his men from immediately exploiting and maltreating the Indians, who was even then being treacherously abandoned by one of his seconds-in-command—what are we to make of this man who could be so charmed by this earthly paradise as to want to subject it promptly to the hell he was bringing with him? Yet he was well-meaning and careful, hoping that those who would stay among the Indians would "know how to govern themselves," himself doing his best to be generous to the natives (although secretly pleased each time he made an outrageous bargain with them)—a man who, according to the Dominican Las Casas, "had assuredly much reason and spoke as a prudent man and almost as a prophet." Yet without being ruthless like the conquistadores who came after him, he was no humanist like More who could see Utopia in the life of these Indians, or Montaigne who could rise to their eloquent defense. No, immediately after praising them, Columbus refers to the Indians as "naked and without arms, and very cowardly beyond hope of change." Another Indian tribe, of whom he hears that they come as cannibals and enslavers, seem to him "fearless people, not like the others . . . who are cowardly . . . and without weapons." These cannibals must "have greater intelligence," he thinks, "than they to capture them," *they* being the gentle-voiced, ever-smiling ones among whom "all took a share in what any one had. . . ." How small a great man can be.

But the Journal is also an account of what it feels like to become a god (for the Indians believed the Spaniards came from heaven) and also Man in his first freedom and glory, with a whole world to explore, to feast on, to name and define. Much of this sense of limitless potentiality comes through in the words, even though Columbus, as he readily admits, lacked the skill to do his experiences justice in writing. Yet at least the writing is so simple as to be transparent, and we can visualize, as it were, behind it the superb land and seascapes, the figures of the Admiral, the noble and devoted Indian prince, Guacana-garí, the feckless Pinzón of the *Pinta*, the clumsy cabin boy who lost the *Santa Maria*, and the various deeds, motives, and relation-ships. In this we are greatly helped by the many excellent contemporary maps and prints, some of which are quaint and amusing, and some of which are genuine works of art. Most fascinating, though, are the deductions to be made from seem-ingly harmless statements made in perfect innocence, like "the admiral believed that he was very near the source of the gold and that Our Lord would show him where it originated." Or the revelation that when, on the return journey, a terrible storm threatened their lives, Columbus and the crew of the *Niña* four times drew lots to determine who would undertake four great pilgrimages if they were not to be drowned—and three times it was the Admiral who drew the chickpea he himself had marked. After a great triumph, the great humility, too, must be his.

Perhaps the one thing lacking from this tale, besides nightingales (though Columbus happily mistook the New World's mockingbird for the bird he so missed), is humor, something both the Admiral and his men were extremely short on. Yet even this sneaks into the Journal inadvertently, as when Columbus observes "the land is so rich that there is no need for them to labour much to get themselves food and clothing, especially as they go naked." So, too, the Admiral comments on some manatees he glimpsed that these "sirens . . . were not as beautiful as depicted, for some-how their faces had the appearance of a man."

"Où est le Christophe Colomb à qui on devra l'oubli d'un continent?" wondered the poet Guillaume Apollinaire, to whom it seemed more important that continents be forgotten than discovered, for there was so much of the old in our world as to choke off the new. The Columbus to whom oblivion of a continent was to be owed, however, was precisely this Don Cristóbal Colón who began a shift of emphasis toward a New World, much of whose glory was to stem from its ability to forget, however in-completely, the existence of the Old.

■

Here Comes There Goes You Know Who

■

In the early nineteen-thirties Americans were being saturated with "tough" writing: *Studs Lonigan* was going strong, as was Dos Passos' *U.S.A.*; on a higher level there was *Death in the Afternoon* as well as *Sanctuary* and *Light in August*; on a lower, *Tobacco Road*. Upon all this hardness, rawness, and ache a volume of stories descended in 1934: *The Daring Young Man on the Flying Trapeze,* by a young man of 26, William Saroyan. It descended almost like a balm, for it was a mixture of love and pity and humor: pity and humor for everyone, especially bums and prostitutes, and love for life, no matter how preposterous. This was so different from the other writings of the day that it was readily forgiven its sentimentality and cuteness, even its occasional mawkishness. If it was writing that perhaps lacked bite, at least it did not gnash its teeth at you; if the prose was not exactly muscular, it had plenty of heart, and the heart, as everyone knows, is an involuntary muscle, and cannot, need not be flexed.

Since 1934, Saroyan has turned out generous quantities of short stories, novels, and plays—some of them delightful, some of them arch; and not a few—especially the more recent ones—lifeless. At his best, when dealing with children, Armenian Americans, assorted odd-balls and poets without portfolio, he has won himself a modest but lasting place in our literature; at his worst, whenever he gets involved in Issues or Ideas (both with capital I's), he falls flatter than Bahgh-arch, the Armenian flat bread. There is a third capitalized I that has proven fatal to Saroyan: the plain, unsimple I of his boundless ego. It is to this, and to his considerable tax debt, that we owe his new book, *Here Comes There Goes You Know Who,* which the publishers hopefully label "an autobiography," but which belongs to a genre somewhere in between Bulfinch and Paul Bunyan (the latter, judging by that final -yan, doubtless also of Armenian extraction).

The book consists of 52 vignettes, partaking in form of the short-short story, the pseudophilosophical essay, and the mnemonic exercise. It may be that the number 52 is significant beyond the fact that it was Saroyan's age at the time of writing, and that the pieces were intended as Dr. Saroyan's sermons for the new year, one for every Sunday. The writing, at any rate, is that of a Sunday writer, but one who can do a fairly good take-off on William Saroyan. He tries, moreover, to improve on his original by means of a slight admixture of avant-garde spice. The result is apt to read like this: "I began a moment ago by implying there was something to say, something to be said, something to *have* said after half a century since the arrival of memory in my life, since the arrival therefore of myself into it. I have tried to say, I have meant to say, I have believed I might say, but I know I haven't said, and while it doesn't trouble me, or at any rate not violently, as it would have troubled me thirty-five years ago when I wanted to say everything in one swift inevitable book, it also doesn't please me, and I feel that I must try again."

The vignettes ramble through Saroyan's life in no particular order, but they tend to bunch up at both ends, thus dealing mostly with his childhood and puberty and the present, i.e., his early fifties. The years in between are virtually absent. In the first half of the book we are treated mostly to anecdotes from the family album, from the author's years in an orphanage, and, later, school. There are anecdotes also about his first employers, various quaint acquaintances and frenetic friends. The latter part of the book, much less interesting, deals with the author's unpaid income tax, gambling, life and death, popular metaphysics ("The guileless are by that very fact not less *capable* of guile but more. And I am not sure that *having* guile is not finally much more guileless than not having it."), Saroyan's son and daughter, travels and life abroad, and those two great mythic figures, The Tax Collector and William Saroyan the Universal Genius ("My plays *are* the human race. And most of the plays of the other playwrights aren't." "My own [writing] which nobody's writing will outlive . . . will be discovered again and again. It will speak . . . as long as any writing speaks to anybody." "To sum up, I am great, and I am proud to be great. It is quite a responsibility."). But for all this genuine conceit Saroyan makes up with an equal amount of false modesty.

Other sections of *Here Comes* might be classified as "An Armenian Cookbook" containing invaluable recipes, and "The Correct Letter-Writer," containing sample letters showing how to answer a chiseling movie producer, the Passport Office, and teen-age fans.

This is not to say that here and there a bit of the old, good Saroyan does not peep through. There is the speculation on what Saroyan senior must have done immediately upon Willie's arrival: "I suppose he was picking grapes, and I hope every now and then he was stopping to eat them." Or this, part of a lengthy numerological meditation: "3000 hasn't got that little extra something that is the difference between a great piano player like Richter, for instance, and a poor piano player like my cousin Hoosik, who is actually a lawyer." Or: "You are never under any circumstance to speak discourteously to your mother, as that is not only un-American, it is un-Chinese." But the old, pure, wonderfully hammy love for all humanity is lacking. Saroyan writes: "In the end, anything worth anything comes from love," but continues: "even when it looks a lot like hate." And, sure enough, there is no lack of hate in *Here Comes*. Herewith, in alphabetical order, a list, probably incomplete, of Saroyan's pet peeves: actors, Sherwood Anderson (in his later years), bankers, Bernard Baruch, best sellers, great men, high-school principals, insurance policyholders, lawyers, leaders, Mount Rushmore, New Yorkers, playwrights (Saroyan excluded), psychiatrists, Shakespeare (not altogether), Shaw (ditto), successes, tapioca, teachers, the world.

There are, of course, those (Saroyan included) who will remind you all the same what a great lover of humanity Saroyan is. One thing is certain: with a lover like this, humanity needs no enemy. To say more against *Here Comes*, and interfere with Saroyan's paying off his debt to Uncle Sam, would be not only ungracious, it would be un-American.

■

From Waste to Wonderland

■

Some people write books; others, palimpsests. Foremost among English palimpsest writers are Joyce, Pound, and Eliot. What are *The Waste Land*, the *Cantos*, *Finnegans Wake* if not layers over layers of literary fragments shored against our ruins—bodies of myth coated with universal history coated with personal experience? To these three names must be added, though not quite on equal footing, that of David Jones, the Anglo-Welsh painter and writer, whose first work, *In Parenthesis*, was issued for the first time in America in 1962, an even quarter-century after its original publication.

In Parenthesis is the account of seven months with the Welsh Fusileers from the winter of 1915 to the summer of 1916: from the author's enlistment to his getting wounded in the Battle of the Somme. Death, thought E. E. Cummings, is no parenthesis; but the death-in-life of trench warfare, to David Jones, was the most constricting and pointless of parenthetic existences—although a glorious one, too. "For the old authors," Jones writes in his preface, "there appears to have been no such dilemma"; no dilemma, that is, between "the embrace of battle" and "the embrace of a lover." For Jones, the dilemma did exist: he suffered acutely, but the experience of war united him with the world of epic, legend, and myth, which his Welsh temperament embraced with the same mystical glee with which it later espoused Roman Catholicism. Out of this was born In Parenthesis, a poetic narrative that interweaves with personal recollections of war, scenes and passages from the Mabinogion, the Morte d'Arthur, The Song of Roland, Anglo-Saxon heroic poems and Icelandic Sagas, the Bible and Jessie Weston, Catholic ritual and The Golden Bough.

When Jones started working on In Parenthesis in 1928, The Waste Land was six years old, the Cantos had been appearing at irregular intervals since 1919, and the installments of Finnegans Wake had been coming out for some four years. Jones, a fastidiously snail-like worker, was to spend several years on the 187 pages of In Parenthesis, and it was not till 1937 that the book saw publication—for which, it seems, its author never intended it, but yielded, at last, to the pressure of friends.

From Eliot, Jones seems to get, along with certain highly characteristic cadences, the concept of the mythical, historic, and literary parallels, as well as the idea of appending explanatory notes—34 pages of them—often of a fairly cryptic nature. In one of these he refers to Eliot as "the greatest English poet of our own time," a compliment which Mr. Eliot handsomely repays in his introduction to In Parenthesis, which he calls "a work of genius," thereby legitimizing his intellectual offspring. From Pound, Jones derives what I would term "creative archaism": using words from various phases or dialects of the English language in order to incorporate the twin exoticisms of the past and the pastoral. Setting down one's highly personal experiences in a kind of shorthand, and assuming that this will be of universal comprehensibility and significance, is another Poundian trait, as are such mannerisms as the inversion of word order, the frequent omission of articles and auxiliary verbs, and the prodigal use of the ampersand. From Joyce would appear to come the macaronic mingling of languages: Jones inserts a good deal of Welsh and Latin and —it seems almost a language—Cockney; though all this is as nothing compared to the difficulties of his later, longer, and much more demanding "autobiography," *The Anathemata* (1952). From Joyce, also, come the humorous, picaresque, lowbrow figures who become comic or grave counterparts of legendary heroes. Eliot, too, uses this device, but with little or no sympathy for such common types; in Jones, as in Joyce, these characters are treated with gusto and a nice, unsentimental compassion. Indeed, Jones's autobiographical protagonist is named John Ball, like the leader of the 14th-Century Peasants' Revolt. As for the poetic exploitation of the Catholic liturgy, Jones might have gotten this from either Eliot or Joyce (or neither); with Joyce, the fellow Celt, he has in common, at any rate, that "intoxication of style" which Matthew Arnold considered the hallmark of Celtic literature.

After this, one might wonder whether there is any major original contribution left for *In Parenthesis* to make. There is: its very form. For the book, considered a poem by some and a novel by others, is neither; nor is it, like *Finnegans Wake*, an extended prose poem; nor yet is it what medieval literature knew as *prosimetra*, works in which prose and poetry alternate. Still, it is this last form that *In Parenthesis* comes closest to, with one important difference. Here it is not passages of pure prose and pure poetry that jostle each other jarringly, but a highly poetic (even if often slangy) prose that, at appropriate moments, is heightened into extremely free verse. Thus the transitions are neither so ostentatious as to become disturbing, nor so discreet as to disappear altogether. And what could be more apposite for a work that deals both with the chaos of modern warfare and with evocations of ancient, epic heroism than to be *both* novel and poem, each at the proper time. Thus Jones's work fulfills the basic requirement for a work of art: the perfect fusion of idea and expression, the oneness of content and form. Herewith a typical prose passage ("he" is the enemy, who holds the opposite hill):

> The other slope was still sun-lighted, but it was getting almost cool on this east-facing hill, and the creeping down and so across so gradually, gath-

ered to itself, minute by minute, the lesser cast-shadows, the little glints and smallnesses, garnered all these accidents of light within a large lengthened calm. Very soon the high ridge-line alone caught cast lateral ray. But for long after, his shrapnel bursts, away beyond, were gauffered at their spreading edges with reflected gold. Across the evening, homing birds, birds of the air with nests cawed on high above them waiting, and the preparation there. Oddly stirred winds gusted coolish to your face, that might have borne things webbed and blind, or the grey owl suddenly. And some people began settling down for the night or at least to snooze before this talked-of bombardment loosed off to make it difficult. Some of them were already fallen to sleep, but the more solicitous disposed themselves and stood about on that hill, and rather tended to speak in undertones as though to not hasten or not disturb, to not activate too soon the immense potential empoweredness—and talk about impending dooms—it fair gets you in the guts.

We can follow the parabola of this prose which curves from the poetic and slightly archaicizing, through the folksy, into the deliberately, anticlimactically plebeian.

Presently, however, there will appear a verse passage such as this, from the description of an infantry charge:

> No one to care there for Aneirin Lewis spilled there
> who worshipped his ancestors like a Chink
> who sleeps in Arthur's lap
> who saw Olwen-trefoils some moon-lighted night
> on precarious slats at Festubert,
> on narrow foothold on le Plantin marsh—
> more shaved he is to the bare bone than
> Yspaddan Penkawr.
> > Properly organized chemists can let make more riving
> power than ever Twrch Trwyth;
> more blistered he is than painted Troy Towers
> and unwholer, limb from limb, than any of them
> > fallen at Catraeth
> or on the seaboard-down, by Salisbury,
> and no maker to contrive his funerary song.

But it is not only in sustained passages of prose and poetry that *In Parenthesis* scales such heights. (The notes, by the way, contain just enough explanatory matter to make the abstruse verse passage almost, but not completely, comprehensible.) Often it is on a single line of poetry or prose that Jones's words impale the very core of being: thus we read of a place "where adolescence walks the shrieking wood"; or hear an injunction to stretcher-bearers, "You mustn't spill the precious fragments, for perhaps these raw bones live." And by provocative couplings of the Anglo-Saxon and Latin elements of our language, by juxtapositions of obsolete words and neologisms, Jones achieves both a feeling of timelessness and a poignant verbal music.

Sometimes, however, the language and rhythms lapse into pastiche. So we get some pure Hopkins:

> Slime-glisten on the churnings up, fractured earth pilings, heaped on, heaped up waste; overturned for throwings; tottering perpendiculars lean and sway; more leper-trees pitted, rownsepykèd out of nature, cut off in their sap-rising.

Or sheer Joyce:

> It's twins—and doing well. But let's have it the Marathon kid—cut it out, Mr. Mercury Mystogogue.

Or this, which out-Eliots Eliot:

> Where's the sergeant-major
> I know where he is
> where's the old squire—he's been foully murdered
> where's Rosy
> where's Pendragon
> where is his anointed face in all time of our necessity . . .

Nevertheless, for the most part, the rich verbiage of *In Parenthesis* envelops—tart, warm, bright—the crisp, spare narrative. It is verbal Welsh rabbit: marvelously creamy and tangy on top, solid and crunchy underneath.

And so the book takes us from the humorous and satirical atmosphere of the early scenes, behind the lines or in dismal but relatively safe trenches, to the final, decimating, nightmarish attack. And throughout, the bygone and the numinous intermingle subtly with the immediate, or rear up menacingly before it: a sudden quaint echo from Geoffrey of Monmouth, the

Bible, Herodotus; a sorrowful warning from Shakespeare or the Offices of the Catholic Church; a supernatural terror out of Malory. Jones proceeds in the spirit of the old Celtic tales: you are never sure in them whether you are confronting the quick or the dead; the background is always some nebulous region which turns out to be the Country of Death. So, too, the scenery of *In Parenthesis* shifts bizarrely and brusquely: now it is the Waste Land, now Wonderland. In the end we realize that the two are the same.

But, however irritatingly un-Celtic of me it may be, I am inclined to doubt that *In Parenthesis* is the "work of genius" Mr. Eliot has dubbed it, or the "masterpiece" Mr. Auden has declared it to be. And I doubt even more seriously that the "average reader" will follow Auden's precept: "I would advise him to do as is best to do when reading *The Divine Comedy*: read it first straight through without bothering about allusions he does not 'get,' then a second time consulting the notes, after which, before a third reading, he might well do some homework on his own." Even a *better* reader is more likely to go through the book once, with mingled interest, admiration, and exasperation, and see in it what Frank Kermode called "the sacramentalism of some Roman Catholic aestheticians, like Mr. David Jones." The main difficulty lies in Jones's assumption about army life: "The 'Bugger! Bugger!' of a man detailed, had often about it the 'Fiat! Fiat!' of the Saints." It takes some pretty advanced sacramentalism to accept that particular transubstantiation. Which is why the reminiscences of Robert Graves (in the same fighting and with the same regiment) in prose such as *Good-bye to All That* and verse like "Recalling War" are ultimately more valid—humanly as well as artistically. As remarkable prose poetry, situated somewhere among Hopkins, Pound, Eliot, Joyce, and Dylan Thomas, *In Parenthesis* deserves honorable mention. But as sustained imaginative recreation and exploration of war, it strikes me rather as the Charge of the Light Brigade did the official French observer: "C'est magnifique, mais ce n'est pas la guerre."

part three : theatre

■

Novels into Plays:

■ *A Passage to India*
The Aspern Papers

There is a simple law governing the dramatization of novels: if it is worth doing, it can't be done; if it can be done, it isn't worth it. Trash can be just as trashy on the stage as in an armchair, but when an artist has conceived of something as a novel, let those who think they know a reason why his matter should not be married to his manner forever hold their peace. In every literature course in every college, students today are being told that the form and content of a work of art are one and inseparable, that the form in a very real sense *is* the content, and that the old notion that you can peel the form right off the content like the skin off an orange is worth about as much as a piece of old orange peel. But in every class of every college there is at least a handful of students who can be taught nothing, and some of them, in due time, are sure to become adapters of great novels for the stage. Let whoever doubts this proposition name one distinguished novel that became an equally distinguished play. The exception, of course, is when the novelist dramatizes his own novel; even then, as in the case of Giraudoux and Brecht, the writer ends up not just rewriting, but rethinking.

Great playwrights write their own plays and cannot, will not, meddle with dramatizations. The person who undertakes to dramatize a major novel is either a greedy hack who cannot write a good play and resorts to this kind of legalized parasitism, or a simpleton as unaware of his own littleness as of the novelist's greatness. To extend to Santha Rama Rau the courtesy to which her sex may entitle her, I shall allow of one more possibility: blindness to the meaning of the novel. On the evidence of Miss Rama Rau's own printed statement, she has no more understanding of what *A Passage to India* is about than do the reviewers who loudly praised her dismal dramatization.

Here is what Miss Rama Rau tells us (*Theatre Arts*, February, 1962) she sees in Forster's novel. (1) "The courage to look at the colonial British from the outside, in the harsh but understanding light of truth." (2) "Real Indian characters, acting in genuinely Indian ways, thinking as Indians. . . ." (3) "Memories of colonialism and the position of the subject and the ruler." But to locate *A Passage to India* by this paltry triangulation is like conceiving of *Don Quixote* as a novel dealing with the oddities of an elderly man whose senility is, moreover, accurately observed, the whole thing an eloquent plea for the advancement of geriatrics. Actually, E. M. Forster's novel has at least four other, more important, strong points. (a) The almost complete ambivalence and consequent ambiguity that governs all human relations—the misunderstandings that breed love as well as hate, friendship as well as enmity. Even the magistrate, Turton, at the point when he is presumed to hate the Indians, says sadly, " 'I don't hate them, I don't know why,' and he didn't hate them; for if he did, he would have had to condemn his own career as a bad investment." In the adaptation, Turton, like the rest of the colonials, is just a nasty and ludicrous pukka sahib. Similarly, Aziz' and Mrs. Moore's great fondness for each other, standing for the best *intuitive* understanding of East and West, is based, in the book, on mutual misapprehension and ends in the preposterous cult of Esmiss Esmoor. As for the attempted *rational* friendship between Aziz and Fielding, it too is doomed, not so much by the gulf between Orient and Occident as by the gap between one human ego and another. Even the romance between Adela and Ronny feeds only on the incidental and coincidental, and collapses under the aspect of eternity gaping out of the Marabar Caves. (b) The supreme importance of the Marabar Caves. In the play, they become a mere quaint episode, eliciting hysteria from one woman and a dreadful apathy from another. In the novel, they stand for the shocking realization of the pathetic smallness of all life as against the void that surrounds it; for the absurdity of patient, dutiful self-abnegation on behalf of a transcendence that does not exist. (c) The hopeless relativity and mutability of the human condition, which makes Aziz, who personifies India for the first two thirds of the book, as complete an outsider as Fielding, in the last third, among Godbole's Hindus. The novel wears a benignly ironic smile whenever it contemplates a seemingly absolute "truth"; Miss Rama Rau, however, is hot for certainties, and we get the dusty answers. (d) The passages of poetic prose and profound but charming insight in which the author speaks to us directly. Miss Rama Rau either omits them or, occasionally, puts them into the mouth of some character, where they do not belong. Another adapter might do the same, but that is no excuse.

What, after all these subtractions, is left? A pageant of cardboard figures emitting some civilized talk as they fade into genteel oblivion. To that half of the book which she has chosen to adapt, Miss Rama Rau is slavishly faithful, which may explain why it took India so long to shake off English domination, but does not make for very good theatre: dialogue and plot (especially when reduced by half) are the least important elements in Forster's masterpiece. As for Donald McWhinnie's staging, it seems to come posthaste out of some obsolete handbook of directing: the scene in which various figures emerge in mathematical order in response to Godbole's song is typical of the bloodless schematism of his approach; so is the upward-pointing posture atop a rock which the guide is forced to hold for minutes on end in Act II, Scene 1, like a foolish figurehead that has lost its ship. Equally inexcusable is the casting of Saeed Jaffrey as Godbole, turning that venerable but weird old pundit into a smarmy young swami, or the recruiting of the Indian extras from what looks like the staff of Vic Tanny's —including one particularly unlikely golden-haired untouchable. Only three performers survive their surroundings. As Aziz, Zia Mohyeddin is every bit as delightful, mercurial, and absurd as Forster conceived him. Gladys Cooper exactly embodies the crotchety, crumbling dignity of Mrs. Moore, and the insight she affords us into the cooling of her sympathy into final, uncaring solipsism is almost as terrifying as if we saw the sun above us growing cold. And as Ronny, a somewhat contradictory figure in the book and an almost impossible one in the play, Louis Edmonds achieves real credibility and distinction. But Anne Meacham's Adela Quested is alternately tedious and demented, and Eric Portman's features and voice recede into the greyness he exudes, like an English sheepdog's face into his coat. The rest of the cast is feeble, but Rouben Ter-Arutunian's sets are not without charm, except for some curiously Art Nouveau boulders and caves.

I seriously urge anyone who still believes in the adapting of great novels for the stage to compare Forster's book carefully with the play. The confrontation should prove highly stimulating.

Most of what I have said about the dramatization of *A Passage to India* holds true for that of *The Aspern Papers*. The one ostensible difference in favor of Michael Redgrave's adaptation is that *The Aspern Papers* is only a novella, and thus needs less injudicious pruning than a novel—allows, in fact, for the *addition* of some dramatic incidents in the available playing time. But addition proves just as deadly as subtraction: either because it makes something that should be merely suggested, brutally explicit; or because it is inferior to the original, and is thus not only bad in itself, but also infects with its unworthiness the surrounding bits of the original. And not only is Redgrave no James, but even by any standards his writing is shoddy. Thus his idea of humor is that tired, anemic little joke "How shall I begin?—At the beginning" (there were actually a few desperate souls in the audience who found this funny), or the creation of a Brooklyn-Italian comic maid who in a British production doubtless speaks Cockney. And for serious writing he gives us "I'm a traveler, a migrant bird, and with each change of season I seek a new nest," or "He'll hang high up in the heaven of our literature," or "Don't be rash, Harry, patience and kindness win in the end"—and every other triviality and platitude that would have made a stronger-stomached aesthete than Henry James turn a quite unfashionable shade of green.

As for plot, Redgrave has Miss Tina (his folksier equivalent for James's Tita) running like a faithful dog each time she hears the ringing of her aunt's bell (one does not know whether, in true Pavlovian fashion, she is also salivating); or old Miss Bordereau having a mad vision of a ball in the days of her youth, and jabbering away in French, apparently the language of her native America. Such things merely accentuate the hopelessness of trying to trade second-rate action for first-rate style.

Assisting in the undoing of Henry James are Margaret Webster's thoroughly routine direction, a miscast Françoise Rosay, some inappropriate or ineffectual supporting players, and, above all, Maurice Evans. I can think of several reasons, all of them bad, why Evans should have been the hit he is in this country, but even so, to my mind, never have so many successes been owed to so few talents. The likeliest explanation is that Evans combines the most unfelicitous aspects of British and American acting, and that the bargain-conscious American public therefore feels it is getting two things for the price of one. The salient feature of Evans's acting is a slippery competence, weighted down with such a superstructure of smirking smugness, off-the-sleeve feeling, and insistence on dapperness at the cost of all else, that the whole performance assumes the quality of a television commercial assuring us that *this* brand of margarine is just as good as the high-priced spread.

The three extenuating circumstances are Wendy Hiller's Tina—not one of her most inspired performances, but one that has none the less moments of heartbreaking truth even in such details as the angle at which she holds her spine; Ben Edwards's setting (Mr. Edwards is surely the master-composer of scenic dilapidation, encompassing every note from shabby gentility to garish squalor) which confines itself to the higher, more elegant, register of disrepair, and conveys much of the Venice James has evoked; and a rather nicely managed storm, handsomely stylized and suggestive. Few, if any, other things about Redgrave's experiment reach us "through the beautiful circuit and subterfuge of our thought and our desire," as James defined the meaningful indirectness with which a romantic work insinuates itself into our awareness.

Ultimately, however, the proof is in the pudding, and there is no more pudding-headed dramaturgy around town than in *A Passage to India* and *The Aspern Papers*. In fact, I seriously doubt that either adaptation was leveled at the audiences (who seemed to me, in both cases, thoroughly bored), but only at the reviewers, whom one can always bamboozle with a sufficiently great novelist's name. And once the reviews have sold the play to the audience, the play can cheerfully sell the novel down the river.

■

Boredom in the Theatre

■

The theatre, though it is becoming harder and harder to believe it, still deals with people. And even though the playwright may not want them to be ordinary—any more than they themselves do —most people are precisely that, which is to say (kindly) of limited interest, or (unkindly) boring. The problem is how to render the conversation of such people without dishonesty creeping into the dialogue or audiences creeping out of the theatre.

People, and this often includes dramatists, are apt to forget that in a novel the ordinary person may emerge fascinating simply because of the author's brilliant analysis and comments; but the playwright, who must rely on his character's actions and words exclusively, must make the ordinary seem extraordinary. Now there are always those who insist that people are infinitely absorbing creatures, or that, at the very least, they and their friends are quite unique, and that nature, having made them, threw away the mold. Yet it would seem to me that nature, tossing them out on the ant heap, threw *them* away, and kept the mold in order to produce their replicas ad infinitum. For if these optimists were to record on tape their words during work, cocktail parties, and love-making, I doubt that they could keep their best friends listening to more than a few minutes of it. Assuredly even these friends would not pay for sitting through two hours of it. They might, in a pinch, pay to get out. And so, to escape from themselves—or from themselves as reflected in their friends— people go out on the search for boredom-killers, which brings them, among other places, into the theatre.

That boredom has always been a very real disease in life and literature is demonstrated by the many terms for it that have become timeless and universal by-words: the *taedium vitae* of ancient Rome, the *vapours* of 18th-century England, the romantic *ennui* and symbolist *spleen* of 19th-century France. Perhaps nowhere did boredom become so crucial as in the drama of the Byronic-romantic tradition, which produced such colossal sufferers from it as Musset's Fantasio and Büchner's Leonce. But in their awareness of their malady there is something cathartic (now we would say, therapeutic) and a spur, ultimately, to unboring action. I am, therefore, chiefly concerned with plays whose characters are unable to recognize the boredom they endure or inflict, the boredom they personify. It is here that the dramatist is up against a real punching bag: the harder he hits his problem, the harder it is likely to bounce back in his face.

This is a comparatively recent danger in the theatre, for as long as most drama was larger than life-size, the heroic protagonist was, by definition, at odds with deities or destinies that took both action and diction out of the parenthesis of dullness. Not until the coming of realism and naturalism did the atmosphere of boredom materialize in all its unbreathableness around the unheroic heroes and heroines of our age.

The current Broadway season abounds in attempts at escaping from the problem. There are, first of all, musicals and more musicals, with which the theatre shirks not only the difficulty I am talking about but any and all difficulties that crop up when one faces reality. But there are also plays like Graham Greene's The Complaisant Lover, in which the entire action luxuriates in a warm bath of adulterous sex, and others, like Frederick Knott's Write Me a Murder, in which the ice-cold shower of murder is supposed to keep the nerves tingling. An item like A Shot in the Dark tries to be even more foolproof: sexual titillation and murder are sagaciously blended, and, amid all these hot and cold shivers, we are expected to be blissfully unaware of the presence—or absence—of anything else. Still another way of shirking responsibility is the flight into nonsense, currently exemplified by Harold Pinter's The Caretaker. But while these methods provide alternatives to facing squarely the ordinariness of plain, indeed dull, men and women, the result is spectacles of even greater boredom. For, as Alberto Moravia wisely observes in his newest novel, The Empty Canvas, boredom is not simply the opposite of amusement, but a lack of reality. Let us turn away, then, from the more or less fraudulent nostrums of the moment, and consider the prototypical answers with which some contemporary dramatists have parried, or failed to parry, the question of dramatizing our everyday dullness.

There is, to begin with, the playwright who makes an honest, foolish frontal attack on the problem. He picks the dreariest, most cluttered part of the home, the kitchen, and squeezes the big scene, if not the entire play, into it. His characters will have the commonest occupations: the father will be an insurance or dry-goods salesman, with dreams—not even delusions —of grandeur; the mother will be, of course, a housewife, and she will be doing homely chores while lecturing her two children (the perfect number for simple, basic differences or conflicts) on what a fine fellow their boring failure of a father is. If the play is the hit of the 1948-49 Broadway season, the mother's harangue runs:

> . . . I don't say he's a great man. Willy Loman never made a lot of money. His name was never in the paper. He's not the finest character that ever lived. But he's a human being, and a terrible thing is happening to him. So attention must be paid. He's not to be allowed to fall into his grave like an old dog. Attention, attention must be finally paid to such a person. . . . And you tell me he has no character? The man who never worked a day but for your benefit? When does he get the medal for that? . . .

If, on the other hand, the play is the hit of the London season nine years later, the mother's homily will go:

> . . . Your father wants to be a farmer. He hates [his] job; he's always wanted to be a farmer. You have no idea how much that means to him. He hates it and he's done it for you. For you, do you understand? He's a fine man. He's been through a great deal in all sorts of ways and you will treat him with respect. With respect! (*She sits.*) With respect! With respect! (*She puts her face in her hands and weeps.*)

It would be very nearly possible to transpose these speeches from Arthur Miller's *Death of a Salesman* and Robert Bolt's *Flowering Cherry* without in the least disturbing the insignificance and dullness of the respective scenes. And this is not to say that Miller is a hack or Bolt a plagiarist; only that both of them are dealing with a commonplace that neither Miller's fancier (though not necessarily better) language nor Bolt's naked simplicity is able to redeem. Significantly, *Flowering Cherry*, which Kenneth Tynan called "a remarkable new play," and which was both a critical and audience success in London, closed within a week in New York. *Death of a Salesman*, which was grovelingly worshiped in America by press and public alike, was accorded a barely lukewarm reception in London.

The point is that boredom—dullish characters in their everyday surroundings—is perishable indeed, and cannot readily be exported. We work up enthusiasm for our own, our recognizably national boredom, simply because it captures our personal blemishes and rut. In *The Picture of Dorian Grey*, Wilde spoke of Caliban's rage *at* seeing his face in the mirror; there is also, as Wilde knew, Caliban's rage *for* seeing his face there. Provided, of course, the lighting on the face is favorable, so that its dreariness has, if not grandeur, at least pathos. The important thing for the playwright is to portray the endemic boredom and frustration in which everyone recognizes himself or, preferably, his brother, and to spray the picture with a little human dignity for fixative. So it is that Willy Loman's greyness and monomania can be both deplored and sold, and Miller cashes in on his Picture of Boring Grey. But the moment that either Loman or Cherry is uprooted from the public out of which he sprouted, unwatered by audience tears and scathed by withering reviews, he perishes. Perishes, ultimately, of his own dullness.

Frontal attack, to be sure, is not the only way. There is the expressionists' manner of portraying boredom, as in the party scene of Elmer Rice's *The Adding Machine*. Seven couples, whose names range from Mr. and Mrs. Six to Mr. and Mrs. Zero, exchange disa and data:

> Mrs. Six: I like them little organdie dresses.
> Mrs. Five: Yeh, with a little lace trimmin' on the sleeves.
> Mrs. Four: Well, I like 'em plain myself.
> Mrs. Three: Yeh, what I always say is the plainer the more refined.
> Mrs. Two: Well, I don't think a little lace does any harm.
> Mrs. One: No, it kinda dresses it up.
> Mrs. Zero: Well, I always say it's all a matter of taste.

This is exaggeration: an enormous enlargement of boredom and also a caricature, but one that is more frightening than funny. It has the fascination of hyperbole, for the unit of conversation is no longer the word but the platitude. In this way boredom becomes interesting through sheer horror. But the difficulty with caricaturing boredom is that it requires almost superhuman skills to sustain it through a whole evening. This is why Eugène Ionesco, the current master of representing boredom by artful distortion, by suggestive nonsense and *reductio ad absurdum*, usually limits himself to short plays. His frenetic, surrealist humor is at times almost too successful in communicating blind, blustering boredom; in a play like *Rhinoceros*, his customarily perfect balance between excruciation and amusement swings a little too much toward the latter, and the barb turns into a barbiturate.

If Ionesco's plays tend to monumentalize the boredom in ordinary social situations, our other great master borer, Samuel Beckett, erects a more cosmic boredom, in some extraordinary, antisocial, mysteriously metaphysical ambience. In Beckett's *Endgame*, we meet the blind Hamm and his servant Clov, apparently the last inhabitants of the universe—except for Nagg and Nell, Hamm's aged parents who live side by side in two ash bins. At one point Hamm says:

> Hamm: Go and see is she dead. (*Clov goes to bins, raises the lid of Nell's, stoops, looks into it. Pause.*)
>
> Clov: Looks like it. (*He closes the lid, straightens up. Hamm raises his toque. Pause. He puts it on again.*)
>
> Hamm: (*with his hand to his toque*): And Nagg? (*Clov raises lid of Nagg's bin, stoops, looks into it. Pause.*)
>
> Clov: Doesn't look like it. (*He closes the lid, straightens up.*)
>
> Hamm: (*letting go his toque*): What's he doing? (*Clov raises lid of Nagg's bin, stoops, looks into it. Pause.*)
>
> Clov: He's crying. (*He closes lid, straightens up.*)
>
> Hamm: Then he's living. (*Pause.*)

But not many scenes of this short play are as eventful as that. One way or the other, however, such treatment of universal boredom makes its devastating point so quickly that it cannot last out three acts, no matter how great the wit and ingenuity. Beckett's longest plays are two-acters (and at that they may be too long); when Ionesco, in *Rhinoceros*, attempts a full-length play, proceedings begin to pall. So, too, the disciples of these two masters, Americans like Albee and Richardson, Britishers like Harold Pinter and N. F. Simpson, find it hard, or do not even try, to write three-act plays.*

As opposed to this travestying of boredom, there is the attempt by another school to idealize it: the endeavor to sell us insignificance, general human repetitiousness, and monotony of existence as supreme virtues. This is the approach of Thornton Wilder. Whether it is ninety Christmas dinners in the life of a family, fifteen years in the life of a town, or umpteen aeons in the life of the human race, Wilder reduces everything to a sweet suburban formula of familiar family felicities and infelicities couched in cultural slogans and homespun homiletics. Everything blurs into everything else—particularly evil into good, which always triumphs because it is really omnipresent—and everybody merges into everybody else because there are no significant differences between bodies, and isn't that just wonderful? The most wonderful thing about it is its success, but even that isn't so extraordinary: it is merely Caliban, equally exasperated by seeing and not seeing his face in the glass, jumping with joy before a mirror that shows him Ariel's face as his own. Of course, Wilder uses every trick of the Pirandellian, expressionist, surrealist theatres to add zest to his litanies of dullness, and enjoyment of his technique and drolleries has reconciled people who should know better to his content. But he does not fool the shrewd observer; the German poet and critic Gottfried Benn writes about *The Skin of Our Teeth*: "Such datedness and such dullness . . . all this talking-into-the-audience, these narrators, this promiscuity with the orchestra pit is, eventually, utterly provincial. . . ." But Wilder is, at any rate, more honest than Saroyan, whose bores express their improbable magnanimity in impossible flights of sentimental prose poetry.

Another solution is to surround tiresome people in boring situations with so much authentic feeling for their plight and helplessness, reproducing their predicament with such genuine compassion or indignation, that we cannot but be moved. This can be the social thesis play as once written by Clifford Odets, and now by Arnold Wesker; or the plays with less or no clear-cut

---

* Since this writing, Albee has proved with Who's Afraid of Virgina Woolf? that he can sustain a full-length play, but only by making his dramaturgy more conventional, and his characters considerably less so.

social purpose of John Osborne, William Inge, and various others, ranging to such a curious work as Marguerite Duras's *The Square*. In this interminable duologue between two idiot savants which at once repels and hypnotizes us, we experience the same spiritual equivalent of ingrown toenails from which Mlle Duras's characters, as well as her style, are suffering.

A more common approach to alleviating boredom is to set off one or two superior, or at least more sensitive, characters against a background of gaping dullness. Of course, if the superior figures can carry the whole play, as in Tennessee Williams's two or three true successes, the problem of boredom is automatically by-passed. But often the background characters preponderate. Thus Denis Donoghue recently criticized *Look Back in Anger* "because it allowed eloquence and energy only to one attitude, Jimmy Porter's; rival attitudes were assigned to nitwits." Such an objection seems more applicable to Osborne and Creighton's *Epitaph for George Dillon*: the second act, where the intelligent Ruth clashes with the complex Dillon, is totally absorbing; but the commonplaces, vulgarities, and squabbles of the Elliot family which make up the bulk of acts one and three are wearying.

Still another way of mitigating boredom is to put the dramatis personae into an unusual milieu, an extraordinary position. Jack Gelber's *The Connection* exploits to a large extent junkies, hypodermics, jazz, and hipster jargon; but for all its sensationalism, heightened by a fancy Pirandellian play-within-a-play and even movie-within-a-play, the painfully paralyzing boredom is there—for us, at times, as much as for the characters. Yet *The Connection* succeeds because Gelber's play has the benefit of language: the hip talk that blends with the more philosophical passages into a hallucinatory syncopation.

Indeed this is the fundamental way of making existential boredom theatrically valid: a language must be found that will turn tedium into poetry. Think of O'Neill: no playwright had a harder time finding his language, his style; but when, in some of his very last plays, he finds it, it is superb. Now, by poetry I do not mean the sort of thing that T. S. Eliot does in *The Cocktail Party*, where languorous pseudo-poetry is meant to express the ennui of high-class, highbrow bores. No, the poetry I have in mind is something other than the worrying of words and conceits into verse that is merely circumnavigating its navel.

Compare two speeches from two different plays in which two girls, one, to be sure, more promiscuous than the other, voice their none the less identical, unassuming happiness. Girl number one is talking to her girl friend:

> I think I'm happy, Marilyn. I can't tell you how I feel in so many words, but life seems very pleasant to me right now. I even get along with my mother. I think I'm in love. Seriously in love. I feel so full sometimes it just wells up in me, my feelings for him. He went away for three days on a business trip to Detroit, I thought I'd die before he came back.

Girl number two, in a garden, is talking to her baby:

> Me, Polly Garter, under the washing line, giving the breast to my bonny new baby. Nothing grows in our garden, only washing. And babies. And where's their fathers live, my love? Over the hills and far away. You're looking up at me now. I know what you're thinking, you poor little milky creature. You're thinking, you're no better than you should be, Polly, and that's good enough for me. Oh, isn't life a terrible thing, thank God?

It is a stock situation, but the first girl, Paddy Chayefsky's Betty Preiss (in *Middle of the Night*), has only a stock way of expressing it. Dylan Thomas's Polly Garter (in *Under Milk Wood*) also utters banalities, but their happily slapdash juxtaposition, with just a sprinkling of poetic spice, makes them transcend their triviality. It is not easy to do, but a child can do it—if that eighteen-year-old child is called Shelagh Delaney. In *A Taste of Honey* we recently had a play in which humdrum people in standard grubby predicaments manage to be endearing, novel, and true—and, best of all, far more interesting than the characters our quotidian reviewers daily refer to as "endearing, novel, and true."

It does not matter whether our dull, ordinary life is conveyed in this manner or that, whether the boredom is physical or metaphysical, whether we are waiting for Lefty or for Godot, as long as a language is found to make us—not stand up and cheer, only sit up and take notice. This is where the dramatic imagination of the sixties might well busy itself. But, like the lover of Chayefsky's heroine, it seems to have gone on a business trip to Detroit. And we may be gone by the time it comes back.

■

Seasons of Discontent

■

Fall 1960

Of the five productions I am about to review, two were superior, one fair, and two poor. There would be nothing remarkable about this breakdown which is just what one would expect the law of averages and Broadway to produce, except for the interesting co-incidence that the two good productions were, in their fashion, improvisations; that the middling one was the work of an estab-lished, respected playwright; and that the inadequate pair were both adaptations of not exactly choice novels. And as it so often happens with coincidences, this one has nothing coincidental about it.

To start the season, Marcel Marceau returned with a program that introduced one of his company's mime dramas to American audiences. The first half of the evening was the usual solo performance by Marceau. Some of it was old material, but all of it confronted the audience with a true artist whose move-ments are as basic, as beautiful, and as soothing to the eye as the waves of the sea. It is now fashionable among the cognoscenti to decry Marceau's "repetitiousness" or "lack of growth" because, it seems, there is little in his repertoire that wasn't there ten years ago. What of it? It is like objecting that one has heard Starker play Kodály's Sonata for Unaccompanied Cello before.

Pantomime is both the biggest and the most limited art. It is big because, dispensing with words, it is the true Esperanto for bridging all times and all space; because gesture was there before speech was invented and is still there when words fail. But mime is also the most limited art because its range is restrained by definition: stray just so far from what everybody does and everyone recognizes, and you have lost your audience. If the com-mon denominator is to be of any use, it must be the lowest one. Marceau's genius does full justice to the bigness of mime. There is no human situation that his grimaces and muscles cannot com-ment on, shedding light and love on all our actions. What is petty in mankind becomes the subject of much kinetic merriment, and what is evil or sad seems transmuted into the dignity of a tragic mask. And it is precisely in a number involving masks—all of them, of course, simulated by the naked face—that Marceau throws off the limitations of pantomime, which as a rule does not, like words, offer images of the new but only *aperçus* of the quotidian. In this number, a mask-maker rapidly slips on different masks one after another (in itself requiring spectacular facial flexibility and timing) until one, a particularly euphoric mask, gets stuck on his face. The man's desperate efforts to remove it, turning into the agony of failure, are expressed to perfection by Marceau's anguished arms, legs, and body in counter-time to his beaming face. I need hardly spell out the meaning of the parable.

But the group effort, *The Overcoat,* based on Gogol's tale, was a failure that let down not only a superb short story but also the audience. Group pantomime, which, obviously, cannot depend on the rare, if not unique, genius of an individual, dissipates its effects into what is merely a cross between modern dance and ballet. But an earthbound ballet done in lead shoes, and a modern dance performed for puritans who cannot stand the sight of the human body. (How pale this looked compared to, say, the Jooss Ballet's *Green Table*.) Still, the music was pleasant; but it is sad pantomime that should be heard, not seen.

The reviewers who were vying with one another to find the source of Brendan Behan's *The Hostage* (with Brecht, I believe, getting the largest number of votes) were no less misguided than those who, sighing or snorting, announced that it was absolutely unlike anything else. *The Hostage* is distinguished by the fact that it is absolutely like every other play—all other plays that ever were, rolled into one. What a marvelous "mélange adultère de tout"! Everything is here from Pirandello to Jean Genet, from Ernst Toller to the later O'Casey, and if anyone went looking in it for *Everyman* or Strindberg's *Damascus* trilogy, I'm sure he could find them too—just as Noel Coward, despite Behan's jibes at him, is likewise present. For this is truly a *Summa Theatrologica* for our time. And what you cannot find in the printed text is bound to be in the changes, additions, and ad libs which can be savored in the performances, whether put there by Behan, Joan Littlewood, the superbly imaginative director, or the actors themselves. I am sure that, like madras shirts, no two bleeding *Hostages* are alike.

Behan's play is about a lovable dolt of an English soldier held as hostage by some Irish Irregulars who have billeted themselves in an even more irregular Dublin establishment with a number of no less lovable Irish dolts for in- and cohabitants. If a certain Irish boy is hanged by the British in Belfast, the dopey little Cockney will be shot in Dublin. And this is the first respect in which *The Hostage* triumphs: the one kind of play it has nothing, but nothing, to do with is the Irish Patriotic Play, or even the Irish Irish Play, as once manufactured by Yeats, the young O'Casey, and the rest. If the play has any fundamental kinship with anything, it is with the *commedia dell'arte,* or its latter-day avatar, the burlesque skit. Even those of its lines that are the *sine qua non* of every printed and produced version, such as Miss Gilchrist's, the "sociable worker's" remark, "I'm pure as the driven snow," to which Meg Dillon (fractured Irish for Mary Magdalen) replies, "You weren't driven far enough," smack of stage or, more precisely, barroom improvisation.

Improvisation, surely, is one of the most appropriate genres for an era of the absurd such as we are, or think we are, living in. In *The Hostage,* the dead may rise to sing a song, the pansies take over the leadership of the police, or (in the American version) a faggoty Negro boxer carry a sign reading "Keep Ireland Black." For if the play, like all art, is to be a little more real than reality, it must, in our time, be a little more absurd than absurdity. This is by no means easy to do, and various approaches have been tried: Beckett anatomizes, as it were, the interstices between events that never quite occur; Ionesco takes an impossibility, treats it as if it were the most ordinary thing in the world, and works from there; Behan keeps the audience, actors, and playwright unprepared for and flabbergasted by what happens next, and so feels that he has a working model of our world. There is even a cue for the author to appear on the stage and deliver his own immediate feelings if his intoxication is sufficient or business at the box-office insufficient. If Genet, in *The Balcony,* saw the brothel as a world in which our libidinous dreams come true, Behan, in *The Hostage,* sees the world as a brothel in which every sort of happiness is possible—except ultimate fulfillment.

Joan Littlewood's direction performs a stage miracle: chaos is given shape without ceasing to be chaos. Miss Littlewood has integrated disorder into patterns: her art is an order that conceals itself. And the cast is as apt and balanced as a virtuoso chamber orchestra. Whereas *Face of a Hero* has an Ellen Holly, *Becket,* a Marie Powers, *The Wall* everyone but the two principals to contend with, here there is virtually no slack anywhere. And if I needed any additional evidence to substantiate the thesis of the world's absurdity, there was a group of businessmen sitting behind me who laughed and laughed and enjoyed themselves hugely, but who, when it was all over, exclaimed: "What a lousy play!"

In the career of Jean Anouilh the critical point when a dramatist begins to imitate himself has been reached some time ago. L'Invitation au château* was still a valid, fresh play—until Christopher Fry wallowed in it and left a ring around it. It has taken Anouilh's later plays all the running they could do, to keep in the same place. True, there have been exceptions, like The Waltz of the Toreadors; Becket, alas, is not one of them.

When Anouilh was younger (in plays like Roméo et Jeannette, Le Voyageur sans bagage, La Sauvage, Thieves' Carnival—even in movies like Monsieur Vincent and Pattes blanches), he saw life intensely, brilliantly: it was all black or pink or both. The world was a sweet pill coated with a thick layer of wormwood, and somewhere in the middle of one's choking on the bitterness there would be one fleeting, unforgettable soupçon of sweetness. Out of such black and rose madder are fairy tales made—made, surely, by very young people who remember their childhood, or very old ones who have regained it. But there is no such thing as middle-aged bitterness or mellow pink-and-blackness. In this his middle-aged phase, Anouilh resorts to the paradox. It is an institution dear to Frenchmen, and Anouilh may have picked it up where it dropped from Giraudoux's hands. In any case, Becket is full of witty, epigrammatic paradoxes: blacknesses that are really pink, rosinesses that are actually black. The only trouble with whirling these parti-colored globes around with prestidigitator's speed is that what then meets the eye is merely grey.

Becket is civilized, skillful, theatrical, and almost never uninteresting. But it has very little light to shed on either the specific chapter of history with which it, presumably, does not even purport to deal, or on human nature, with which it does. Such clever paradoxes as that a person's morality may be only aesthetics, or that the rich may be God's poor lost sheep, though adroitly handled by Anouilh, have long since ceased to startle. The thought underlying Becket is still the old Anouilh theme of pure young lovers so envied and hated by the corrupt world that they are driven into death, though not without leaving a luminescent trail behind. In Becket the lovers happen to be Henry II and Thomas Becket. Henry loves Thomas, and Thomas almost loves him. When

* This play is known here in Christopher Fry's version as Ring Round the Moon. Wherever I am unaware of an adequate English translation, I have preferred to use the French title.

Thomas finds his true lover in God, the king's crude sense of loving cannot keep up. But both loves are doomed by the pettiness and brutality of mankind. It is a theme too young, too slight, and too naïve for the huge gear of the historical drama—and insufficient to flesh the great myths either (how pitiful are Anouilh's *Eurydice* and *Médée*); but by very careful translation into middle-aged terms —with dabs of bittersweet cynicism on a small greyish canvas, as in *The Waltz of the Toreadors*—it can still be effective.

Looking at *Becket* is like watching one of those charming Parisian ladies of indeterminate age and occupation about whom one cannot quite tell whether she is a whore risen to respectability or a socialite flirting with the gutter—both of whom, of course, would be dressed by the same *couturier*. Yet the soiled elegance, the cynical graciousness, cannot, in either case, leave us wholly unfascinated. And the production, appropriately enough, takes its cue from the play. Peter Glenville has directed with a sense of style, which, however, depends a little too much on trickery, such as an excessive zeal for geometric arrangements; scenery, costumes, and lighting are clever to a fault; and the music is remarkably effective except that it is not music. The acting, too, is strangely ambiguous. Anthony Quinn's Plantagenet king, despite the fact that he belongs on neither side of the Channel so much as south of the Pecos, and even though his mouth suggests the presence of potatoes well ahead of Sir Walter Raleigh's importing them to England, manages to grow in stature as the play progresses. Laurence Olivier, as Becket, in spite of relying rather too heavily on his old device of showing the whites of his eyes (as a sign, no doubt, for the close-up shooting to begin), and raising his voice to a falsetto pitched at the dogs, is still surpassed at this sort of bravura acting only by himself when he is better. The fault of both these men, like Anouilh's, is that they are a little too old for this job, a little too tried and tired, a trifle jaded.

All the same, except for some early disquisitions about Norman versus Saxon which might have come straight from the wastebasket above which Scott wrote *Ivanhoe,* and some embarrassing conversations between Becket and God that would befit Bing Crosby or Barry Fitzgerald in some movie about the puckishness of the priesthood, there is much pleasurable urbanity to recommend this play and production. And the evening has one glory: Lucienne Hill's translation. Abridged though it be, set it beside something like Lillian Hellman's adaptation of *The Lark,* and you have the most shattering object lesson. Where Miss Hellman gave us fractured French and fricasseed Anouilh, Miss Hill preserves admirably intact both Anouilh and the English language. She has got *Becket* down to a *t*; it is not her fault that it is not a double *t*.

There is always something wanting in a stage adaptation of a novel. Most recently Ingmar Bergman has warned against "filming existing literature"; what is even worse is staging existing nonliterature. To turn a good novel into a play is usually the equivalent of making a comic strip out of it, as comic books have frequently done. It is the admission of barrenness on the part of the dramatist, and the assumption of mental sluggishness on the part of the audience. To turn a bad novel into a play is merely to prolong an outrage. That there should have already been two such adaptations this season (three if you count the deservedly ephemeral *Valmouth*) is an evil omen. Let me start with the lesser of two evils.

Face of a Hero, which Robert L. Joseph has fashioned out of his own television play out of Pierre Boulle's novel, and which he will doubtless adapt into a movie, concerns a fighting young district attorney who knows that the town wastrel happens to be innocent of what appears to be murder, but hangs him anyway in what looks like the cause of humanity but is actually sheer vicious ego-propaganda. The way a more or less idealistic young man is corrupted into an egomaniacal demagogue by the sight of power and of the polluted world around him could lend itself to a decent novel or play. But there are three serious flaws here. First, the central incident is a piece of improbable coincidence: the D.A. is present at night on the private pier from which one of the playboy's spurned and pregnant playmates hurls herself—and there is also the coincident improbability of the fine young hero's neither stopping her nor coming to her rescue. (This begets a series of improbabilities with which I shall not burden you.) Secondly, a basic deterioration in the hero's character which, in a novel, can rely on the dimension of time as rendered by the very length of a book, requires, in theatrical foreshortening, greater skill than Mr. Joseph has, or better writing than M. Boulle has provided him with. Which leads into the third failing: that despite being spiked with some Madison Avenue lyricism, the language is stock (the intellectual young Negress speaks of "mah people," whereas the teen-age, poor-white-trash girl asks her wearied lover for "a side order of mercy, maybe")—either incredibly obvious or improbably cute. Add to this the schematic nature of the characters (the adoring secretary, the rich-boy-hating cop) and situations (a short but clumsy scene in which a neglected wife, weeping through her smiles, bids farewell to her overambitious husband), and you have the taste of this baby-formula for adults.

But *Face of a Hero* is saved from sub-mediocrity by several astounding performances. George Grizzard, one of the extremely few younger actors of whom our stage need not be ashamed, makes out of the overprivileged juvenile delinquent a character a little larger than life-size, which, considering the pint-sized writing, is a personal triumph so noteworthy, and so satisfying to watch, that no one who recognizes that acting is an art will want to miss it. Scarcely less impressive are Albert Dekker and James Donald among the older, and Kip McArdle and Edward Asner among the newer names. With five such wholly artistic performances to recommend it, *Face of a Hero* deserves to run beyond the petty pace of its dramaturgy.

As *Face of a Hero* capitalizes on the "prejudices and corruption of the backward South," John Hersey's *The Wall*, adapted by Millard Lampell, cashes in on the tragedy of genocide and the Warsaw ghetto of World War II. Mr. Hersey is the kind of novelist who has a sure eye for spotting obvious social problems (*A Bell for Adano; The Child Buyer*) and the great human calamities (*Hiroshima; The Wall*). But writers who are artistically ill-equipped, i.e., morally unqualified, to deal with these situations are merely lice in the hair of such disasters—and what is more peripheral, and farther from the heart, than hair? The best and the worst one can say for Mr. Lampell's adaptation is that it is worthy of the book.

The method of this work, as of so many others like it, is to follow carefully the atrocity *cum* suffering *cum* heroism recipe: one grain of horror to fifty grains of colorful folk in sad, jolly, or edifying circumstances, and not one grain of truth. We get, then, a number of cliché plot situations told in stereotyped language, the whole sprinkled with the flattest specimens of so-called Jewish humor. Now for a few samples. Horror: a young couple being married and bravely joining with family and friends in a wedding dance, while off-stage we hear large numbers of their neighbors being dragged off to Auschwitz—to be noted especially is that the horror off-stage is sweetly palliated by love and stubborn courage on-stage. Humor: a kindly rabbi being offered a gift of shoe polish by a fellow-prisoner in the ghetto observes: "To shine these shoes is like feeding chicken soup to a corpse." Psychological insight: the passionate but unglamorous heroine to the cynical but golden-hearted hero: "You have such tenderness locked inside you, why don't you show it?" Poetic truth:

the heroine to the hero, ecstatically, just after she broke through his defenses and he through her overripe virginity: "What is your favorite color? What were you like as a little boy?" On second thought, all these specimens should have been listed under one heading, "horror."

Put it another way: a bit actress is dragged across the stage by a bit actor; for this to image adequately something as big as the abominable destruction of tens of thousands of people, a word, a gesture, or at least a special kind of silence has to be found with which to lift this picture from the level of a snapshot to that of a symbol. In *The Trojan Women,* Euripides did it with poetry; in the Polish film *Kanal,* its brilliant creator, Andrzej Wajda, did it chiefly with certain movements, sounds, and still-nesses. But the pretentious platitudes and superficial posturings of *The Wall* merely add another heavy insult to one of the world's greatest injuries, and the atrocity of such writing is aptly seconded by the fatuousness of a comfortable audience, commenting, after an evening of alternate tsk-tsking and guffawing, on the magnificence of this drama. I cannot help thinking that people who can feel purged and uplifted by *The Wall* would be themselves capable of instigating just such unuplifting purges as those with which the play ostensibly deals. And to adapters like Mr. Lampell I would suggest that the next job worthy of their talents might be to adapt *Leaves of Grass* into a sonnet sequence.

What are we to conclude from this sampling of the Broadway season's firstlings? That realism has outlived itself? That only foreign productions have merit? That whimsy is the order of the day? I think not. Only this: that if we want the domestic products to prove as viable as the imports, we must have dramaturgy, not decalcomania; we must find actions and words that fill something bigger than stages and auditoriums: the imagination.

Winter 1960-1

Until recently one could have answered the question "Who is the best American playwright?" with the pseudo-Gidian rejoinder, "Tennessee Williams, alas." After *Period of Adjustment* this view may need readjusting. The main denigratory epithet for Williams's more recent works has been "unhealthy," but this somewhat philistine label is misleading; "cowardly" and "untruthful" seem to me apter words to describe *Cat on a Hot Tin Roof, Suddenly Last Summer,* or *Sweet Bird of Youth.* But no full-length play of his before

Period of Adjustment could have been called dull. Vulgar, biased, pretentious, jejune, oversimplified, unreal—all of these, if you will, but not boring. Which, regrettably, does not even mean that *Period* is free from that first sextet of sins, to which, however, it adds the seventh and deadliest, dullness. I am not saying that there were not some members of the audience who guffawed fitfully throughout the evening, but I cannot help feeling that they were the sort of people who would laugh to see their grandmother slip on a banana peel, and split their sides if she were unable to get up again.

Williams has lately been announcing with a complaisant snigger that *Period of Adjustment* represents a breaking away from his "black" plays toward a new-found serenity, gained with blood, sweat, and fifty-dollar checks for his analyst. I doubt that *Period* is serene, or that it is healthy; but I use the word not as most people, critics included, seem to use it. For it is an error of long standing to assume that the subject-matter or the verbiage of a play is what renders it healthy or unhealthy; to the extent that these terms have meaning, they refer to intentions and implications. *Period of Adjustment*, though superficially harmless, falsifies truth in two ways typical of Tennessee Williams. First, it asserts that the seemingly controlled, stable, functioning people are just as badly off, when the full truth is out, as the flagrantly disturbed ones; and, secondly, it implies that a little good-will and effort can set the gravest emotional conflicts aright. As concerns the latter, since I cannot feel that Williams is stupid and believes in the preposterous Hollywood happy ending, I can only surmise that when a frigid, hysterical girl at the end of this or that play of his reaches out to a sadistic and homosexual husband, and an orchestra all but intones "Home, Sweet Home," what the author is cravenly suggesting is, "Of course there is no hope for such as these, but I'll be damned if I'll come out and say it!" This is Williams's dishonesty: he could love the audience twice as much, loved he not the box office more. And as regards the implication that the difference between human functioning and malfunction is roughly zero, this simply isn't true. Doubtless it is not, as puritans would have it, a difference in kind, but only in degree; it does, however, exist. To minimize it or rationalize it away is the stratagem of a guilty conscience. The heroine of *Period*, a student nurse, describes the world (shades of the forest of Arden!) as a giant neurological ward, and herself as the nurse in it. This is, of course, Williams seeing the world as a psychiatric ward, and himself as its male nurse. But no amount of wishing, even with all of Williams's brilliance and libido behind it, will make it so.

There is one sort of truth in *Period of Adjustment:* clinical truth. Whenever a character reveals the cracks of his psyche, this is done with the accuracy of a psychiatric case history. But there is surely another view of man which perceives him as something that cannot be contained in a manila folder, and this the play fails to provide. In short, there is something lopsided about a play where in each of three married couples the woman takes the aggressive role and initiates the principal events. There is something suspect about a play in which the only intense warmth is generated in the relationship of the two younger husbands. There is something the matter with a play in which the supposedly healthy, solid citizen can readily fall in with an infantile get-rich-quick scheme of a markedly neurotic wartime buddy about whom he feels curiously warm. And all this becomes even more sinister when we consider that the entire action takes place in a house built above an enormous cave, and it is announced repeatedly with a subtlety that I can only call cymbalism that the house is slowly but surely crumbling and sinking into the abyss. Whether this metaphor should be applied to the world or merely to Williams's art remains debatable.

Even in his style Williams is becoming baroque. The beautiful language of the earlier plays has been supplanted by heavy-handed gongorism. In *Cat on a Hot Tin Roof,* for instance, there was obsessive play with the word "mendacity." In *Period of Adjustment,* "obfuscation" in Act One, and "dignity" and its cognates in Act Two, receive similarly compulsive kicking around. But perhaps it is time to stress the one good thing about this production: the splendid performances of the four principals. Barbara Baxley, in particular, creates enough truth and beauty to inscribe the largest Grecian urn; it is too bad that it has to be wasted here on a vessel of quite a different sort.

Robert Brustein has archly suggested that *Period of Adjustment* was not written by Tennessee Williams, but by some hack usurping his name. This seems to me all the more likely as Mr. Williams must recently have been busying himself with a play called *Hedda Gabler,* which David Ross, the producer-director, unwarrantedly ascribes to Henrik Ibsen. In this production which was fulsomely praised by every newspaper critic in the business, Hedda is played by Anne Meacham, a talented actress who has magnificently portrayed one Tennessee Williams heroine and understudied several others; unfortunately the part of the young girl in *Suddenly Last Summer* which seemed to fit Miss Meacham like a glove was no glove at all, but a shirt of Nessus. It has encased her, and her Hedda, in such a ranting agony of Tennesseean frustration that even as simple a statement as "I don't care," in which Hedda voices her gelid boredom with her husband, has to be turned into a taunt bordering on a tantrum, as if she wanted Tesman to rape and disembowel her on the spot. Miss Meacham wears enough green eye-shadow to make a Gorgon envious, has her hair up in a Bloody Mary hairdo, and stalks, stamps, and shrieks as though she were playing all of Dracula's brides simultaneously. Add to this a simpering Tesman who is clearly a mama's, or auntie's boy, mincing his words and patently incapable of making love to a woman; a Judge Brack (Frederick Rolf) who sucks every syllable he utters as if it were an obscene lollypop and who at any moment might apply the corncob to Hedda; an Eilert Løvborg who looks uncomfortable without a torn T-shirt and whose manuscript must have read like something by Kerouac; a Thea Elvsted who flutters like one of Williams's odious "good girls"; an Aunt Julia straight off the nearest decaying plantation; and you have a pastiche of Williams that on Broadway would have made the angels weep, but off-Broadway is considered art and rakes in money. By the way, Elizabeth Colquhoun, an English actress who plays the part of the maid, with some dozen lines to speak, puts all the rest of the cast to shame.

The translation by Michael Meyer is of a kind all too frequent in England, a sort of tea-and-crumpets Ibsen in which "you are a year senior to me," "today she's been taken especially bad," "we visited to Rome," and "if *the* worst comes to *the* worst" things are "intriguing." Mr. Meyer came over from England to see this production, and went home in dismay. Even for such a translation as his, the punishment seems too severe.

While we are off-Broadway, three more productions should be noted. The least painful of these was Molly Kazan's double bill of short plays, *Rosemary* and *The Alligators*. Both pieces are slight and less than finished works: they seemed somehow Actors' Studio improvisations rather than plays, and Actors' Studio improvisations seem, in turn, less impromptu dramatic sketches than group therapy for actors. All the same, in *Rosemary* Mrs. Kazan latched on to a good idea: a young married couple of struggling vaudeville performers act out for publicity shots their little-boy-and-little-girl routine in kiddie clothes on a near-deserted beach. A middle-aged, middle-class couple who happen to be there are persuaded to snap a camera the vaudevillians have rented and lugged along. The young couple is having difficulties centering on the husband's unwillingness to accept paternal responsibilities toward his baby daughter. The bourgeois couple, who at first bantered pleasantly with the artistes, now egg them on to greater efforts; finally the vaudevillians, possessed by their act, become garishly real, squabbling, mean children. When the bourgeois pair is outraged and retreats in a dudgeon, the now united "kiddies" retort with jeers and cat-calls; but this moment of euphoric solidarity is followed closely by a depressed awareness of the flaws in their respective childhoods caused by the selfishness of their parents, and of the resultant damage to their adult lives. Thereupon the young husband (flavorsomely played by William Daniels) promises to live up to his new duties. Thus in the conclusion of *Rosemary* Mrs. Kazan successfully blends three elements: the battle of the sexes, or the Shavian view of man; the hostility between the artist and the bourgeoisie, or the romantic view; regression, reliving of childhood experiences, and self-realization, or the psychoanalytic view. If the rising action did not rise at an angle of a mere ten degrees, and if Piper Laurie, as the young wife, possessed the rudiments of acting, this would have been a provocative vignette, but, in any case, no more than that.

The Alligators offers us a rather more conventional plot, in which an ambitious young TV and film producer wants to make an "enlightened" movie biography of a dead gangster, showing that gangsterism is not so much sheer moral evil as a regrettable result of certain social and psychological factors. The old-fashioned ethical views of the gangster's frightened but shrewd widow merely elicit the producer's condescending smugness, but a jar of acid thrown by the dead gangster's mob into the producer's actress-girlfriend's face presumably awaken, belatedly, his understanding. As the gangster's widow, Jo Van Fleet gave a bravura performance which will be long remembered by the fortunate few who saw it, but Miss Laurie trying to simulate a totally ungifted actress managed to be ludicrous. Had she played the part absolutely straight, her natural badness would have been quite convincing. It is a little worrisome, also, to find on the same bill two plays by the same author, one of which is Freudian, the other anti-Freudian. But I suppose such scruples had best be reserved for works of greater literary consequence.

The Rules of the Game is minor Pirandello which could have made an effective one-acter (a form in which Pirandello excelled), but drawn out to a full evening's length this tragicomic little marital triangle becomes a rather untidy trapezoid. In the hands of actors who dragged out what ought to be crisp and sophisticated as far as ponderous histrionics could stretch it, matters became unbearable. Indeed, the trio of principals and the three main supporting players seemed to me six characters in search of an assassin. Perhaps the most trying performance in a close contest was that of Joanna Merlin, the blaring monotony of whose presence was relieved only by the astounding changes in the size of her bosom from act to act, not, I daresay, ascribable to natural causes. But it was an evening in which one had to be grateful for even the slightest form of variety.

Before discussing anything The Living Theatre puts on, it behooves one to say grace for the existence of a repertory company willing to serve up plays that are out of the ordinary. Let us now consider this said, and get down to the unhappy business of *In the Jungle of Cities* by Bertolt Brecht, just added to the repertory. From the moment the first text is flashed on the screen and we spot that catachrestic *w* in "Don't wrack your brains," an effect of alienation sets in undreamt of by Brecht. But though Gerhard Nellhaus's translation does not manage to cope with the curious blend of elevated, almost legalistic, formalism and plain-spoken toughness that is Brecht's style (or one of his styles), it is still the best thing about this production, and free of the howlers that crop up in a Bentley translation. This early play, written in 1924 when Brecht was 26, belongs to his symbolist-expressionist period, of which the uneven but impressive *Baal* is a much more distinguished example. *In the Jungle of Cities* concerns the fight between a poor young intellectual who works in a Chicago lending library and a rich Malayan lumber dealer who wants to buy and corrupt him by foul means or (if necessary) fair. The plot would be too complicated to summarize—even if it were not too obscure to grasp—but as far as I can make it out, it deals with a kind of Self and Anti-Self, two aspects of the individual: that which in the name of honesty, self-fulfillment, and freedom is willing to be both destructive and self-destructive, and that which in the name of the world and the devil is willing to indulge in mock generosity, sham self-sacrifice, and a relentlessly hounding pseudo-solicitude. This is truly Brechtian; for Brecht was a man whose most sinister views were couched in cleverness and charm, and whose decencies went always somehow against the grain of his asperity. But to elevate one's own slightly puerile perversities into an image of man, to pretend that an extremely idiosyncratic inscape is a great universal symbol (as we now see Tennessee Williams doing), is arrogant falsification. Brecht actually recreated the situation of *Jungle* in a later, maturer play, the excellent *Puntila* (which Nellhaus translated even better for Repertory Boston), and The Living Theatre would have been well advised to do this riper work.

Matters are not helped by a shoddy and threadbare production, lighting that slashes faces in half, music that enervates the ear, scenery that is cluttered and un-Brechtian in spirit, uncertain staging and acting, and, above all, as unattractive a set of players as I have ever seen assembled on any stage—what price naturalism? There is, to be sure, a superior performance by John A. Coe, and here and there a good moment from Marilyn Chris, Grant Code, and one or two others, but the turbid mass of the play comes alive only by fits and starts—not so much epic as epileptic theatre.

Returning now to Broadway, we find there two attractive theatrical events. It is a little saddening that they should be the only good things to report on at this time, and that they should both be imported: it is a painful thing when the truth sounds like snobbery. It is even more painful when one has to share it with *Time* magazine.

A Taste of Honey would be a good play by anyone; by Shelagh Delaney, an English teen-ager, it is extraordinary. It is a small, charming, tender play: for the first half you think it will be hard-boiled and winsome by turns, or even both at once. But presently you become aware of an overwhelming loneliness, and of the gallant, pathetic striving of a couple of deeply dented but wholly lovable young people not to succumb to their aloneness in a big, ramshackle one-room apartment which, though rather smaller than the world, appears just as grubby and impersonal. Then you are utterly drawn into the play and to these two not quite innocent innocents. In the early part of *A Taste of Honey*, the humdrum life of a very young girl in the north of England who goes from pillar to post with her sluttish and boozy but ribaldly amusing mother elicits some interest by its authenticity of voice, but it does not command our undivided attention. The girl's wearily wise acceptance of her mother and even wearier gestures at rebellious self-assertion lead to her schoolgirl romance and affair with a Negro sailor (this part is written and played a trifle too prettily to ring true). There follows the mother's desertion: the old girl goes off with a rather classy young gigolo (presented, likewise, more jovially than might be, but saved by Nigel Davenport's stylish performance which perfectly balances the fellow between polish and putrescence). All this has interest and nicely shifting emotional appeal, but it still fails to be absorbing. When, however, the girl is left alone in an apartment she hates, has had to quit school, supports herself by working in a shoe-store and bar, is pregnant by the Negro sailor who'll probably never come back; when she takes in, to share her loneliness, a pleasant, artistic young boy, who, alas, is a homosexual, and they both would like to be lovers but can summon up no more than devotion and bickering; when her advanced pregnancy forces her to stay at home, with the young art student, himself impecunious, looking after her—then, at last, a warm, understated, exquisite sadness descends on the play. From then on to the end, A Taste of Honey shimmers with the funny, wistful, awe-inspiring spectacle—set down without any self-pity—of two children trying to face the grimness of an all too precipitous adulthood with the greatest degree of adolescent humor and grace.

The truly surprising skill that this play commands is the way of making language do double duty: for, in a play about ordinary people, language must be simple enough to be appropriate and believable, and yet also special and fine enough to rise above the ordinary, indeed, to go beyond prose into a kind of poetry. O'Neill labored all his life to acquire this know-how, but achieved it only in his very last plays. Shelagh Delaney seems to have been born with it. "And me, I'm contemporary," says her heroine. "I really am, aren't I? I really do live at the same time as myself, don't I?" expressing thus in simple and fresh words a universal problem and her anxiety concerning it. And how touching it is when the young invert tries to be casual in justifying his living platonically with the girl whom he would like to marry: "Oh well, you need somebody to love you while you're looking for someone to love." But such lines are much more impressive when heard in their context which gives them their slightly raucous, bittersweet vibrancy. And even the humor in Miss Delaney's play is rich in suggestive ambiguity. Thus when the silly mother remarks: "I don't care for the cinema any more, it's getting more and more like the theatre," this is a three-pronged barb, puncturing simultaneously speaker, screen, and stage.

It is to be regretted that what was in England a more understated and subtle production, has been broadened and blunted here. Or just bloated: thus what the gigolo was pleased to pick up in England was "a couple of grapefruit on a 32-inch bust"; in the American version this becomes 38 inches, though, happily, the number of grapefruit remains two. Angela Lansbury's portrayal of the mother contributes nicely to this loss of subtlety. Miss Lansbury is comical enough, but one of the two directors should have explained to her that the stage of the Lyceum is not the Hollywood Bowl. As the daughter, that often superlative actress, Joan Plowright, is sometimes forced into exaggeration, as a man beside a waterfall must shout to make himself heard. But even so she manages, especially when Miss Lansbury is off stage, to rise to that overpowering simplicity which comes only from a profound understanding of one's art. But perhaps the most compelling performance of the evening is that of Andrew Ray as the troubled young artist. Mr. Ray accomplishes something as wonderful as it is economical: he simply plays the homosexual as a human being first, and envelops the incipient femininity in a youngster's angularity of movement, so that a wholly apposite coltishness overshadows the lack of masculinity. It is a performance both unusual and credible. This is the nature of the playwright's excellence, too: the quickening of the ordinary with an injection of the atypical that makes it survive the dangers of obviousness.

Irma la Douce, too, started out as a smaller, more delightful show in Paris, became bigger and more predictable in London, and has been divested of additional refinements for the benefit of Broadway. None the less, compared to the new domestic musicals, it is a work of towering genius. It has its stretches of unfunniness, but achieves also a measure of genuine artistry. There is, first of all, the neat, all-encompassing, resourceful direction of Britisher Peter Brook, whose authority and ideas are ubiquitous and inexhaustible. Even when he resorts to old tricks, which he frequently and unashamedly does, they emerge rejuvenated by expertise. He is helped considerably by Rolf Gerard's sophisticated sets which move with the poise and agility of dancers, and by the evocative lighting. Seldom, moreover, have I heard such sure-fire orchestrations and vocal arrangements. Some of the songs are quite good, the lyrics are acceptable, the jokes and puns properly outrageous, in a few instances even making use of such big words as "André Gide." The plot happily manages to laugh at itself, and the musical wisely resolves itself into a series of loosely connected songs and skits. Part of its charm lies, for me, in its macaronic quality. Confronted with a song that begins: "There's no kyuah, foh lamooah," one feels at first in the realms of Lewis Carroll and Edward Lear. When reprised, "foh lamooah" becomes "follow *moi*," and only at the next reprise (luckily all good things in *Irma* are milked and milked) does one unscramble the whole thing as: "There's no cure for *l'amour*." All along, one's ears are tickled by an aural Franco-English *entente cordiale*, with some Americana tossed in for good measure, and there's a feeling of well-being which is almost as much political as theatrical.

Nearly all the performers are talented and prepossessing, but Irma, played, sung, danced, and exuded by Elizabeth Seal, is an absolute peach, and if we weren't all such inveterate Prufrocks, would have been eaten long ago. The program lists sixteen men and one girl, but the moment Miss Seal appears on the stage, the ratio is reversed. From every cranny of the scenery Miss Seal crops up all at once, and when she is smack before you, splits up by near-atomic fissure into the most winning bevy of enchantresses. She was well on her way toward the Royal Ballet, we hear, when an injury to her ankle brought her to musical comedy—truly a case of the fortunate fall. Neither the unimaginative choreography nor the lapses in the writing can keep Miss Seal from proving that the artist, as Molière said of himself, takes his due wherever he finds it.

I shall mention briefly two insignificant comedies, *Under the Yum-Yum Tree*, and Arthur Laurents's *Invitation to a March*. The first is interesting only insofar as it demonstrates that however shoddy, disingenuous, indeed, vulgar a play may be, a masterly director (Joseph Anthony) can salvage with the help of a few snatches of comic dialogue and one or two able players enough fun to make one grant the play the indulgence usually reserved for an ingratiating B-grade movie. A similar reprieve might have been earned by Laurents's play, were it not that *Invitation to a March* is shot through with delusions of grandeur and pretends to offer answers when it does not even comprehend the questions adequately. Neither such poignant bits of dialogue as "Schuyler, I rather love you.—I rather love *you*, Mother," nor such epigrams as "Maybe one day West Point will be a dancing school" (presumably the day after the world has become a giant neurological ward), do much more than shed light on the author's problem, and the whole notion of a contemporary Long Island setting for the Cinderella story with pseudo-Freudian overtones, is as dubious as it is creaky. The chief merit of the evening (besides some more than competent performances) is that it holds out in Jane Fonda the promise of a major actress to come, though she is already a delight to watch. Despite her studies with Lee Strasberg, Miss Fonda emerges as an individualistic, non-"method" talent—thanks, no doubt, to the paternal influence—so that the several cubic feet of American theatre surrounding her light up deliciously. To anyone choking on a surfeit of rasping-voiced, disheveled, hysteroid actresses, I offer Miss Fonda as that rare thing, a health-diet that is not less but more savory than the regular fare.

This brings me to the biggest blot on the scutcheon of this rather smudgy Broadway season. I refer to Tad Mosel's dramatization of James Agee's *A Death in the Family* under the title *All the Way Home*. Mr. Mosel, producer Fred Coe, and director Arthur Penn have all proved their mettle on previous occasions; here, however, they have combined to lay a roc's egg. About the play there is little to say except that novels do not gain by being dramatized, that complex, psychological novels bordering on prose poetry lose even more, and that Mr. Mosel simply wasn't up to the task. Much of what is moving in the book is—not always inevitably—missing, or coarsened, or painfully "explained." The play is largely alien to the spirit of Agee, obvious, and neither poetic nor dramatic. Scenes involving the older generations are handled creditably, but the middle-aged, the young, and the very young fare less well. The director must take the blame for, among other things, casting such inadequate players as Lillian Gish and the excruciatingly inept Tom Wheatley; and also for entrusting the female and child leads to Colleen Dewhurst and John Megna, who, though skilled, are devoid of all charm. Among the principals, only Arthur Hill and Aline MacMahon are impressive, and there is a foursome of boys not one of whom would, in older and better days, have escaped the Tarpeian Rock.

More than anything else, *All the Way Home* is uninteresting. What is interesting, however, is the bullying of the public into deferring to a coalition of pusillanimity, meretriciousness, bad taste, and sentimentalism. First the title was changed to *All the Way Home,* because one was scared witless that the word "death" would keep audiences away. *All the Way Home,* though an insipid title, would do very nicely because the initial A keeps it at the top of alphabetical listings. (This, of course, meant obscuring Agee's intentions and share in the work, thus actually decreasing the box-office appeal.) Next, because Fred Coe was unable to raise all the money, a co-producer was called in:

Arthur Cantor, a press agent with the mentality of a press agent. The moment that the play, in spite of the reviewers' undiscerning and undeserved praise, began to fail with the audiences, Coe announced its closing. But Cantor's public-relations genius began to stir. He took out, together with Coe, large newspaper ads headlined "The Miracle on 44th Street," and proceeded to tell people what a superb play *All the Way Home* is, and that if only the cheering audiences would pass the word on, etc. etc. After every performance of the play Mr. Cantor began making curtain speeches about the beauty and fearlessness of this work and the glory it brings to the theatre, and if only everyone in the audience would tell all his friends, etc. etc. Direct mail campaigns were undertaken, Ed Sullivan was prevailed on to give plugs at regular intervals on his TV show, and, as far as I can make it out, theatre people were invited to come and see and help this brave, lovely show.

I attended what was to have been the fourth and last performance. Needless to say, there were no press seats available to me, and Mr. Cantor assured us that even his grandmother had to pay, etc. etc. The names of those present would—to use a phrase doubtless dear to Mr. Cantor's heart—have read like a show-business who's who. Everybody seemed primed and forewarned that this was his chance to do his bit for his profession and colleagues, for the glory of the theatre, for the good of mankind. When Lillian Gish came on stage, herself the living proof of how sentimentalism can magnify into a star a saccharine silent-screen personality whose only skills are batting her eyelashes and uttering nauseating homespun truths in a voice dripping with prairie cuteness, a two-minute applause stopped whatever action there was in the play; similar outbursts occurred elsewhere, and Mr. Cantor's unctuous oration to praise the play, not to bury it, was greeted with more frenetic applause.

For it seems that in the interest of the theatre we must love everything, and if it is pretentious, vapid, and invokes high-sounding abstractions (and cost some goats a pretty penny), we must prostrate ourselves before it. Already the Cantor Plan has spawned similar campaigns, and several ghastly plays have tried or are trying to buy and browbeat their way to success. I can foresee the day when every street from Bleecker to 59th will have its own miracle, and the quality of plays will be determined by the amount and frequency of space bought in the newspapers. Current ads of Mr. Cantor's keep us regularly posted about how marvelously the word-of-mouth campaign has been working. As the late Professor Karl Viëtor remarked when Jaspers brought out his 1200-page book, *What Is Truth?*: "If that fellow knew what the truth is, he wouldn't need 1200 pages to tell it." When will Americans everywhere see through the public-relations and ad men who protest too much? When will the word of mouth be superseded by the word of brain?

Spring 1961

One play I always avoided reading was Denis Johnston's *The Moon in the Yellow River*. I had discovered at a tender age that there are only two Irish plays. There is the modern one about the I. R. A. and the Black and Tans and the poetic hero who dies spouting poetry, and his girl friend who is too good a Catholic to go to bed with him, but not so good a one to escape being impregnated by the villain. There is also a brave mother who, almost without stopping to stir the stew, loses countless sons, and a braggart father who guzzles and gabs with his cronies, and the younger son who betrays the movement and is shot, and the good priest who knows everything and everyone (and especially his housekeeper), and the bad priest who understands and tolerates nothing (least of all the heroine's pregnancy or the need for planting a harvest of bombs). This more or less takes care of the plot, but for the sake of the local color there are assorted drunks, brawlers, liars, keening crones, provocative widows, and a tremendous number of participial constructions introduced by the word "and," and "herself" and "himself" proliferating. The other play is the historical one about a beautiful queen and her hero lover and the aging, jealous king who sets obvious traps for them into which they fall with heroic stupidity. Sometimes, to be sure, it is the queen herself who is jealous, and sometimes there is a chorus of beggars or strolling players—especially if the play is in verse, which it usually is, meaning that it has a few participles less and a few more references to Maeve, Cuchulain, Conchubor and other figures famous for not being pronounced anywhere near the way they are spelled.

Well now, I had the highest, and most desperate, hopes that *The Moon in the Yellow River* was the *tertium quid*: the one Irish play that was not one of the other two. If there is incontinence in it, I prayed to myself, it surely concerns consumption of opium; the poetic hero surely spouts haikus or, at worst, pantoums; the lovely heroine is surely seduced by an unfrocked

Buddhist monk; and if anything gets blown up, it is a sampan with home-made fireworks. Imagine if you can my horror when, after years of religiously saving up this play, I was finally confronted with it at the East End Theatre. There was the same poetic hero shot in the process of I.R.A. activities, the same comic tipplers and termagant housekeeper, and the same electric works being blown to kingdom come. No, you cannot imagine my consternation. Not even the unwonted presence among the dramatis personae of a comic Austrian and a misanthropic scientist could make up for this orgy of *déjà vu*. There was not a single sampan in sight—just the usual junk.

Nevertheless, the play has a modest charm which was well served by the decent direction of David Fulford and scenery by Mary Ann Reed that successfully defied the tightness of both space and budget. Most of the acting was commendable, except for the scientist of Roy Poole, a hulking clod of an actor for whom it is about as easy to enter into the subtleties of a character as it is for a camel to pass through a needle's eye, and the poetic rebel of Jonathan Frid, whose mouthings and posturings were deplorable. (His notion of diction is to make the final consonant equal in length all the foregoing vowels rolled together.) But casting the roles of intellectuals will always be a problem while our actors nurture their ignorance like a delicate, exotic fruit.

By way of contrast: Gustaf Gründgens brought his Hamburg troupe to the City Center, and they gave us a *Faust* (unfortunately only Part One) of such overwhelming intelligence and elegant spareness that one almost missed a little old-fashioned schmalz here and there. The sets by Theo Otto were impressive by their very omission of detail, and Mark Lothar's music was equally effective whether derived from German folk song or New Orleans jazz. Its association of the *Walpurgisnacht* with the American dance hall was as thought-provoking as the image of Faust's study with retorts and alembics ominously built up into a sort of atomic reactor. Tasteful economy presided over the cutting of the text, too, enabling the Deutsches Schauspielhaus to reduce the running time to three hours. But it was the direction that was particularly lean and sinewy: the movement, though often intricate, was always purposeful and swift: handsomely stylized for Faust and Mephistopheles, pleasantly raffish for the simpler folk, and conspicuously absent from the inhabitants of the empyrean. Lines were delivered with the ease and precision of German gymnasts at the Olympics: neat, efficient, speedy syllables intricately performing on the high bar of poetry. But a little cool, a little lacking in heart; thus the most celebrated bravura passages were delivered particularly casually and trippingly: Gründgens, a somewhat hoary Mephistopheles, throwing away debonairly such lines as "Staub soll er fressen, und mit Lust" or "Ich bin der Geist, der stets verneint!" and Will Quadflieg, an extremely intelligent Faust, vying with him in underplaying lines like "Verweile doch! du bist so schön." But, mind you, all this was done with utmost finesse and deliberateness, as if the actors wanted to illustrate the Goethean apothegm that the master reveals himself only within self-imposed restrictions. I was fortunate, however, in seeing both Gründgens and, on another day, the American-born Ullrich Haupt play Mephistopheles; for Haupt's slightly broader interpretation, though it had not Gründgens's grace of movement and general *raffinement,* added some welcome earthiness to the part, and made a scene like that with the doltish student considerably more comical. I must admit that I rather missed the poodle and Gretchen's spinning wheel; the former may have been a victim of quarantine regulations, but the latter's absence was surely emblematic of rabid streamlining.

The handful of plays from the repertory of the Comédie Française, which followed the Germans into the City Center, was an *hors d'oeuvre* of a different color. Though it was pleasant to see and hear this venerable aggregation once again, how sadly it falls short of what it was no more than, say, a dozen years ago (I am not even talking of periods when an entirely fresh outside influence, such as Barrault's or Jean Marais's, took over). Nowhere to be seen now a *jeune premier* like Jean Chevrier, a young leading lady like Renée Faure, a mature leading man like Jean Davy, a wily, subtle character actor like the late Aimé Clariond. True, Jacques Charon and Robert Hirsch have tried to infuse some new spirit into the proceedings, but Charon gives us burlesque, which, at best, has limited application, and Hirsch introduces a Marlon Brando-Tennessee Williams note, which has its curiosity value, but strikes me rather like going to the Tour d'Argent and ordering hamburger and California wine.

To get down to particulars, *L'Impromptu de Versailles* was done in a routine, faded fashion, rather like the set and costumes that badly need redesigning. And as Georges Descrières played Molière without imaginativeness or delicacy, this charming little play flapped haplessly around a wobbling pivot. No one was credited with the direction, perhaps because no one in the present company could remember that far back. *Les Fourberies de Scapin* suffered greatly by comparison with Barrault's famous production. Where Robert Hirsch's Scapin was different—Actors' Studio with French dressing—Barrault's was prototypical and moving; where Hirsch's décor and costumes were agreeable, Christian Bérard's were works of art; where Jacques Charon's staging was hearty and rambunctious, Barrault's was also poetic and wisely humane. A typical difference: Géronte, the ornery curmudgeon, was played by Michel Aumont, a by no means untalented but very young and physically slight actor, made to look like a dyspeptic Santa Claus. When he gets into the bag and mercilessly beaten, one almost feels sorry for this frail and rather introverted miser. In Barrault's production, Charles Mahieu, a wheezing, blubbery whale of a man, was Géronte, and to see such a mountain of meanness get its just deserts releases those atavistic satisfactions in an audience that good *commedia dell'arte,* or Punch and Judy shows, are meant to sublimate. The current production was further hampered by Micheline Boudet's factitious and unprepossessing Zerbinette—her big laughing scene was downright amateurish. (Mlle. Boudet went on to confirm this poor first impression in her subsequent appearances. The Français has fallen on bad times indeed if this is the best leading lady they can muster.)

Tartuffe, as directed and played by Louis Seigner, was another stock, stale affair (in this case no one was credited with scenery and costumes, and for good reason), which, in turn, suffered horribly from comparison with Jouvet's last production of it. Seigner, who in the right part can be unbeatable (for example, as the turnkey in the movie Christian Jacque made of *The Charterhouse of Parma*), is neither physically nor psychologically suited to the role of Tartuffe. Whereas Jouvet could make both the holiness and the unholiness of the man larger than life-size, so that we stared into his hollow aspect as into a cave inhabited by an oracle or monster, Seigner's petty, fatty, bourgeois nastiness hardly conveys the sinisterness of hypocrisy's eponymous hero. The difference is like turning on your television set expecting Bishop Sheen, and getting Cardinal Spellman instead. There were, however, two entirely satisfying performances by the charming and sensitive Annie Ducaux as Elmire, and the thoroughly dependable Lise Delamare as Dorine.

The high point of the engagement was *Britannicus.* Here there was extremely suitable staging by Michel Vitold (whom one remembers as a distinguished actor, and one not trained at the Comédie), noble scenery and costumes by Francine Gaillard-Rissler, and some good performing. In the part of Nero, Hirsch's "method"-acting came into its own, and contrasted meaningfully with Annie Ducaux's grand, but not too grand, style as Agrippina. Danièle Ajoret's Junie, though vocally a little limited, was exquisite visually and histrionically; François Chaumette, rather undistinguished in other parts, had an interestingly skeptical, flaccid interpretation of Narcisse. It would have been a notable evening but for Michel Bernardy's effeminate, awkward, often ranting Britannicus, hell-bent on proving himself the second-noblest Roman after Winnie Ille Pu. What struck me especially was how much sturdier Racine's genius is than Molière's: how much more readily than Molière's often dated buffoonery Racine's poetry triumphs over an offensive performance such as Bernardy's. What struck me also was the ignorance and rude noisiness of the audience. Little did they appreciate that they were in the presence of that ultimate beauty "whose novelty survives," as Cowper put it, "Long knowledge and the scrutiny of years."

The last bill was Feydeau's Le Dindon, which translates into English as a turkey. Those who enjoy bedroom farce, i.e., all Frenchmen and, apparently, most Americans, found these more than three hours of straining toward various beds into which hardly anyone finally falls, uproarious. I laughed intermittently, but thought the notion that bedroom farce can be paced and stressed in much the same way as Corneille questionable. Two things stood out: the unmannered and thoroughly believable performance of Catherine Samie as a tart, and the flitting, mincing, and strutting of the entire male contingent except for Louis Seigner. It was as though they had needed shots of adrenalin for this change of tempo, but received, by mistake, estrogen. One wonders whether Le Dindon really lends itself to production by an all-female cast. But, if for nothing else, we must thank the Comédie for corroborating the dictum of the boy Rimbaud: "Racine est le pur, le fort, le grand."

Let us turn now to a rather different France for a look at Ionesco's Rhinoceros. There are several objections one can make to the play: that it far outstays the welcome of its imaginatively satirical point; that the switch from fantasy to realism in the last act is clumsy; that, being an attempt of Ionesco's to befriend the bourgeois whom he used to flabbergast, it ends up, like most compromises, unsatisfactory to both parties, Parnassus and the pit, alike. The fact remains that it is wittier, richer in ideas (even if some of them merely rehash former Ionesco trouvailles—the Logician, for example, is only a paler version of the Professor in The Lesson), and more genuinely theatrical than almost anything written these days. The production, likewise, is not quite up to what we have come to expect from that artful director, Joseph Anthony. Whereas Ionesco tried to bring the play down only to the level of the French public, Anthony has attempted to reduce it further to the catchment basin of Broadway. Though the staging has his usual nervous inventiveness and bristles with ferocious fun, the play's deeper, oracular voice is gagged by the gags. The performances are creditable, some outstanding, though the acting styles, unfortunately, do not blend as well as they might. All in all, *Rhinoceros* is not magnificent, but it *is* art.

How sad, by comparison, is a play like *Advise and Consent,* which also concerns political and personal morality. To see a good deal of directorial skill, some very able acting, astonishing sets (Rouben Ter-Arutunian has designed bold semi-abstractions, mostly rectangles, that slide from one position into another and transport you with them from Senate chamber to bedroom) wasted on a piece of sensationalistic and tendentious writing that bears only the faintest, most gimmicked-up resemblance to political or psychological truth, is, to put it mildly, saddening. It seems to me that in the America of the future (where Loring Mandel's play and Allen Drury's best-selling novel on which it is based take place) the attitude toward a single, youthful homosexual experience would not be medieval. Yet the "guilty" senator's devoted wife is scared nearly out of her wits by it, and he himself dares not confess it to the fellow-senator nearest and dearest to him and who could be of considerable help in the smear campaign that is about to begin. That the protagonist's only recourse, rather than striking back at his vile enemies, should be prompt suicide, makes him into an intellectual, if not moral, coward. But it is clear that the author (I shall not try to distinguish between Mr. Drury and Mr. Mandel, who seem to me nothing if not interchangeable) is disingenuously playing both for sympathy for his hero and for the endorsement of the broader public, which, presumably, demands that any deviation from the straight and narrow be fully expiated. Again, it seems unlikely that a president of this country and some of the highest office-holders would be "fellow-travelers," as the play would have it; what seems more likely is that a good many of them will, as always, be ignorant and stupid. But the author, with typical middle-brow sanctimoniousness, can conceive of corruption in high places, but not of imbecility. And the corrupt ones, of course, lose out in the end. It is, again, a total misrepresentation to show the American people as reacting to Russian successes on the moon with terror and desperate craving for appeasement; at least until the bloodletting begins, the people will always be on the side of the warlike swagger. I find the author's motives highly suspect, but since I am not concerned with his politics but with his writing, suffice it to say that this is on the level of "We have a marriage, haven't we?" and "Stranger things have happened—like the Grand Canyon." But he tries to make up with redundancy for what he lacks in other areas: people are asked to speak "succinctly, with brevity," and minds are described as "tough, strong," and so forth.

All this would not have bothered me so much as the audience reaction. The absurd seriousness with which this play was discussed during intermissions and explained to one's neighbor during performance ("He is a homosexual, you see. . . ." "Let me think, in the book it was the other one who. . . ." "*That* is meant to be Stevenson, don't you know?") was enough to fill one with a far greater contempt than one could muster for the novelist and his adapter. Though that, too, was not inconsiderable.

If I marveled at the audiences of *Advise and Consent*, it is the reviewers of *A Far Country*, who, with their raves, took my breath away. This play about Freud's discovery of psychoanalysis is to drama roughly what the Great Moments in Medicine posters displayed in the windows of drugstores are to art. Or, for that matter, to science. The notion that great scientific discoveries make superb theatre is based on the confusion of the momentous with the dramatic, and all of Henry Denker's embellishing his subject helps about as much as if, had he been writing a play about Newton's discovery of gravity, he had upped the number of apples to a thousand. It may be, of course, that Mr. Denker was merely trying to complete the triptych the Warner Brothers had begun with *Pasteur* and *Dr. Ehrlich's Magic Bullet*, but there is a likelier reason: at Easter, Mr. Denker gave us a television play about Barabbas. Obviously, if one writes about such ecumenical father figures as Christ and Freud, one is comfortably wafted into realms beyond the reach of mere criticism. It is relevant to point out here that Mr. Denker could have learned something from those ineffably boring passages in Milton's epics when Divinity is brought on stage. But it was ever so nice to see that Freud was greatly helped in his discovery of the labyrinthine nature of the mind by toying with a ball of wool his wife left in his office, and that the good lady was equally ready with helpful cups of black coffee as with insights into her husband's psyche which could only be called Freudian. But, don't worry, the path of genius is never smooth: there is plenty of opposition from foes, and incomprehension from friends, family, and patients to provide as generous a quota of platitudes as you'll find kicking around any of the city's stages. Freud himself once explained the success of one of Sardou's historical plays with "The French love such oversimplifications." It seems they are not the only ones.

Norman Twain, the producer of *Roots*, was ill-advised in picking out the middle part of the deserving Wesker Trilogy. He was probably misled by its being the most successful of the three plays in England, but then there it had Joan Plowright —here there was only the hard-working but less than convincing Mary Doyle. Either the first or the third play would have gone over better in this country, because both the accents and the personalities of London's lower-class Jewry are within the grasp of American actors and audiences. Norfolk, on the other hand, might just as well be Sirius. The Babel of tongues, or, at any rate, accents that went into this local attempt at reproducing Norfolk peasant life is indescribable: there was everything from purest Hollywoodese to Third-Avenue Irish, as well as several brogues that came and went like spectators at a seven-day bicycle race. Perhaps the best performance was that of a superannuated, carious farm radio, which delivered sickly-sounding music along with extremely robust static. It was through just such static in the acting and ponderous staging that Arnold Wesker's message had to reach us. But this touching tale of a human being trying to teach her fellows a fulness of living and thinking she herself has not yet learned, and finding that, while she loses all her potential students and even her teacher, the man she loves, she at least succeeds in teaching herself, is sincerely and intelligently enough told to survive both its slight inherent sluggishness and the adventitious heaviness of this production. Yet I wonder how much this play can mean to audiences unfamiliar with the other two: the aims of the three plays are carefully interwoven and need one another's proximity to achieve their full impact.

One truly delectable and absolutely adult entertainment was briefly to be seen off-Broadway: a pair of short musicals by Jay Thompson which appeared under the collective title *Double Entry*. His book, in both cases, was pleasantly inconsequential; his tunes, completely endearing and, in some cases, even gifted with a wholly individual idiom; his lyrics could be tender or, what is harder, at once devilishly clever and innocently funny. To judge from this his first independent work, Jay Thompson is a man of such overwhelming talents that, if he is not struck down by the combined envy of everyone else in the field, he should soon become its uncontested champion. Why with excellent direction by Bill Penn, lovely performances—except for Jane Connell's hamming—such as one almost never encounters off-Broadway, and a good press, *Double Entry* should still have failed, will remain one of those curious, heartbreaking theatrical mysteries.

Not mysterious at all is the success of *Mary, Mary* by Jean Kerr, whom I can best describe as the Madonna of Larchmont Notions. Mrs. Kerr is just so much more intelligent and literate than the average suburban matron as to be able to paste together with some handy household glue five or six hundred wisecracks caught on the wing somewhere between the cocktail table and the kitchen sink. The three specialties of the house are the pseudo- (and, of course, anti-) intellectual joke like "He was writing long intellectual articles proving that Shakespeare was a homosexual—sort of the intellectuals' answer to *Photoplay*"; the joke that tickles the alert housewife's sensibilities: "I thought of you as the Golden Couple smiling over bowls of steaming Campbell's chicken soup"; and, most meretricious of all, the clean dirty joke: "I edit the letters to *The Ladies' Home Journal*.—They need to be edited?—It does seem rather like incest, doesn't it?" All of these, along with the embryonic characterizations and stock situations around which they are wrapped, seem to have been written in spilled Bloody Marys on white formica counter tops. But Mrs. Kerr has ascended, if not to heaven, to the cover of *Time* and to the over $20,000 income bracket, which, as she herself has said, makes her a serious writer. Twenty thousand dollars, like fifty million Frenchmen, cannot be wrong. Still, what made *Mary, Mary* moderately endurable for me was some good acting, especially from John Cromwell, and Joseph Anthony's devastatingly ingenious direction.

What to say of *The Devil's Advocate?* A play that treats sympathetically the Jews, the Catholic Church, pederasts, promiscuous women, and alcoholics, clearly has all of today's most powerful pressure groups behind it and can make light of the objection that an interesting situation is treated in it with the utmost banality and ineptitude. However, the fact that this adaptation of a novel by Morris L. West was written by one of our very worst playwrights, and directed by one of our very worst directors, both of whom happen to be Dore Schary, may outweigh the advantage of the aforementioned allies.

The two main export articles of Bengal are its tigers

and Tagores. The trouble with the latter is that, though almost as loud, they lack the former's bite. Sir Rabindranath's *The King of the Dark Chamber*, given at the Jan Hus Playhouse with fanciful trappings, enthusiastic staging, and vehement performances, is no exception: its platitudes are as pale and profuse as was the beard of that Indian sage. Under Western eyes, these mystic profundities (even when they are played, as a third of this play is, in almost pitch dark) shine with the unmistakable glow of tinsel. A case may be made, I think, for Tagore's folksy lyric poetry; his philosophic drama is elementary as philosophy and exiguous as drama.

Lack of space compels me to postpone discussion of Edward Albee's dishearteningly bad twin bill now at the York Playhouse, and of a few other plays on and off Broadway that, to some degree, suffer from the same malady. But at least I can end on a cheerful note: Jack Richardson's *Gallows Humor* at the Gramercy Arts is, despite a certain schematism and overstatement, amusing, literate, and, in its second half, a substantial piece of tragicomedy: as when a ludicrous Othello, white of face and liver, tries to strangle his domineering Desdemona; when he inquires pleadingly whether she isn't at last finding it difficult to breathe, she answers, all choked up with mirth, "This is as close as we have come to sex in years." The difference between Richardson and Albee—to disentangle names that are often carelessly bracketed—is that Richardson is not a perennial, self-indulgent, compulsive autobiographer. Though he has yet to write something as furibundly poetic as *Zoo Story*, his intellectual equipment, schooling, and self-discipline will never permit him to plummet to the level of Albee's subsequent plays. Equipped with George L. Sherman's perceptive direction and inexhaustibly creative performances by Julie Bovasso and Gerald Hiken, *Gallows Humor* offers an authentically new twist on the old theme of life-in-death and death-in-life—even if the twist is that of a rope around our necks.

Fall 1961

The one show that could run forever on Broadway would be a big, vulgar musical about Jewish Negroes. The author would have the reviewers, audiences, and Pulitzer people eating out of his little hand, and would not even have to consider all the perfumes of Arabia. Unfortunately, our showmen seem to be incapable of appropriating more than two of these useful ingredients at one time: thus *Milk and Honey* is a big musical about Israel, *Kwamina* a big musical about Africa, and *Purlie Victorious* has its Negroes celebrating Chanukah in their church. Yet a score of two out of three is hardly a negligible achievement, and I trust that all three shows are reaping their just rewards, though I can as of this moment report only on the third.

One of the characters in Ossie Davis's *Purlie Victorious* says, "Some of the best pretendin' is done in front of white folks," a maxim whose truth is corroborated at the box office of the Cort Theatre. The play is a kind of *Abie's Irish Rose* in blackface with somewhat heightened social consciousness and an author who has heard of Brecht. The humor of this farce, except for a few brighter moments in the second scene, consists of jokes in which a wife tells a husband who is retreating toward the stable, to look after the mule by all means, because, she observes, he and it are two of a kind; or of hilarious speeches in which the hero boosts the heroine's morale by assuring her she should be praised in all the languages of Africa, from Swahili to Bambulan, and proceeds to name every last one of them. (If only the encyclopedias could teach you as much about play-writing as about African dialects!) But because the huge topic of integration and social justice is treated farcically, the spectators can, if their sense of humor is as sophomoric as their social awareness, see themselves as a liberating army marching on its belly-laughs. Hence *Purlie Victorious* has been hailed with the subliterate encomia befitting another *Uncle Tom's Cabin*. But I doubt that it will succeed in bringing about another civil war, because it is so much less witty than Mrs. Stowe's immortal classic of *humour noir*.

The play is, however, admirably acted, and all the players whip up such a storm of performing that one can almost miss the vacuum at the eye of the storm. There is Ruby Dee's ability to make benightedness take on heroic proportions, Alan Alda's mastery in ringing changes on one note, Sorrell Booke's skill in making outrage look like a household commodity, and Godfrey M. Cambridge's marvelous black Falstaff without the assistance of Shakespeare. These and a couple of others manage to turn *Purlie Victorious* into somewhat less of a fiasco.

But if the success of *Purlie* is at best a national scandal as yet, that of the Greek Tragedy Theatre is well on its way toward being an international one. I saw the double bill consisting of the two final plays of the *Oresteia*; it was also a double translation: into demotic Greek and plebeian performing. Though we were assured on all sides of authentic recreations of classical drama, Mr. Rondiris, the founder-producer-director, not only failed to give us the true accouterments of Greek tragedy, but also defied ancient Greek practice by making the chorus speak—not just sing —in unison. (Of an intelligent modernization, he evidently cannot conceive.) The avoidance of masks in the *Eumenides, I* could, to be sure, understand: Mr. Rondiris, who in one respect at least seems to be as Greek as can be, has picked a chorus whose resemblance to women is close to absolute zero, and their naked faces achieved a bloodcurdling likeness to the Furies' which even the most terrifying masks could only have palliated. The dancing reminded one of an amateurish imitation of Ruth Draper doing her celebrated take-off on eurhythmics; the music might do in a pinch for toy soldiers or circus horses; the costumes, identified by the more than usually illiterate program notes as "products of the famous Greek textile handicraft," made the people and nobles of Argos look like a second-rate leper colony performing an Offenbach operetta.

A few random snapshots: the great recognition scene of the *Choephoroe* played like a rather jolly meeting between two Tenth Reunionists on the old Quadrangle; Orestes leading Clytemnestra to her death as though he were about to rebuke her for having neglected to water the aspidistra during his absence; the body of Aegisthus carried on stage from right to left on a litter covered with a threadbare orange shawl—and, a few minutes later, Clytemnestra's body carried on: same litter, same bearers, same thin orange shawl, only now, of course, from left to right. And what of the Orestes who appeared to have come home not to claim bloody justice but his old age pension, the Apollo who looked and sounded like a cut-rate catamite, the Clytemnestra who was a sort of faded Melina Mercouri without benefit of *bouzoukia*—but why go on? The one authentic touch was the zippers on the costumes of the Eumenides: they were the zipperiest zippers I ever saw. In short, small acting and less Greek.

The director, Dimitrios Rondiris, who arrogated the only full program note to himself (well ahead of Aeschylus), is to be commended for sparing no effort to appear at the theatre in time for curtain calls after every performance, matinees included, and taking a wholly unsolicited bow—though for some reason denying us the sight of the three decorations which the program says he was awarded—thus proving that, like chivalry in France, hubris is not yet dead in Greece. It may be worthy of note also that this *Oresteia* was warmly received by our reviewers, both by those who, following the program, gave its date as 45 B.C., and those who declared it three thousand years old.

Another excursion into ancient Greece was afforded us by Maurice Valency's *The Thracian Horses,* a retelling of the Alcestis story. Mr. Valency was kept waiting twenty years before he could see his play put on in New York, but, as if in compensation, he had to wait no more than one week to see it taken off. I was secretly hoping that all the wit and charm Mr. Valency had removed from his adaptations of Giraudoux and Dürrenmatt might have been stored up in his own play, which would then have been very rich indeed. But Mr. Valency is no embezzler. And no playwright, either. But he may draw some comfort from the fact that even such more Herculean Americans as T. S. Eliot and Thornton Wilder have failed to bring Alcestis back to our stage alive.

Mr. David Ross continues his Ibsen cycle by giving us a production of *Ghosts* that marks a small step up from his *Hedda Gabler.* Robert Brustein and even Walter Kerr have so cogently criticized the gross and wanton cutting, the many specific misinterpretations, and the general mis-staging, that I can content myself here with filling in a few minor gaps.

The quality of an Ibsen translation increases at an inverse ratio to the number of *fancy's* used—I mean, of course, the verb and interjection, not the noun. Well, this version by Mrs. Ross out of R. Farquharson Sharpe does not pass the *fancy* test, not by a long—or Archer's—shot. It features, furthermore, such tidbits as "What do you want to pay any mind to that for?" "Are you trying to humbug me?" "Indeed I set myself very definitely against that!" "I can get that much for myself if I have a mind to," "When Oswald was first born," "I'm speaking only as a kind of a metaphor," and many more.

But the production had other curiosities. Thus there was the utterly extraordinary pacing of the first-act scene between Pastor Manders and Regina, in which Staats Cotsworth and Carrie Nye religiously maintained from line to line an insane and excruciating rubato: presto, adagio, presto. Moreover, the whole cast indulged in a spitting contest which Miss Nye won hands down. Her every syllable, obviously too precious to be entrusted to the flimsiness of mere air, was floated down a little ocean supplied by her salivary glands. Leueen MacGrath's interpretation of Mrs. Alving as a *grande dame* did not quite hold water (in another sense), but at least it was accomplished, lively, and, at times, affecting. Mr. Cotsworth was one-sided, and Miss Nye narcissistic. As Oswald, Joseph Marino looked and acted Gregor Samsa to perfection; his eye-popping bit as he surveys Regina's charms could have been condoned only by a director of Mack Sennett's or David Ross's stature. Incidentally, Mr. Ross fired most of the original cast well after rehearsals had begun, and hired a new set of actors. Why? The dismissed cast, I fancy, could scarcely have been more unfaithful to Ibsen's intentions.

Those who complained they were not getting enough experimental drama, found themselves suddenly bombarded—well, pelted, anyway—by it from all directions. Off-Broaday came up with a Beckett world première, *Happy Days*, and with N. F. Simpson's *One Way Pendulum;* Broadway offered another English import, *The Caretaker,* and a German one, *Do You Know the Milky Way?* By far the most provocative, if not entirely satisfactory, member of this quartet is *Happy Days,* whose days, I hear, are unhappily numbered. Beckett, the old fox, is becoming more and more acrobatic—or is it Aeschylean? He is steadfastly exploring how much the theatre can do without and still be theatre. He has already written a near-monodrama for actor and tape recorder, as well as a brief act without words; in *Happy Days,* as in Aeschylus's *Suppliants,* we are reduced once again to two characters, one of whom does almost all the speaking. And this protagonist is, like Aeschylus's Prometheus, immobilized. For Beckett's unfortunate heroine who stands for the human condition, stands for it buried up to her waist during act one; in act two, life has inhumed her up to her chin, and only her head is still distinguishable from the landscape. The image is striking, both visually and symbolically, but it does rather cramp one's dramatic style. Of course, it is very much part of Beckett's scheme to inhibit dramatic, i.e., human action, but the maneuver is extremely dangerous. Beckett the acrobat has hung on to his dramatic thread first by his feet, then by one hand, next by his teeth, and now he proceeds to take out his dentures in mid-air. Needless to say, he is performing without a net. And there are moments, indeed minutes, when the play lapses into *longueurs,* when the existential *ennui* becomes plain old-fashioned boredom. All the same, the play is full of that Beckettian strategy which presents the most innocuous trifles of human existence dripping with blood and bile, and the most unspeakable horrors rakishly attired and merrily winking. The heroine who keeps blithering about the great mercies of existence as she is pressed deeper and deeper into the sod is an egregiously valid theatrical metaphor—particularly as portrayed by Ruth

White, whose performance is formidable in its broad outlines, and irrefutable in the accuracy of its deadly details.

One Way Pendulum is a less easily describable quantity. It is made up of satire, sophomoric jokes, malefic humor alternating with absurd drollery. There is a good deal of Ionesco and Beckett in it, and not a little of English domestic comedy with a strong odor of Terry-Thomas and Alastair Sim, which is quite all right, but also, alas, much that is labored and lumpish. A good many of the jokes are to drama what Marcel Duchamp's ready-mades are to art: at least as tiresome as they are supposed to be amusing. But behind the "honest idiocy" one often glimpses a genuine comic talent which can wrest relevance from the bizarre. Consider this exchange: "Does he have any Negro blood?"— "He does have one or two bottles in his room, but he doesn't tell me what's in them." Casually and incidentally, this dirty kick in the groin of racial prejudice accomplishes more than a thousand *Purlie Victorious's* with their Queensberry rules. Again, when a mother questions her daughter about a skull, a gift from the boy friend, which sits on the mantelpiece, Daughter explains: "It's supposed to remind one of death." Whereat Mum mumbles: "It hasn't worked since he gave it to her!" Could there be a more modern way of questioning Death as to the whereabouts of his sting? And for those who do not weaken along the way, N. F. Simpson has reserved one of the loudest and most cathartic laughs from any playwright's medicine chest—too bad that he disburses nothing like it until the end of the play. By that time, despite some fine performances (especially by Audree Rae and Barbara Lester) and Douglas Seale's knowing direction, a veritable exodus from the auditorium has begun. Even I, as I watched the company around me getting fewer and fitter, nearly yielded to wanderlust. But I am glad I fought it back.

. Not since Joanna Southcote announced that she would give birth to the Messiah, have there been such public pangs and heaving—and such a failure to produce even a *ridiculus mus* —as at the Lyceum (operating) Theatre, where Harold Pinter's *The Caretaker* tossed and moaned like a parturient Ingmar Bergman heroine. We have heard this play explained by assorted mystagogues as a tragicomic excursion into the Kafkaesque realms of human non-communication; as a salty satire on the British middle class with all its prejudices, pretentions, and absurdity; as a Manichaean parable of man's existence; and as an insoluble conundrum full of fascinating and funny details. One of the producers freely admitted that he does not understand it, which, however, did not keep him from producing it; the reviewers, though they admitted nothing, gave ample evidence in their reviews of equal incomprehension, which, however, did not prevent them from praising the play to the skies.

One trouble with the various explications is that they are either too parochial or too cosmically vague; another is that they do not fit. The play abounds in every kind of mystification: disconnected speeches, non sequiturs, red herrings, paradoxes for the sheer hell of it, withheld information, unexplained oddities, and, above all, unimpregnated silences. Most of the time, the speeches seem to be carefully constructed so as to have all the superficies of sense, but a big hole where the meaning ought to be; and whatever connecting thread may have held the minuscule incidents together, has been carefully allowed to rot away. When the language happens to deviate into sense, as in the elder brother's description of how he was given shock treatment, the drabness and triviality of the writing become manifest in spite of Robert Shaw's immaculate reading of the lines.

The Caretaker, I am afraid, is very much the work of an actor who relies on his knowledge of the externals of theatre and his shallow awareness of contemporary trends in drama. For whereas the better experimental writers in today's theatre have mastered the uses of language and symbol, Mr. Pinter, a once and future thespian, though occasionally amusing and sometimes resourceful in thinking up effective things for his three brilliant actors to do, has no style, no ideas, no poetic fantasy with which to hold us. "Vacant and idiotic as an actress," Lawrence Durrell says of a mirror in one of his poems. This is unfairly discriminatory. For it can be applied with equal rights to most *actors,* at least when they overstep the narrow boundaries of their competence.

This brings us to our last experimental play, *Do You Know the Milky Way?* Its author, Karl Witlinger, is, according to a recent survey, the most performed contemporary playwright in Germany. This in itself does not constitute a condemnation, but *Do You Know the Milky Way?* does. We are treated (at least in this adaptation), to a Hellzapoppinish circus, nightclub turns, a play-within-a-play, a film-within-a-play, a dream-play—everything, in short, except a play-play. While Wolfgang Borchert's more interesting, though imperfect, attempt to deal with Germany's collective guilt, *Draussen vor der Tür,* still awaits viewing here, despite yearly promises, Witlinger's more commercial, saccharine confection is given a relatively opulent, overblown production.

I am not saying that this amalgam of everything from expressionism to epic theatre, from cabaret to cinemascope, does not have good intentions with which it tries to pave the way to heaven; here and there, briefly, it manages to be engaging even. But I wonder, first of all, whether diverse but hoary things can ever be slapped together into something new: plunder the nests of the most exotic birds—cassowaries, lapwings, birds of paradise—for your omelet: stale is stale, however you scramble it. Countless jokes whose point is that the psychiatrist's and patient's roles should be reversed, that the so-called sane are the truly unhinged, that the world is one big lunatic asylum, have little kick left in them. And what they have, should be directed toward the director's pants: Herbert Berghof is a master of ponderous cuteness, and his staging proceeds by a series of clubfooted pirouettes. But even if Witlinger were more of a dramatist, and Berghof a director, what could one do with lines like "He is your milkman, bringing you every morning liquid, pasteurized imagination"? Or, "If God lost sight of all his stars, if he shut his eyes even just for forty winks, they might all begin to fade. But he won't. At least, he didn't yet." I don't think that even simple faith has any business being *that* simple. As enacted by Hal Holbrook, it is positively simpering. And what of George Voskovec's tour de force? You'd never think that those dozen parts were all played by one actor. I didn't even think they were played by *an* actor. The most cheerful aspects of the evening were Colin Low's sets, and his handsomely photographed film sequence (which did, however, seem overlong —but then, what didn't?), Bill Baird's masks, and at least one of Alex Fry's melodies.

An interesting question is posed by the English translation, or adaptation, which the program credits to no one. It was, we hear from reliable sources, begun by Mr. Berghof, polished by Lyon Phelps, and revised by Gore Vidal—as well as garnished in places by still other hands. It is regrettable that so many cooks could not keep the liquid, pasteurized imagination from curdling.

We come, finally, to something that might also be considered vaguely experimental, *From the Second City*. It is cabaret done in a theatre, and in a country where there is almost no cabaret in cabarets, I suppose this venture should be welcomed. And yet production in a theatre, in which these eight young people with their often slender material seem like fighting cocks in a jousting hall, was not a felicitous move. Not only is there a difference between the company's little showcase back in Chicago and the Royale Theatre, there is an even greater difference between the

Second City and the First, where competition is tougher and expectation, however foolishly, higher. Some of the material in the show is, to be sure, quite good; one number, "Museum Piece," a meeting at the Chicago Art Institute between a guitar-playing Beat and a repressed U. of Chicago co-ed, is almost flawless fun. It goes on rather long for such a sketch, and yet manages to maintain a consistent, concentrated humorousness that, without being wholly social satire or high comedy, comes close to being both. Barbara Harris and Alan Arkin perform this ultramodern museum piece like old masters; they, along with Howard Alk and, occasionally, Severn Darden, are the bright lights of the troupe. But only two or three of their other numbers can even approximate this sumptuous jest, and there are not a few items that are simply, or complicatedly, embarrassing. Nevertheless, these young people have talent: if *they* grow and their hall shrinks, the results ought to be gratifying indeed. At that point, any debate about whether or not this is theatre will become perfectly otiose.

Winter 1961-2

Since there could be such a thing as a *Son of Lassie,* it is perhaps not altogether surprising that a *Daughter of Silence* should have come along. Let me see if I can figure out exactly how this out-of-wedlock accident occurred. At one point in the play, an Italian lawyer who from an impecunious peasant rose to a prince of jurisprudence, and who is given, quite unaccountably, to quoting Palgrave's *Golden Treasury,* utters the line "Thou still, unravished bride of quietness." I can assume only that Morris L. West, the Australian playwright, misread this beloved verse as "Thou *still* unravished bride of quietness," and hastened to make amends for this neglect by raping hell out of the unfortunate lady. So much for the genealogy of *Daughter of Silence.*

For those who care for plots, however jerry-built, let me say that the plot concerns an Italian village girl whose mental development was arrested at the age of eight, when she witnessed the rape (you see!) and murder of her mother by a vicious partisan leader, now the mayor of that village. Vowing vengeance, she manages, at the age of nineteen, to bump him off, and faces the full severity of the law, the mayor's villainy being a closely guarded secret. She ends up being defended by a bright young lawyer who is terribly unsure of himself, made a cuckold by his sophisticated wife, and patronized by his father-in-law, the aforementioned wealthy and celebrated advocate. In the course of the play, our hero brilliantly uncovers the truth, moves the judges, and wins the girl's near-acquittal. He also wins his young client's love, but must give it up because she proves as demented as a Donizetti heroine and because we have a Catholic playwright. But starting with the case (I refer to the trial, not to the hapless girl), he goes right on winning: his wife's ardor, his father-in-law's admiration, his own self-respect. Under the circumstances, it would be asking too much to expect him to win over the critics and audiences as well. To convey the nature of the writing, I give you three proto-typical specimens: "Well, I know too there are women who need to rob their lover of his manhood!" "Well, then you must know what a rough one he can be!" which probably sounds better in the original Australian. Lastly, "I'm going to follow you into what-ever twilight country you're living in now and I'll drag you back with me."

Besides being the most boring and pretentious play of the season so far, *Daughter of Silence* rates two other firsts: one for the absolutely worst performance by a leading male actor, which goes to Rip Torn, who has been known to do rather better; and one for the worst direction, going to Vincent J. Donehue, who has been known to do every bit as badly. Mr. Donehue groups his people as though they were about to compete in a barbershop quartet contest, lets them move aimlessly or not at all, and pro-duces dramatic tensions as a child might make his toy locomotives collide. Mr. Donehue must also be allowed his share in Mr. Torn's booby prize: it has to take at least two persons to evolve such an elaborately rotten performance. Gazing yearningly out into the audience *à la* Olivier (but somehow always managing to forget to pull his gaze back), throwing away lines like Orson Welles at his slatternliest, and doing his best to look like Henry Daniell's death mask, Mr. Torn allows words to revolve wanly in his mouth like a jingling key chain in a bored man's pocket. Marlon Brando, another one whom Mr. Torn emulates, cannot, even in the midst of his most narcissistic silences, produce such an illusion of a non-functioning soundtrack as Mr. Torn conjures up throughout most of his speeches.

As for the rest of the cast, the superbly human Joe de Santis and perhaps a couple of others deserve better, but William Hansen and Joanne Linville, to mention only two, should be condemned to lifelong tours in Morris West plays, preferably in Australia and Oceania.

In *Take Her, She's Mine,* Phoebe and Henry Ephron have taken a California father's slow burn over his daughter's potential deflowering at an Eastern girls' college, and stretched it to two hours, which makes it easily the slowest burn on record. Since daughter knows that it is better to marry than burn daddy up, it is also the most unwarranted burn on record. Unwarranted? Inexcusable!

The play purports to deal with the problems of sex and education as they affect the young and terrify their parents. Yet at the fictitious college the heroine attends, not a single student gets nearer sex than some slimily suggestive hinting about, and we are treated to the spectacle of a Hawthorn College girl who has apparently never been kissed telling an Ivy Leaguer whose dastardly activities include petting: "Even by the loose standards around here you are a sex maniac. Why don't you find some reasonable vice, like dope, alcohol or boys?" As for the parents, they wonder what activity to engage in now that daughter is off to college. "Something we could do at night," Mom suggests. In comic outrage, Pop retorts: "Are you about to make an indecent proposal to me?" Whereat Mom, soothingly: "Oh, I wasn't going to give *that* up. . . ." The implications are that, among young and old alike, sex is rare or nonexistent, decidedly extracurricular, conceivably indecent even in marriage, and something a wife might well be thinking of giving up. With such plays around, small wonder if the ingénue's advice to a boy to take up boys were readily followed both on and off the stage. Of course a sex comedy can—and in America almost always does—exist without sex; what it cannot exist without is comedy.

Theme number two is "Education," and the Ephrons come out with equal vigor against it. The scene in which the heroine takes her visiting father to a lecture by the English prof with whom she is smitten surpasses in anti-intellectualism anything we got even in those beloved "campus pictures" of the era when movies were not quite yet better than ever. Here we have a flabby, ludicrous professor bumbling from platitude to platitude about a poet named Liam McTeague. (The Ephrons lack the courage to identify Dylan Thomas whom they are trying to lampoon, but the choice of an alias out of Frank Norris at least clearly indicates the point at which their literary development was arrested.) After a brace of banalities, the professor intones a poem by McTeague —a parody of Thomas as untelling as it is unfunny. Whereupon Dad points out the absurdity of the whole thing, and his California horse sense demolishes McTeague, the prof, and daughter's infatuation, thus saving her from the even more sinister seduction of the mind. There is, of course, nothing wrong with horse sense, except when, like the Ephrons, one is reduced to scraping the bottom of the horse.

One might expect the authors to be able at least to create some consistent comic characters. Nothing of the kind. The same parents who allude casually to Hegel's theories are revealed in a Webster-ransacking tizzy when daughter uses the word "ambience," and, to top it all, Dad cannot grasp even the dictionary definition. But, needless to say, it is these parents' values that triumph in this supreme piece of Ephrontery. Take one further example of the play's dishonesty. The girls and boys of our exclusive Eastern colleges are shown undergoing a veritable frenzy of philo-Semitism. All the Christian girls at Hawthorn are strumming and singing Jewish songs, one girl is told she is "so lucky to be Jewish," all talk about how divine it would be to have a "third year in Israel, learning the *hora*" because Jewish men, like Leonard Bernstein, are so frightfully attractive. When the telephone interrupts this meditation, the gentile heroine picks up the receiver with a ringing *"Shalom!"* and presently whispers to her chums, "It's Clancy Sussman," and so on. Now whereas this sort of thing has a meretricious fascination for certain playgoers— notably those who are ashamed of being Jews or anti-Semites —the fact remains that philo-Semitic gags are in no better taste than anti-Semitic ones and do not even have the melancholy virtue of corresponding to an unsavory but undeniable reality.

It is regrettable that such charming and gifted players as Art Carney and Phyllis Thaxter should be trapped in this morass, but as for the younger members of the cast, they are, with the exception of Stephen Paley, a thoroughly unprepossessing bunch, and slosh about in the mire as though they were to the burble born. George Abbott has directed with his customary expertise that goes back to the Twenties, and forward to 1930. The Eckarts have designed ponderous sets which roll onto the stage like grim Juggernauts straining to crush everything beneath them —unfortunately without quite succeeding.

"Now more than ever," says Art Carney in the play, "the world is shaped by ideas." If so, *Take Her, She's Mine* is definitely out of this world.

A minute and malodorous prize must be awarded to *A Gift of Time* for keeping more types of dishonesty flying through the air than have ever been juggled before. *A Gift of Time* is Garson Kanin's adaptation of Lael Tucker Wertenbaker's *Death of a Man,* in which she told how her husband, journalist C. C. Wertenbaker, discovering that he had incurable cancer, preferred to spend his last three months not in a hospital but in the Basque country with his wife and children, administering morphine to himself while he could, enjoying life with his family while the going was bearable, and then, with his wife's help, cutting his wrists and dying like a man.

The dishonesties of this play have a way of coming in pairs, which already puts it well ahead of any competitors for the Dishonesty Award. Thus the play can establish W.'s claim to greatness only by showing how tough and brave he is in the face of the terrible, but it can make the terrible palatable to Broadway audiences only by making it as mute or cute as *can't* be. So the play is forever straining to be tragic out of one corner of its mouth and full of wisecracks out of the other; the effect is roughly that of the Marx Brothers playing some hitherto unknown Maxwell Anderson adaptation of Sophocles. Yet the play is dimly aware that *three* months of relative mobility in a charming Basque cottage, complete with all the morphine, whiskey, music, and other comforts money can buy (to say nothing of an adoring wife and worshipful villagers), when chosen in preference to *four* months of being immobilized, cut up, and neglected in a New York hospital, may not guarantee a passport to immortality. Hence other proof of W.'s greatness must be found. What? Well, he was a writer; true, not a good writer, but, after all, he was only fifty-three and might yet have become one. In the hospital, just before the fatal diagnosis, he was reading, his wife says, "Montaigne, of course," and, failing that, the *Partisan Review.* He was friends with Harold Ross and Irwin Shaw and other such greats, could quote the second-best-known quotation from Gertrude Stein, and enjoyed writing his novels greatly, even if they did read poorly. But unable to fob off W. as an artist, the play turns about and tries to palm him off as an "artist in living." Discussing a dud of a book he wrote, W. says, "This passion for being original . . . God! It's like looking for a new way to screw! What's wrong with the old way, as long as there's love in it?" So, the pitch is LOVE, and it is directed, indiscriminately, at running year after year before the bulls at Pamplona, being told by one's wife that one's love-making is "miraculous, as always," bequeathing upon one's son the injunction to use all five senses every day of his life, hitting the bottle with euphoria (a word W. needs the whole morning to remember), recognizing, at death's door, that "falling in love is different from loving," learning, to the last, to play the guitar with one's son, and making an effort to have sex once more even though, as W. says, his "right nut has swollen to the size of an apple." All this so that one may speak one's own epitaph in a manner befitting Holden Caulfield: "I have had a perfectly goddam wonderful life!" And one's eulogy, which is the play's curtain line, is spoken appropriately by one's small, smart, and oh so unsentimental son: "Yeah, he was O.K."

In short, the problem is how to make W. both ordinary and extraordinary, literary and above mere literature, having the violence of a sick man but also the gentleness of a lamb, suffering the pains of the damned yet having also as jolly good a time as the theatre audience is supposed to have, teaching a lesson yet avoiding pompous didacticism, and so forth. There must be at least twenty pairs of chairs, therefore, between which the play manages to fall. Even the final cutting of the wrists, which, in the book, emerges as gruesome as Mrs. W.'s limited talents permit, is made, in the play, as clean, swift, and painless as a Palmolive shave. And W., needless to say, dies with an epigram on his lips.

The ultimate dishonesty lies in Mrs. W.'s writing the book in the first place. A wife cannot be objective in telling *this* story, and only a very great artist can make subjectivity become truth. Furthermore, by implying, indeed having her husband spell it out, that it was really *she* who was the hero of the two (and I agree that, if anyone was, it was she), the book and play became a tribute, largely, to herself. This is morally intolerable, as is the implicit assumption that, confronted with *real* people in *such* a situation, the critic must be respectful or hold his tongue. And so it was: the one objection most reviewers dared raise was that if we know ahead of time that the hero must die, there is no drama—a consideration that seems never to have occurred to the authors of *Antigone* and *Julius Caesar*. No, the objection, in its briefest form, is that there is no excuse for a badly written piece—sentimental even in its self-conscious attempts to avoid sentimentality—about a mediocre man who lived and died heedless of anything greater than his and his family's enjoyment, and believed in the immature ideals of a Hemingway without having any of Hemingway's talent.

Since at this writing I am just recovering from a joyous holiday named after him, I shall begin with Noël Coward, whose *Sail*

Away is so burstingly full of the spirit of the Thirties, and so utterly devoid of everything else. It is sad to see the grand master of witty dialogue lapse into a theatrical climacteric; to find the supreme magician of the English non-art song in his musical menopause. *Sail Away* uses some songs from previous Coward flops such as *Pacific 1860,* but even the new ones are as chilling as warmed-up leftovers. In this musical cruise, there are the customary jokes about tourists, Americans, Englishmen, natives, ship's personnel and their relations to the passengers—"They get V.I.P. treatment. You know: Captain's table and extra fruit in the cabin." With all those homosexual gags, unattractive girls, and gorgeous chorus boys, the one thing the show could do without is extra fruit. The things it cannot do without include jokes that are not vulgar like "It's Josh Logan's *Fanny* on a wide screen," or superannuated like "Ever since I retired from the stage on popular demand. . . ." Nor can it spare better lyrics than these which rhyme "rallentando" with "you're no Marlon Brando," or catchier songs than "Don't Turn Away from Love" with its completely tuneproof insulation. Add to this—or, rather, subtract from it—Joe Layton's choreography which ranges from the amateurish to the insipid, and a cast either uncharming or untalented or both. Nor was I particularly delighted by Elaine Stritch in the male lead. Can any of this be the work of Noël Coward, whose witty and poignant fancies once were legion? Noël, Noël, *redde mihi legiones!*

Seldom has a musical been more maligned by the reviewers than *Subways Are for Sleeping.* Granted, the book is awful, or, at any rate, nonexistent. But suppose that someone thoughtfully offered you Brigitte Bardot for Christmas, would you have the churlishness to ask him to be sure to throw in some brains? Who in the heyday of George Gershwin and Jerome Kern would have noticed the absence of a mere book? But it is our curse to live in an age which has seen musicals based on such literary and cultural landmarks as the stories of James Michener and the pages of the Trapp family album, and promptly we expect a musical to have a book. Next thing we'll be demanding that it oblige Sir Charles Snow by reciting to him the second law of thermodynamics.

As it is, *Subways* has a few amusing lyrics and bits of repartee by Comden and Green (when has this hugely overrated team been good for much more than that?), a couple of thoroughly pleasing songs by Jule Styne, rousingly old-fashioned dances by Michael Kidd, and—a rare thing these days—a talented and personable chorus line that can do justice to them; also eminently suitable settings by Will Steven Armstrong, and two incomparable performances by Orson Bean and Phyllis Newman. Mr. Bean's technique is built on a basic dichotomy (to borrow a word from the David Susskind collection): something in his movement or delivery is always contrary to the sense of the situation or statement; even his mouth opens to different shapes from those required by the sounds he is making—rather like a perverse lip-reading instructor venting his sadism on his students. Mr. Bean seems to have a sinisterly calm and complete control over the Spirit of Comedy, and even though he is one and inimitable, he makes the whole show full of Beans. Miss Newman, playing the girl who lives inside a towel as in a carapace, because, however insolvent, she cannot be ejected from her hotel room while she is in the near-altogether, is an altogether charming bit of fluff, her gestures and utterances dimming at the edges with amiable benightedness as she accomplishes the difficult task of making a dizzy dame with no talent come to life with perfect collectedness and a superabundance of skill.

Given all these assets, and in particular Mr. Bean and Miss Newman, *Subways* needs no further *Apologia*.

Kean boasts three librettists: Dumas père, who wrote the original play, Sartre, who adapted it, and Peter Stone, who made a musical out of it. It boasts also a remarkably handsome production designed by Ed Wittstein, and a star who boasts all over the place. Alfred Drake, whom we remember as perhaps our greatest musical-comedy talent, has become one enormous swagger; charm and poise still come with the fustian, but it is all not so much bravura as bravado. Drake plays an Edmund Kean tormented by his lack of status: he is the foremost man of his day on the boards and between the sheets, but subordinate to the least twerp of a gentleman in the drawing room. Tortured by this enforced duality, he exclaims something to the effect of "O Shakespeare, how much kinder author you had been,/ Had you but written me a role called Kean!" This seems rather inappropriate in a production into which the kind author Alfred Drake (apparently the fourth librettist) has written a positively monolithic part all but called Alfred Drake. Drake, his voice prematurely grey and his ambitions belatedly Gielgudian, usurps every nook and cranny of the show, and even commits the strategic error of playing a scene from *Othello* in his grandest Stratford, Connecticut manner and still wishing us to take him for Edmund Kean. I have no more disbelief than the next person, but the suspension was killing me.

Out of the two leading ladies one truly splendid one could be fashioned if Joan Weldon's rousing good looks could be wedded to Lee Venora's ravishing voice. The music has its moments: in a delightfully comic trio, "Civilized People," in which Drake's timing and wit are at their zenith; in a roisterous but not wholly integrated number, "The Fog and the Grog"; and in a limpid, Dr. Arneish period piece, "Penny Plain, Twopence Colored." But, for the most part, composer-lyricists Robert Wright and George Forrest have written a brashly obvious score, obviously in need of the collaboration—as in their previous musicals —of Villa Lobos, Grieg, or Borodin. Jack Cole's staging and dances are agreeable, and some performers seem to have talent, however much they are forced to let it fust unused; still, it is a long way from Sartre's comedy about illusion and reality to this "serious" musical comedy with delusions of reality.

How to Succeed in Business Without Really Trying has the most engaging first fifteen minutes of any current musical. Through that exemplary number, "A Secretary Is Not a Toy," everything satisfies us. The plot promises to be genuinely cynical, Abe Burrows's direction and Robert Fosse's musical staging yield tongue-in-cheek tableaux and movements that interlock with ratchet-like precision and hatchet-like satire, all this framed by Robert Randolph's sly scenery that knows how to be tastefully tasteless. Robert Morse, looking like some kind of floppy Mickey Rooney doll, lists more thoroughly and in more directions than the Tower of Pisa, and tosses smiles over his shoulder like a putty faun. The Machiavellian teddy bear is pitted against Charles Wilson Reilly's sissified snake-in-the-grass, a performance that has more vocal, kinetic, and histrionic know-how than I have seen combined in some time. But after a while everything flags: the satire becomes persiflage, and uninventive at that, Hugh Lambert's choreography proves banal, the costumes miscarry. Our hero's tricks congeal into a Morse code less dashingly dotty by the minute, the other principals disappoint us, and Frank Loesser's score wasn't much to begin with. In less time than it takes to say "How to Succeed in Business Without Really Trying," it becomes evident that show business is no exception.

In *Ross*, Terence Rattigan examines what caused the author of *The Seven Pillars of Wisdom* to turn into a pillar of salt, and finds that the answer is sodomy. While I do not wish to dispute Mr. Rattigan in matters on which he is an authority, the fact remains that the Lawrence Mystery never struck me as much more interesting than, say, the exact nature of the young Henry James's relationship to his bicycle (believed to have been quite racy); in fact, I was not, even in my youth, so moved by Lawrence of Arabia as I was by Scott of the Antarctic—possibly because Scott never messed around with Homer. Anyway, Mr. Rattigan has not kindled any belated enthusiasm in me. The greatness of his Lawrence is horizontal rather than vertical—by which I mean that it is all in the victorious sweep across deserts and enemy lines, in the conquest of a will over far-flung obstacles, and as such far more suitable material for the movie camera than for the dramatist's and theatre-goer's eyes, which can thoroughly look a man up and down but cannot follow him very far across.

Mr. Rattigan is like a singer who has an admirable middle range, and can cope with the lower, darker register reasonably well; but when the *tessitura* gets sublimely high, can only fake it in with a falsetto. When the going in *Ross* approximates drawing-room comedy, as in Allenby's and Lawrence's battle of wits, the writing purrs along urbanely over half-sheathed claws and we have a good show. When things become serious and we hear philosophical utterances like "There's nothing clean or dirty but thinking makes it so," we can, at best, toy nervously with the old school tie and mutter, "Good show!"

It is a far cry from *Ross* to *A Man for All Seasons,* a play that comes off as biography, as drama of ideas, and, quite simply, as entertainment. It may be that Robert Bolt's Sir Thomas More is not exactly a man for *all* seasons: not for the heat of July, for instance, or for the gambols of May. But what better company for the bittersweet glow of Indian summer, or during winter's restless rattling under the eaves?

"What has nature ever fashioned softer, or sweeter, or pleasanter than the disposition of Thomas More?" asked his friend Erasmus. "Where is the man of that gentleness, lawliness, and affability?" wondered Robert Whittinton, and Robert Bolt has taken these rhetorical questions perhaps a shade too literally. It should surprise no one who sees *A Man for All Seasons* to learn that Mr. Bolt was a schoolteacher: there is a good deal of the Senior Common Room about the play. I do not mean this unkindly: it is intelligent and literate and has such a blend of high-toned idealism and artful dodging as, in our day, only the denizens of faculty rooms can—and must—evolve. There is wit, grace, courage, common sense, and dignity in Bolt's Thomas More, but he does ultimately emerge as a schoolmasterly hero, a man who will advise an impoverished young man of dubious character to become a schoolteacher, a man who watches with scholarly condescension as Henry VIII, showing off in Latin, turns "it is most well" into "optimus est," and, in general, gilds his baser emotions with a gentle, donnish irony. Accordingly, he shows much less affection for his uneducated wife than for his daughter whom Master John Colet has taught Greek, and is not seen, like the real-life More, publishing polemical tracts that hounded poor Tyndale to his death. But this is not to say that Bolt's More is unlovable or even unbelievable; and there is something eminently winning in the way he reluctantly backs into greatness: "We have to stand fast a little, even at the risk of being heroes," or in the manner he sums up the perfect courtier: "The basic syrup with just a soupçon of impudence."

As a play of ideas, *A Man for All Seasons* has to operate against considerable odds. There is the fact that the protagonist is never challenged by an antagonist of commensurate intellectual stature, and there is the difficulty that More's unbending Catholicism which causes his martyrdom may not seem so ineluctably compelling today. No doubt Mr. Bolt wishes us to substitute whatever equivalents are dearest to us, like sitting down in Trafalgar Square or refusing to sign loyalty oaths. But all principles are surely not equally good: lifting the siege of Orléans and freeing one's country from foreign marauders seems a worthier cause for dying than absolute obedience to the Church of Rome. Granted everyone must work out his canonization as best he can, all ways do not seem equally endearing or even stageworthy. All this notwithstanding, Bolt has constructed a drama which is almost always intellectually challenging, and if it is perhaps more of a chronicle play than a tragedy, it manages to make the distinction an academic one: the passing parade and panoply of the history play are abridged and foreshortened, issues and individuals merge in their lowest common denominator—the approach is panoptic rather than panoramic.

But the final excitement of the play lies in its sound dramaturgy: action and idea are fused in just proportions, as are gravity and wit. The metaphysical and the palpable are juxtaposed and staunchly sustain each other; it is what Corot recommended to a disciple: "Next to uncertainty always put a certitude." Thus More can come out after some fancy verbal feints with the Spanish ambassador with such a plain passado as "You live in

Cheapside, Señor. To make contact with a brother in Christ you have only to open your windows and empty your chamber pot." And during More's last interview with his family, following some impassioned pleas and counterpleas, Bolt has his hero say to Mistress More, "That's a nice dress you're wearing," the sort of thing he perfunctorily remarked in better days. In astonishment almost verging on reproach, his wife replies, "It's just my cooking dress!" To which More, with aching tenderness: "It's very nice, anyway." These four words in their particular context are of that simplicity of which greatness is made.

One might possibly object to the figure of The Common Man who, as commentator or participant, fulfills the roles of a lowbrow chorus whose sense is as common as dirt, of a voice from the present providing anachronistic footnotes on what happened to whom afterwards, and of a touchstone, or touchclod, against whom More's greatness and our littleness can be measured. But Bolt has integrated this part so adroitly, and George Rose delivers the apologetics of opportunism with such alternately sniveling and sniggering rascality, that the gurgling of these gutter solos seems plucked on our own guts.

The great performance of the evening, however, is Paul Scofield's Thomas More. Here an actor embraces his part with a genuine amor intellectualis. It is as if a vast, benevolent mind suffused every gesture and every inflection—every wrinkle of a face resigned to its ability to face anything, whether or not it can be countenanced. The voice comes at us with a subdued intensity, as of someone patiently trying to carve meaning out of the obdurate mass of encircling verbiage. The actor's movements have the economy and deliberateness of a man conceiving of locomotion less as displacement than as discourse, and his facial expressions have the unassuming elegance of one whose features serve chiefly to keep his brain clothed.

A word must be said, too, for Noel Willman's staging and Motley's sets and costumes. Both Willman and Motley have a firm hold on essentials, a contempt for the blandishments of irrelevance, and a blessed gift for blending purposiveness with taste. In this way the intelligence of the audible is matched by the comeliness and seemliness of the visible. All of our objections to A Man for All Seasons could be written on the back of the ticket stub, and, with it, discarded; we leave with the awareness of having been not just at the theatre, but in it: extended to its limitless limits.

Many ergs have been expended by critics like Eric Bentley on the discussion of the relative merits of translation and adaptation of foreign plays for the American theatre. Though there is little doubt that translation is much the better method, having against it only—like Christianity, according to Bernard Shaw—that it has never been put into practice, it seems to me that both terms, "translation" and "adaptation," are less than adequate when one deals with recent Broadway history. It would be more relevant to argue the merits of dilution versus adulteration, castration versus decortication, decimation versus pulverization. A fine example of all six of these methods was Gore Vidal's version of Dürrenmatt's *Romulus der Grosse*.

Between Dürrenmatt and Vidal, alas, there is not a shred of that "wonderfull consimility of phansey" that Aubrey tells us united Beaumont and Fletcher. Where Dürrenmatt wrote a trenchant, tough comedy with profoundly disturbing overtones, Vidal gave us a lightweight, mincing farce with occasional mawkish posturing. As Dürrenmatt conceives it, the last Roman emperor plays the empire into the hands of the Germans (or Goths) because he thinks Rome hopelessly decadent, and the Germans under Odoacer such sterner stuff as his dreams are made on. But Odoacer himself, aware of the impending barbarism of Germany, comes not to conquer but to submit to Romulus's superior wisdom and humanism. There is nothing left but for Romulus to say, "Let's hurry up. Once more, for the last time, let us play comedy. Let us act as if all accounts had been settled down here, and spirit had triumphed over the matter called Man." How does Vidal render this? "We shall as sovereigns act as though all the accounts in the world had been finally settled, as though spirit had finally triumphed over matter." Here in a nutshell, are Vidal's two main failings: turning terseness into prolixity, and then missing the point. For the point is *die Materie Mensch*: matter is not something around man, or even part of man, it *is* man. Vidal ignores the *Mensch* and, characteristically, unmans the text. And instead of Dürrenmatt's enlightened emperor, whose cynicism turns out to be the last desperate attempt at hopefulness, Vidal, with the help of Cyril Ritchard, gives us a Romulus who swishes about ("Hail, divine Caesar!—Ooo . . . ooh! You eggs-aggerate!") among other assorted cooers and cluckers. "The part," said a woman behind me, "seems to have been written for Cyril Ritchard." Truer inanity was never spoken.

Since drama critics, unlike fiction writers, do not get whole issues of magazines turned over to them, I cannot itemize the details of the rape of Dürrenmatt's play—if you will pardon this inappropriately virile metaphor. What Vidal contributes is countless vulgar jokes like "Galloped all by himself? Without a horse?" or the "Going, going, gone!" with which an effete art dealer announces his departure, or the imperial chamberlains retiring to write "*Backstairs With the Twelve Caesars*—the sales in Great Britain alone will keep us comfortably in our old age," or "Your empire isn't worth a plugged *denarius!*" and ceaseless "timely" chatter about things like medical care for the aged, graduated income tax, and agonizing reappraisal. What he further adds is dreary "psychological motivation," background matter, explanations, and foursquare foreshadowing—he refers to it in an article in *Esquire*: "I gave as many clues as I could"; Dürrenmatt, it seems, "had neglected to dramatize his situation"! (Shades of the movie version of *A Midsummer Night's Dream*, with its "Additional Dialogue by Sam Taylor.")

By way of dramatizing Dürrenmatt, then, Vidal has added, besides the aforementioned explanations, such zircons as "Sicily should be fun at this time of the year, especially the beach!" (wistful charm); "Life is a river, a flood—you cannot change its course" (Pre-Socratic profundity); "The present, the day, the moment, the instant, *now!*" (pure poetry, direct from that dwelling place of the Muses, Mount Thesaurus, and proudly reiterated in the play). And when all these fail him, Mr. Vidal resorts to a line from Chekhov, Wilde, or Shaw, watered down lest the borrowing become too obvious. Excised, on the other hand, are all the surprises (Vidal: "I even tried to explain some of the ironies. . . ."), the true bitter wit of the play, the verbal music, and, above all, any historical reference for which Biblical spectacles in Cinemascope do not constitute a sufficient educational prerequisite. Excised, too, with the help of the cast, Joseph Anthony's misdirection, garish scenery and costumes, was any sign of Dürrenmatt's sturdy masculinity of approach. *Romulus* closed, appropriately, after 69 performances, hoist, as it were, with its own petard.

"An honest God is man's noblest work of art," said Oscar Wilde, standing Pope on his head; now along comes Paddy Chayefsky's *Gideon*, and God is, well, not exactly stood on his head, just made to fall on his backside. Not a very noble work of art, this God of Chayefsky's who begins as a capricious despot, and develops a kind of locker-room palsy-walsiness with Gideon. And he ends as a bearded (in both senses) autocrat forced to accept the fact that he is no longer top dog and recite some bottom-drawer doggerel about how man may yet become a wisely emancipated being: "You know, he might, he might some day! / With this conceit we end the play." And a pretty awful conceit it is, too, but nothing compared to the one needed to begin such a play.

If God changes from tyrannical to feeble, Gideon —man—evolves from servile and stolid to vain and self-willed. In his effort to humanize both God and Gideon, Mr. Chayefsky, to whom humanity is a kind of Marty-ness, has endowed both of them (since he is aiming for higher literary effects) with arty-Marty qualities. And at no point can we truly sympathize with either God or Gideon, largely because the play lacks a point of view. For two-thirds of the way the idea seems to be "Don't make a cult out of man—not even in fancy!" (I'm not sure how it could possibly be made in anything else), only to switch to the opposite position that Gideon must act "so that man may be a significant creature." To which this God remarks, "This is beyond even God's understanding!"

The prevailing muddledness is manifest in the language. A statement will begin in a grand Biblical tone, "Whoever is fearful and trembling, let them go home!" (note that the grandness does not extend to the grammar), and continue in the flattest present-day fashion, "You may return to your farms." Chayefsky himself undercuts both the Biblical and the modern mode. First it is: "Whosoever shall not follow after Gideon, and so forth, and so forth. . . . Well, it's hard to take that sort of thing seriously." And then: "Some wild farrago of things about the temporal inadequacies of man." So he runs both idioms through his Mixmaster and out come things like "I am but a personation of God" followed by things like "Oh dear, I see this is heavy going for you." I cannot help feeling that a Waring blender does even less to justify God's ways to man than Milton can, to say nothing of beer.

Confusion is evident on other levels too. Consider the stage image in which Gideon is drifting away from God. His ability to see God is rapidly forsaking him, however hard he and God strive to reëstablish ocular communion. The spectacle of Gideon, at the very moment of his emancipation, straining to see God and failing to do so is perhaps contradictory but believable; but the sight of God huffing and puffing to make himself visible, and, despite his omnipotence, failing, is ludicrous and wrong. As is the whole caricature of God. If Blake, according to Humbert Wolfe, depicted God as an old English sheepdog, Chayefsky sees him as a Michelangelo head mounted on top of a Chagall cos-

tume, and behaving like a Pekingese in a tantrum. The loss of
dignity is made conclusive by Fredric March's poor diction and
skittish performance.

I shall not go into all the other vulgarities—the half-
naked belly-dancer, the idiot guard who always mistakes Gideon
for the enemy and keeps taking prattfalls, the stock characters like
the hellfire-and-brimstone prophet and the cynical agnostic, the
gratuitous gags based on anachronism, and all the rest which
Tyrone Guthrie's resourceful but burlesque direction merely emphasizes. My main wonder is that someone with Chayefsky's poor
command of language should have risked such an enterprise. We
hear, for example, of "slipping backstream," where "backstream,"
I suppose, is a solecism for upstream, but one can slip only down-
stream. Again, a puzzling problem is said to "bear attenuation,"
as if attenuation were tantamount to elucidation. Yet, to my amaze-
ment, here are words like "charismatic," "corybantic," and "ses-
sile" being casually kicked around the stage like so many old
shoes—I mean, buskins.

But perhaps, in the spirit of *Gideon*, this may be
explained by a parable. I once let a well-known four-letter word
slip out in the presence of a not well-known Bennington girl. To
cover up my *gaffe*, I said, "Oh, I'm sure you don't know the meaning of that word." Proudly she replied, "I certainly do! It's a
famous German philosopher of the idealist school." I did not know
which to marvel at more: such learning, or such ignorance?

Circle in the Square has come into possession of two cycles of
Thornton Wilder plays, each consisting of seven one-acters.
There is a secular cycle, "The Seven Ages of Man," and a spiritual
one, "The Seven Deadly Sins." By way of a first installment, we
are treated to one sacred and two profane playlets, which, I
guess, is the way trinities come these days.

Thornton Wilder's plays have an inverse-Antaean
quality: the closer down to earth they get, the weaker they are.
Whenever Wilder attempts to achieve imaginative reality and tell
us "truths" about human beings, we get a sentimentalization of
the little guy that is as unbelievable as it is indigestible. "So eine
Altmodischkeit und solch ein Stumpfsinn," wrote Gottfried Benn
of *The Skin of Our Teeth,* and went on to speak of the play's
dilettantism and provincialism. And of *The Bridge of San Luis Rey,*
D. H. Lawrence noted, "I found [it] a dull dough-nut with artificial
jam in it." But let the subject-matter get away from reality—let

it be, for example, what goes on in the rarefied minds of babies, as in *Infancy,* the best of the three new *Plays for Bleecker Street*— and Wilder can be enormously convincing. After all, nobody knows for sure what goes on in the heads of infants, and it may be that Mr. Wilder, who looks more and more like a fat, old baby, and whom I myself have heard utter the infantile dictum that certain plays by Frank O'Hara and Kenneth Koch are "the grass roots of the American theatre," may qualify as the supreme student of the infant psyche on the basis of the venerable apothegm "it takes one to know one."

The first item, *Someone From Assisi,* is helpfully identified by the program as being "*Sins,* No. IV, Lust," without which I might have easily misconstrued it as dealing with the deadlier sin of dullness. It concerns St. Francis, St. Claire, and a madwoman of Assisi who was once seduced by the then worldly hero, abandoned by him, driven out by her noble kinsfolk, and is now something for dogs to bite and the rabble to throw stones at. There is much holy talk between Francis and Claire, much charitable talk between Claire and the madwoman, and much mad and repentant talk between the madwoman and Francis. Three things happen. (1) Francis tends the madwoman's wounds. (2) Francis, whom the animals adore, takes the madwoman home, because by a kind of reverse "love me, love my dog" principle, she too will be safe from bites in his company. (3) Francis is so shaken by this experience that he tells the nuns not to put any of that saffron he so craves into his dinner, after all. The beatific air with which Francis contemplates saffron is, by the way, the closest the play gets to grappling with the theme of lust.

The women in the cast are adequate, but I have my doubts about Lee Richardson's crass and mean-looking Francis. There is a line in the play about the wolves sharing their meals with him because of their love for him. Couldn't it be simply because they mistook him for one of them?

The next play, *Childhood,* is the usual excursion into Wilder's Never-Never Land of adult children and childlike parents who share a dream in which they enact something like a dream version of Wilder's *The Happy Journey:* a trip across a fanciful U.S.A. in a particularly wayward bus made out of folding chairs. After braving together imaginary Indians and experiencing other mysteries of Togetherness, the dream-metamorphosed parents and children achieve a deeper harmony. "You're just people in our game," say the dream-children to the dream-parents, "that's why we can talk to you." And that is, presumably, why they didn't talk to me: because I was not participating in their enchanted dream, though, I must admit, I was far from wide-awake. Of the three children involved, only two invited immediate strangulation.

Infancy is, for the most part, delightful. Two babies, wheeled side by side in Central Park, confess to each other their overweening ambition to learn fancier words, higher mathematics, more advanced geography; their parents and nurses, to shut them up, provide them with such thin intellectual pabulum—or pablum —as the multiplication table and the list of the boroughs of New York City, but they spurn such propaedeutic pap. They bawl out their *libido sciendi* and *libido sentiendi* in ever louder (though, to the stupid adults, incomprehensible) vocables, till one of the babes climaxes this Faustian urge with the cry, "I want to make a baby!" But when we come to the adults that surround all this "striving against swaddling bands," as Blake so aptly put it, they are a drearily burlesque lot and go in for jokes that smell either of the mausoleum or of the bathroom. Thus we have a comic Jewish mother frantically deliberating in mid-park whether the toilet of the Museum of Natural History is indeed the nearest one, and then racing off to it. Or we hear her telling a nursemaid that Baby Moe was giving her husband and her dirty, knowing looks whenever they engaged in intimacies or spoke of personal matters in English. So they switched to Yiddish, but "In two weeks, Albert Einstein got Yiddish!—But he's just a baby, he doesn't understand a thing!—I know that, and you know that, but does he?"

The Night of the Iguana is not vintage Williams, but at least it comes from the same cellar that gave us *Menagerie* and *Streetcar* rather than from the Calcuttan black hole that exuded some of his more recent works. It is old wine in old bottles, which is as should be, but some scenes taste a little of cork, and the wine leaks messily out of the cracked container. There is, first of all, the ramshackle Mexican boarding house with its rickety but randy proprietress, whose star boarder (her evening *and* morning star) is an unfrocked minister turned tourist guide, with a penchant for leading tours down back roads and the youngest female tourists up the garden path ("Statutory rape," he explains, "that's when a man is seduced by a girl under twenty"), and a further affinity for fits during which he has to be tied to his hammock in "a comfortable, a luxurious crucifixion." Into this ghostly hostelry comes, besides a number of noisily irrelevant minor characters, a blind bard in his late nineties, led by his granddaughter, a

New England spinster who ekes out her "Nonno's" meager earnings from reciting poesies of a curiously un-Edwardian flavor with her own equally meager gains from peddling her watercolors. The watercolors we are happily spared—unlike the poems, which contain lines like "The earth's obscene, corrupting love." The body of the play is a duologue between the God-hating "man of God on 'vacation' " and the combination Antigone and Emily Dickinson, to the accompaniment of the jeering Aristophanic chorus of the proprietress who wants her boarder back, and the noble Sophoclean chorus of the grandfather who wants the golden age of poetry back.

The central exchange begins as a mixture of sympathy and defiance which has the spinster and the ex-minister batting at each other little balls of amused tolerance or chilling irony, and sometimes, for good measure, hurling the bat itself. But, gradually, their understanding grows to the point where they pay each other the supreme tribute two Williamsian characters can pay: they tell each other their life stories. The archetypal example of this occurs in Williams's most powerful poem, "Life Story," which, I believe, has not yet been recognized as the source of the similarly futile exchange in the first act of *Sweet Bird of Youth* between the hero and the aging diva. (And what of the turning of a homosexual poem into an ostensibly heterosexual situation in a play?) But unlike many Williamsian characters, the confessing pair in *Iguana* really hear each other and learn something thereby: even if they cannot join their far too divergent selves, they can at least achieve respect for another's antipodal but equivalent misery, and draw from the realization a wistful fortitude.

Other plays of Williams's start from such a colloquy: *Camino Real,* for instance, which, like *Iguana,* grew from one such scene into a full-length play. But whereas this sound kernel of *Camino Real* was smothered by a mighty hard husk to crack, in *Iguana* it manages to impart a lovely, controlledly bittersweet savor to a play which some importunate impurities at times make less palatable, but never wholly distasteful. If only Frank Corsaro's direction were less crude and superficial, and if Patrick O'Neal's showy, mumbling, and undisciplined performance were up to Margaret Leighton's with its beautifully muted radiance—perhaps a trifle too empyreal at times, yet how noble!—but it isn't. Nor is Mr. Williams all he might be and was. But he's getting there.

Considering how badly the American theatre has treated Strindberg—even more so when it produced him than when it merely ignored him—one is at pains to find something to like about *Creditors*. But I am sorry to say there is nothing to praise about this production, unless it be that Paul Shyre, in his adaptation, has turned a one-acter into two acts, thus giving us ten minutes of unforeseen respite. Even this, though, is done at the cost of the cumulative momentum *Creditors* can ill afford to lose. And I am not sure that Mr. Shyre, who considers plays, novels, autobiographies indiscriminately grist for his theatrical mill, was well advised to pick this as the initial offering in his projected Strindberg cycle. The collected works of Strindberg, in the Swedish edition, number fifty-five volumes, and there are far better things in them than *Creditors*.

All the same, something might have been done with this play if, for instance, it had been acted and directed. (I shall not dwell on Mr. Shyre's "adaptation" which contributes lines like "She couldn't tell a bee from a bull's balls, and you know it," constructions like "*One* should learn a little bit about human nature before giving *your* own nature free play," and vulgarisms like "the both of you.") This play about a marriage destroyed by the capriciousness of a wife and the vindictiveness of an ex-husband of hers, requires expert staging and performances. Indeed all of Strindberg does, because his genius was both so chameleonic and so *outré* that even as short a play as *Creditors*, for example, must be played both naturalistically and expressionistically at once, or almost at once, which requires delicate balances, transitions, and ambiguities.

Donald Davis belongs to what I would call the greasy school of acting, where the least utterance is orotund, where every phrase is accompanied by sucking or wheezing noises to denote how juicy it is and how loath one is to relinquish it, and where one's facial expressions and gestures are broad and firm—for example, if one's curiosity is aroused, one's entire face reduces itself to nostrils and lips straining forward; or, if one is to lean nonchalantly on a mantel, one ostentatiously looks in another direction while cautiously exploring the area with the elbow, and, once one has ascertained the exact whereabouts of the mantel, plunking oneself on it with all the weight of one's carefully accumulated casualness. I was much impressed with Mr. Davis's Krapp, but having observed his subsequent work, I have come to the conclusion that his acting style lends itself less well to roles under eighty. As for Rae Allen, her performance is, I should think, of particular interest to the geologist. The top, or Pleistocene, layer, consisting largely of running one's hand up along one's face and of forelock-twirling, shows remains of Geraldine Page; the next layer, or Pliocene, yields a kind of overgrown baby talk and coy little whine, in which one finds well-preserved remnants of Julie Harris; and so on. Eventually, as one descends farther, one reaches certain hip-poundings with either the fist or the open hand, which are fossilized relics of the Triassic, or Bette Davis, period. I cannot in all fairness say anything about the performance of James Ray as the unfortunate second husband, because he is, in appearance and manner, so perfectly brownish-grey that I could not distinguish him very well from David Johnston's brownish-grey setting.

As director, Mr. Shyre was not even sufficiently in command to convince his booming and yelling players that the tiny Mermaid Theatre is not the Colosseum. That noted German drama critic, the late Alfred Kerr (definitely no relation to Walter), once observed that whereas Ibsen was the poet of human destinies, Strindberg was the poet of monomanias. Until now, I would have disagreed.

The Phoenix Theatre rose from its ashes, in which it had been wallowing, and produced the first play by an American film and television writer as its own first new play. This was *Who'll Save the Plowboy?* by Frank D. Gilroy, and it was not only intelligent, sound, honest, enormously promising, but also remarkably good. It interweaves two problems: first, that of the loveless marriage of Albert Cobb, a yokel who had allowed an army buddy to convince him he was meant to be a big, happy farmer—at which he failed ignominiously, to end up as a tiny, urban nonentity; and of Helen Cobb, who had married him as the last alternative to embittered, barren loneliness, and who now helps their marriage along into a quietly ugly warfare based on individual failure and mutual fiasco. Secondly, the problem of Larry Doyle, the old army buddy, who saved this "plowboy's" life at the cost of a wound whose aftereffects are slowly devouring his own. At the brink of death, he arrives to inspect that family happiness which must justify his solitary sacrifice. The play proceeds to show how various kinds of mean pretense—that the Cobbs are a happy family, that Doyle is a normal, healthy man—are gradually absorbed by a more generous pretense. The purpose of this pretense is not merely superficial well-being, but a difficult, desperate assault on the ugliness of life by giving something small but genuine which might bring about—not love or joy, perhaps, but at least a struggling solidarity. Let's Pretend becomes Let's Extend: extend the effort which is only one step up the mountain, with stubbed toes, bloody fingernails, crumbling rocks underfoot, but up: one whole, gallant, pitiful step up.

The two men, Gerald O'Loughlin and William Smithers, performed commendably, but Rebecca Darke, as the wife, was brilliant. She was a smoldering, black flame, almost too indolent even to hiss and sputter, only crackling malevolently. Her voice stung, each sneering syllable drawn out thin and dropping like wormwood from her lips; the volume almost never rose beyond the reach of a muting self-irony—"Death or a new stove, I'll settle for either one." But in this grisly verging on comedy, managed with equal adroitness by actress and author, the woman became both more believable and more appalling. It is too bad that Mr. Gilroy's beautiful play—lacking that last fillip of perfection, but beautiful all the same—was forced off the boards so soon. This happened because the Phoenix, despite efforts in that direction, is not a repertory theatre and cannot keep even a critically and popularly acclaimed play running. If there were no other arguments in favor of repertory theatre, the premature disappearance of Plowboy would be quite a sufficient one in itself.

Having served up such excellent, though plain, meat and potatoes, the Phoenix next turned to a rich, fruity dessert, and came up with Jerome Robbins's production of Arthur Kopit's Oh Dad, Poor Dad, Mamma's Hung You in the Closet and I'm Feelin' So Sad. Kopit's play is a bittersweet prank, made up in part of engaging schoolboy sassiness (it was written while the author was still a Harvard undergraduate), and in part of devices and techniques of the "Theatre of the Absurd" or "anti-drama." But college humor seldom sustains beyond the length of a skit or two in a musical revue, and "anti-drama" is practiced best by writers old enough to have become genuinely embittered, then genuinely disillusioned, and, at last, wafted even above their disillusionment onto a comic Olympus from which to drop lighted matches on the wooden heads of the world.

The play concerns a wizened, stuttering young boy whose mother is a sort of man-eating Claire Zachanassian (out of Dürrenmatt's The Visit) as Walt Disney might see her, and whose girl friend is a nymphomaniacal Little Orphan Annie. The boy's life is spent under maternal house arrest among Mamma's menagerie which includes a Siamese kitten-eating piranha, insect-eating Venus flytraps, and the embalmed body of her late husband whose insides she herself has ingested. The boy is allowed three fabulous collections—of books, stamps, and coins—and only one (1) seemingly innocuous little girl playmate who turns out to be a baby Whore of Babylon. The two more than wife-size females lock in deadly combat over this unhappy manikin, but just as the girl is about to seduce the boy on Mamma's bed, Dad's cadaver hurtles warningly out of the closet, and—well, that is the problem with the production.

Even where the play is witty and gruesome enough to stand on its own bizarrely spindly legs, the ghoulish overelaboration of Jerome Robbins's production and direction comes tumbling out of its cupboard and bowls over the proceedings. Unprecedented for off-Broadway, 45,000 dollars worth of bad taste has gone into decking out Kopit's work with totally uncalled-for film sequences whose style can best be described as "Antique-Shop Moderne," outrageous frippery in costume and scenic design (including a traveling-coffin for Dad that looks like a Biedermeyer candy-box), and some rather queer casting that makes Dad's mummy look no more cadaverous, aged, or even masculine, than a member of the Ballets U.S.A. troupe. The very program, quaintly shaped and printed, suggested a dance-card for a cotillion. Among the performances, only Austin Pendleton's uncompromising honesty in the part of the boy emerged hopefully from this Pandora's box of a production: neither Jo Van Fleet's "method" acting, nor Barbara Harris's equally rigorous "Second City" improvising proved adaptable to the needs of the play.

But the play itself is far from self-sustaining. The scene, for instance, in which the mother, Mme. Rosepettle, vamps the luckless Commodore Roseabove (everyone in the play is called Rose-something-or-other, as if, by any other name, he could not smell so foul), and tells him the story of her life in an interminable monologue that is a pastiche of all the absurder aspects of the "Theatre of the Absurd," is excruciatingly boring and pointless. Still, Mr. Kopit is interesting, and he is very young, and, for someone who got his A.B. in engineering, a helluva engineer. Let him mature a little and give us a show that has less baby-blue and Robbins-egg blue about it, and it may be something worth waiting for.

The Old Vic visited us with three productions, two of which made the "Old" in the company's title seem like typical British understatement: "Superannuated" or even "Prehistoric" would not have been the slightest offense against modesty.

Douglas Seale's staging of *Saint Joan* had enough

tedium, bloodlessness, and stiltedness to make it correspond to my mental image of a Walloon touring-company production of *La Princesse Maleine*. Barbara Jefford gave us a full-bodied Maid, replete with a jolly maternal quality, who tried to compensate for the earthbound opulence of her form by pitching the last word of most of her major utterances as far up as possible. Thus "I see now that the loneliness of God is his . . ." was delivered in a well-tempered mezzo-soprano, but ". . . strength" was floated into an unnerving bit of coloratura. I doubt that this Joan could have raised the Siege of Orléans, but she might have lifted a pair of fifty-pound dumbbells with relative ease. John Clements, as Warwick, was stylish enough, but the general flaccidity of the rest of the cast was only here and there punctuated by an outburst of hamminess, like an old watchdog's sleep with an occasional bark. The director revealed his fine Westphalian hand in scattered bits of unlikely business—Poulengey lovingly picking up the clogs Joan jumped out of in her excitement; two soldiers, after the trial, forming a St. Andrew's cross with their quite unneedfully drawn swords against which Joan is pinioned in a mock crucifixion *pour épater les bourgeois*—for the rest, we get a surfeit of the obvious. John Lambert's music sounded like something even Khachaturian would have seen fit to exclude from *Gayne*, and Leslie Hurry's costumes, though carefully made, did not look quite new enough for any production of *Saint Joan* in the last two decades, nor, somehow, quite old enough to be authentic relics of the fifteenth century.

Michael Benthall's *Macbeth* was an attempt to emphasize the spectacular, the colorful, and the barbaric—but all, rather capriciously, off and on. Thus the banquet scene was played for a maximum of statuesque groupings, swirling capes, a startlingly appearing and disappearing ghost; but the march on Dunsinane and the defeat of Macbeth were kept as colorless, schematic, and "let's get it over with" as possible—or a little more so. There was a good deal of unhelpful cutting as well as some positively disastrous writing in. Accordingly, Macbeth dies on-stage: the entire army (a grand total of fifteen) watches, in a sporting tableau, as a heavily armed Macduff slaughters a bare-jerkined Macbeth, who then rolls on the ground and mutters "Blood! Blood!" as he looks at the murderous hands that slew Duncan. It is a fine piece of homespun philosophy, quite worthy of *Gorboduc* and Michael Benthall.

Benthall's imagination, in fact, ran, I mean, hobbled riot. Thus we had a shy postulant of a girl playing Fleance (by way of preparation, I assume, for Viola or Rosalind); a loutish youth in his twenties playing Macduff's son, giving that usually touching scene a unique blend of the Oedipal and the cretinous; a march on Dunsinane distinguished by not so much as a token of Birnam Wood in the shape of, say, a toothpick; a special choreography for sleepwalking which consists of scurrying like a mechanical mouse around corners, and then, in the straightaway, shifting gears into a dreamy, slow-motion glide; several apparitions sticking their heads out of the witches' cauldron like comic-strip missionaries being boiled for the cannibals' dinner; and so on.

But it is the performances that were particularly painful. Barbara Jefford's Lady Macbeth was a respectable, restrained clubwoman, quite uninspired, but, for all that, preferable to John Clements's Macbeth. Clements scooted and rattled through the part as though the whole thing were an after-dinner speech to a group of Veterans of World War One, but just a few times, to murther their sleep, springing a howl and scowl on them. In the "Tomorrow and tomorrow" soliloquy he did, however, reach certain heights—albeit comic ones. Thus he bellowed his indignation at his dead lady: "She should have died *hereafter!*" ("Damn her!" we almost heard), and roared again, as an afterthought: "Tomorrow!!" which, it seems, would have been the ideal time for her demise. Then, after a pause, came the remaining pair of "tomorrows" in a totally unrelated tone, starting out on a new tack. André Van Gyseghem's Duncan was a high-pitched, fussy old thing that, as far as I was concerned, couldn't have been dispatched soon enough, but I will say that I was amazed to learn that the old man had in him any blood whatever. As for Macduff, played by an American, William Sylvester, he walked through his part in a way which suggested that somnambulism might, unknown to medicine, be contagious, and received the news of his family's murder with a stoicism that can be described only as soporific. The high point here was when Malcolm (ably played by John Stride) had to exclaim "Macduff, this noble passion, etc." after a piece of diatribe from said nobleman that would not have dislodged a fly from his lips. The rest of the cast were, except for the fact that they spoke English, indistinguishable from what one gets at Stratford, Connecticut. Michael Annals's sets and costumes had their moments, but Tristram Cary's electronic beeps and proto-subliminal buzzes did not.

Franco Zeffirelli's *Romeo and Juliet* was, however, a lively and original conception, which, up to a point, was genuinely interesting. Here was a Verona all faded terra cotta (if terra cotta can fade): a city that seemed to crumble before our very eyes and yet spread in all directions to blot out the sky, endless streets full of untidy, unruly life—everything etiolated, drab. This is what Zeffirelli the designer (with the help of Peter Hall's costumes) artfully designed for us, and this is what Zeffirelli the director skillfully populated with a verminous, pullulating life. Such occlusion and such dustiness would indeed shorten tempers, generate loutishness and its counterpart, fastidious nastiness. Under such circumstances, even Romeo must be a bit of a—however likable—oaf; even Juliet—however endearingly—a bit of a hoyden. For if they do not rush into love—angularly, bumblingly, desperately—it will be too late: by tomorrow they, too, might be corroded by the spiritual rust. After all, even Mercutio has become a charming but lewd loudmouth, even the worthy Paris has turned into an effeminate popinjay, the Duke himself is but a harassed bureaucrat dehumanized by his sticky job.

Scenes of violence, farce, youthful bumptiousness and clumsy charm (a balcony scene like a workout in a gym), against clever settings as if out of Renaissance manuals on stagecraft and in costumes that are utterly functional and self-effacing, these things carry us along swimmingly up to Act III, Scene 2. But just when the fiery-footed steeds of poetry should start galloping apace, Zeffirelli's conception begins to totter and, eventually, collapse around the heads of actors, audience, and playwright.

Already the first look into the program had made one anxious, as one read Signor Zeffirelli's program note. How would the concocter of sentences like "It is so difficult for a foreigner to believe that any but British and American people would be able to touch their own cultural heritage, especially with Shakespearian tradition" come to grips with the complex poetic music and frivolous wordplay of this dramatic poem? Well, for half the journey, admirably; but then! Was it that the actors could no longer backtrack from neo-realism into poetry? Or was it that the director did not permit it? Did the cumulative effect of a paunchy, prosaic Chorus, a calla lily-livered Paris, a male fishwife of a Capulet, and all those other churlish grotesques finally accomplish their attrition? Yes. And all those excesses of business that Zeffirelli's *verismo* and archness (blended in him as curiously as in his master, Visconti) appliquéd onto the action began to pall. It is clever for Mercutio to eat an apple through his Queen Mab speech, for Romeo to climb up a tree to Juliet's balcony, for Mercutio to be ignored while dying because no one thinks death can come of these street games, and for the discovery to come all the more crushingly. It is resourceful for Romeo to welter on the floor of Friar Laurence's cell, for Juliet to assume that Romeo has already left her when he is actually still putting on his shoes behind her bed, and, again, for her almost not to notice his dead body as she is about to leave her tomb. But such devices are time-consuming. Hence the text must be cut mercilessly. The wedding preparations which so ominously turn into a funeral? Cut. Romeo's pathetic fight with Paris? A couple of words and one quick stab. The discovery of the dead lovers in the vault? Slurred over by people stepping unceremoniously over Paris's corpse. The Friar's explanation of what happened? Cut. The reconciliation of the clans? Performed as if by push buttons. Despite John Stride's and Joanna Dunham's fetching acting, Romeo and Juliet became a pair of scissors-crossed lovers.

Brecht on Brecht may not be much, dramatically speaking, but it is a miracle of dentistry. Bertolt Brecht, that bitingest of old dogs, has every one of his sixty-four teeth neatly extracted by George Tabori's shameless dentistry. The Brecht that we are offered here could easily pass for Will Rogers, Norman Vincent Peale, Hal Holbrook doing Mark Twain, Jack Paar, or whoever the currently preconized middlebrow humorist may be.

There is, first of all, little or no justification for taking tiny snippets of a man's work in prose, verse, and song, scrambling them insouciantly together, and tossing the whole mess out into the auditorium. This procedure is by no means comparable to what, say, Emlyn Williams did when he read out complete pieces or generous chunks from the works of Dickens or Dylan Thomas, where the tone, moreover, was much more unified, and where the effort was clearly directed at getting across the most representative aspects of an author. Nor have we here a Drama Quartet doing a single, seldom performed, nearly autonomous part of a play in concert fashion.

Secondly, Gene Frankel, the misdirector, and the six histrions involved, flying in the face of both Brecht's ideas on theatre and any valid non-Brechtian practice, give us such a concert of prefabricated smirks and stances, such gazes of mutual and self-admiration, and other cutenesses masquerading as impromptu responses, as to make the late unlamented quiz shows seem by comparison orgies of spontaneity.

But most of all it is the democratic citizen Brecht, the chaffer of bureaucrats, the loyal enemy of whatever is un-

American, the good Joe who loved all little men everywhere, regardless of color, creed, and IQ, that is the great offense, the great lie that Mr. Tabori and his cohorts have perpetrated. If they want to introduce Brecht to American audiences, they should show us a Brecht sniping not only at the straw men of Hollywood, not only at the nasty Nazis who have long since become the target of even such less astute political critics as the Three Stooges. They should show us (and I am sorry if this comes as a shock to Howard Taubman) a Brecht spewing his brilliant, deadly satire on the common man, the rich man, the organization man, the artist, America, democracy, liberalism, religion, and whatever else is enshrined in Washington and Cooperstown, at the YMCA and *The New York Times.*

But that, Mr. Tabori and his team would tell us, would not pack 'em in every night, would not send 'em home smiling, and would not even be a service to Brecht, since no one would come to the theatre to be ridiculed or insulted. To which there is a simple answer: the purpose of the theatre is not to accommodate ignorant audiences, nor to drum up trade for ANTA, Cheryl Crawford, and George Tabori, nor yet to make Brecht well-liked by the American public. Its purpose is to offer us the best truth a serious author is capable of. And however misguided Brecht may have been in some ways, however snarlingly unfair, he was still a thousand times the thinker and artist that those responsible for *Brecht on Brecht* are. There may be some injustice in cattle raisers gelding their livestock, but it is a much more serious matter if the livestock get together to castrate their masters.

Just why *The Apple* is called *The Apple* I can no more tell you than why it is called (not by me!) a play. Perhaps it is not even called *The Apple* on all nights, but is freely improvised as perversely as possible by the seven actors who use their own names, so as to shock and rattle us into buying the greatest amount of lemonade and coffee from the same actors during one intermission, and to bid as high as can be, during another, for an action painting one of the actors has squirted and sloshed before our very eyes. It may be that the intermissions are the real thing, and that the three abominable acts of *The Pear* are merely meant to make us appreciate the entr'actes more fully.

The Banana concerns a Chinese girl, a Negro, a pederast, a whore, a con-man, a spastic, and a typical member of the audience who is the repository of every form of vileness.

They act out a number of anarchist, sado-masochist, and obscurantist charades, some of which contain a little effective theatricality, a couple of which abut on meaning, and one of which is imaginative and affecting. But it would be idle to detail the various scenes of *The Pineapple,* beyond saying that they all amount to a would-be stentorian "Screw you!" hurled in the face of things and people as they are. In its more dialectic moments, *The Papaya* lets out with statements like "Our configuration is like the structure of a nucleus . . . celestial and out of touch with one another"; in its spicier phases, *The Passion Fruit* shows us the spastic being taunted during a fit with the offer of a woman, the homosexual trying to stick his hand in the Chinese girl's crotch (horizontally, of course!), and a couple stuck together during copulation brought out on the stage in a wheelbarrow. *The Casaba* is, however, pertinently directed by Judith Malina, and capably performed by all but Marion Jim and Julian Beck, whose rendition of a homosexual is, quite unintentionally, the most potent argument for heterosexuality yet adduced in a theatre, nay, a society rather in need of one.

It goes without saying, that, for all its paroxysms and bellowing, *The Boysenberry* does, or, rather, undoes nothing —except perhaps the reputation its author, Jack Gelber, achieved with his previous play, *The Connection.*

The Cantilevered Terrace sounds like twenty years' worth of back issues of *Poetry* (Chicago) finely ground together, heavily spiced with Henry James, sprinkled with powdered perversion, and served at sick-room temperature. For poetry we get: "Who would have thought that the dampness on a fingertip would express a father's sorrow?" or "Don't be confused by the sibilant kisses that curve like S's around you." For humor: "You, my poor girl are in your dotage, wearing silk against your thighs in anticipation of Lawrence," and "Don't shout, dear, the Sitwells will wonder.—The poet Sitwells?—No, dear, the potato Sitwells next door." For philosophic profundity: "O how sad that there is no other way of ending life, except death!" That William Archibald's play ran at all seems attributable to Howard Taubman's rhapsodic review—another unfortunate sign of the *Times.*

The word "cynic" comes from the Greek word for "dog." In the revue *Signs Along the Cynic Route,* it finally returns to its origins.

Spring 1962

I can see how the production of *No Strings* could dispense with all but two, to be attached to a catwalk and librettist Samuel Taylor's thumbs. But even that, I suppose, would require ten. Mr. Taylor's book is a concoction guaranteed to give ptomaine poisoning the moment one takes in the situation: Boy—brilliant young American novelist squandering his talent getting potted and fleshpotted in Europe—meets Girl—Negro American top model of Parisian *haute couture,* kept by a rich Frenchman for purposes which do *not* include sex, and thus must be either infamous enough to make the Marquis de Sade sit up in his grave, or preposterous enough to satisfy the American audiences' lust for virginal whores. This heroine who, besides being a model, is a downright paragon, not only tracks down in Paris the hero's out-of-print short stories, which is unlikely, but also reads them, which is unheard of. The novel model and model novelist (a kind of Hemingway on the rocks) go off to Honfleur together, where she, with the zeal of that middle-aged Midwestern patroness of James Jones, puts the delinquent genius to work. But he can't, because the call of the wild parties is too strong for the gay dog. There is a breakup, and the girl returns to her wealthy French mentor who teaches her such useful bits of worldly wisdom as "the red wine must never be chilled," only to be reunited soon thereafter with her novelist. But here *No Strings* pulls a few strings to bring about an *un*happy ending so desirable nowadays in an adult musical (if you'll forgive the contradiction in terms)—especially in one that introduces an interracial romance, which might, if legalized, offend the Southern buyers in the audience.

      So the girl declares, "I want you to write about the things you really know, the things in your bones and blood." To do this, the hero *must* go back to Maine, because his bones and blood, apparently, were not portable; the girl will sell her *couturier* dresses and will live with him in homespun. In Maine, however, one must be married. Very well, even though a minute ago one sang "let the little folk who need their help depend upon vows and such." Just then, though, it dawns on them that the wife could sooner pass through a needle's eye than be admitted to the local Ladies' Sewing Circle where she was going to busy herself while her husband wrote. Realizing this, they say good-bye with breaking hearts. And the show ends as pretentiously and falsely as it began.

      Richard Rodgers is a composer whose scores vary

greatly according to the quality of his lyricist, and since Rodgers the lyricist, who here makes his debut, is hardly another Hart, but can, like anyone else, hammer out a bit of Hammerstein, the songs and lyrics cannot stop the show—only some of its gaps. But Rodgers, unlike Hammerstein, tries to be naughty rather than goody-goody, and so we get lyrics like the heroine's "I just want money,/ And then some money,/ And loads of lovely love"— which, besides being out of character, makes meretriciousness sound as solidly American as Hammerstein made solid American- ism sound meretricious. There are, then, some glibly competent songs, and one rather better one, "Nobody Told Me," which would gain a good deal if Richard Kiley, while singing it, did not look as if his lungs were hemorrhaging.

Diahann Carroll is an alluring and clear-voiced heroine with an attractive vocal style, but her acting is not much more than merely inoffensive. The gyrations, however, with which she tends to garnish the end of a song are offensive in the ex- treme: they make a Presley or Fabian fit for his ab- or subnormal audiences, but on a girl they look like possession by a particu- larly prurient demon. As for Richard Kiley, he is certainly dull enough to pass for a Pulitzer Prize-winning novelist. Polly Rowles is first-rate, despite the appalling jokes she has to spout, such as: "He's a Europe bum. You know what that is?—No.—You've heard of ski bums and tennis bums? Well, he's a Europe bum." (The script never leaves bum enough alone.) Among the other prin- cipals, Alvin Epstein manages to add unauthenticity to the already baseless role of a heterosexual fashion photographer, and Bernice Massi can squeeze additional vulgarity from a thoroughly crude conception of a rich American tourist. The outstanding presence on stage is that of Noelle Adam: this young Frenchwoman is beau- tiful and seductive enough to dispense with talent, but instead she dispenses it freely in various directions. Her dancing, her speech, her *moues,* her very gaze which repays the spotlights in kind are the incarnation of *joie de vivre,* and of that easeful womanliness which our actresses seem to achieve, if at all, only with the utmost difficulty.

Yet in its production *No Strings* exhibits some useful virtues derived from *commedia dell'arte* and the nightclub: David Hays's décor consists largely of oversized varicolored spot- lights and evocative movable pieces, and the orchestra, instead of being damned to the pit, weaves its way pleasantly through the proceedings, actors bantering with musicians. Donald Brooks has designed resplendent high-fashion clothes for Miss Carroll (which, unfortunately, leave Fred Voelpel's tawdry costumes for the chorus all too far behind), and even the occasional lighting up of the auditorium as at a concert provides a welcome whiff of originality. But such things are effectively squashed by Joe Layton's flat-footed choreography and flatter-footed direction. Mr. Layton's dance steps are obvious and ungainly, every one of them—or, to speak with greater mathematical precision, *both* of them. Inasmuch as *No Strings* is unlikely to make any other lasting impression, the best we can hope for is that it will accelerate the desegregation of Ladies' Sewing Circles.

Herewith a bit of dialogue between an incurably ill adolescent and her doting father: "Moof! [*She clutches her chest.*] —What's 'moof' and what's with your chest?—'Moof!' is 'Aiii!' without admitting it, and nothing is with my chest.—Pain?—No. Flat!" If you can imagine a play that curls its lower lip into the most exquisitely wistful grimace while keeping an upper lip stiff enough for *rigor mortis,* you have an exact picture of Robert L. Joseph's *Isle of Children.* If you can't, don't bother. One can grieve for a girl of thirteen who is going to die, but not if she says things like "Just one day of being old—even a day with nice illnesses, like rheumatism!" or "By all rights, shouldn't I leave now, with a hug—while you still love me? . . ." Nor is there much to be said for the girl's parents, though they do celebrate their daughter's birthday by putting on an elaborately costumed Nō play, making it surely the first Nō play within a no-play on record. Patty Duke does as much as one can do with the precocious and prematurely doomed heart patient, but what really undoes her is the author's art disease, as well as the arty slickness of director Jules Dassin. Stefan Gierasch and young James Aubrey are the only ones that come out relatively unscathed. My feelings about the whole thing were "Aiii!"—which is "Moof!" and admitting it.

"Todos los días se matan en New York," wrote Federico García Lorca, "Every day they slaughter in New York/ Four million ducks,/ Five million hogs,/ Two thousand doves to tickle the taste buds of the dying. . . ." On exceptionally fine days, a play by Lorca is thrown in for good measure, *para el gusto de los agonizantes.*

There were three things particularly wrong with Stage Seventy-Three's recent short-lived production of *If Five Years Pass.* The first thing is the translation. Granted that to translate Lorca satisfactorily is virtually impossible, James Graham Lujan's and Richard O'Connell's "official" translations are quite impossible. Here the very title, *Así que pasen cinco años,* is mistranslated: it is not "If" but "As Soon as" or "Thus Five Years Pass." The importance of this is underscored by the subtitle, "A Legend of Time," for in this play Lorca was trying to dramatize by expressionistic, indeed surrealistic, means the oneness of time: the tragic fact that there is no past, present, and future, but that all time is of a piece and immutable: in Eliot's words, "What might have been and what has been/ Point to one end, which is always present." The hero of the play deludes himself with the notion that *as soon as* five years pass he will win his truelove; the play shows the manner of their passing: in a trice, in a dream, in the now-and-forever—*thus.* Since the hero is an ineffectual fantasist, what is to happen as soon as five years pass, never happens.

To illustrate further what Lujan and O'Connell do to Lorca, there are ear-splitting inversions like "My ring of ancient gold/ Has sunk through the sands of the mirror cold," which also makes hash of Lorca's meter; or such insensitivity to words as "A dagger, some scissors last forever," where the "some" errs both through ambiguity and misplaced colloquialism; or, again, "Is the fountain spouting water all right?" where "spouting" is unattractive enough, but "all right" is murderous. And so on.

The second big mistake was the choice of Valerie Bettis as director. Miss Bettis has done very good work in the dance, in musical comedy, and has, on occasion, proven herself a capable actress. But as director of this play, she could hardly wait to get to Act III, Scene 1, which she conceived of as a ballet, but which is in fact a grotesque pantomime or puppet show, and which turned into a misplaced non-ballet for non-dancers on a stage unsuited for dancing. In the other scenes, though Miss Bettis perceived that stylization was called for, she could not hit on the right kind, probably because she failed to grasp the meaning of the play. Thus the Old Man represents the hero as he might be were he to grow old, and the two Friends stand for his sensual Self and procrastinating, back-to-the-womb Self—a multiple identity which the staging nowise indicated. Again, there is no excuse for actors doubling in roles when such doubling obfuscates the author's intentions. The three Card-players, therefore, who symbolize the Fates (in Lorca's fantasy, characteristically, male), should under no circumstances be performed by the same players who earlier appeared as the alter egos of the hero. (Incidentally, actors for whom one role is rather too much should certainly not be cast in two.) In short, Miss Bettis, with the help of her cast, turned a somewhat obscure, metaphysical play into something cloddishly physical and impenetrably dark.

The third error was the choice of this relatively early play by Lorca (1931), which the author wanted neither published nor produced, for, indeed, this drama about the fourth dimension is somewhat deficient in the other three. It would seem that until New York audiences have had a chance to see good productions of Lorca's great plays, it does him little service to dabble with his more tentative, experimental ones. But whereas Franco's Civil Guard merely killed the poet-playwright's body, the American theatre seems determined to annihilate his genius.

In the cast, Virginia Bosler could, at least, dance, and Tamzen Allen had a now brooding, now tempestuous sensuality which provided the one convincing scenic illusion. But to assess whether Miss Allen is a true actress, one will have to wait and see more of her. A child, Victoria Thompson, was thoroughly winsome, and deserves the theatre's nurturing care. In general, however, the cast was distinguished chiefly by its pitifully losing battle with stylization, mime, and diction. Thus one actor was heard referring to "neckid women," and neither hero nor heroine could make it clear whether she was supposed to cut off her braids or her brains.

"A degraded theatre," Lorca observed, "can coarsen and put to sleep an entire nation." The infinitesimal part of the nation that witnessed *If Five Years Pass*, remained woefully un-ennobled and unawake.

To swing between the two extremes, ecstasy of living and horror of living, this is how Baudelaire conceived of life, and this is how a latter-day Baudelairian, Michel de Ghelderode, described the vision of renaissance man which was also his own.

It is a bizarre, inchoate renaissance that this Belgian dramatist and storyteller evokes in his works, a world which, as we have often been reminded, derives from that of Bosch and Brueghel, Goya and Ensor, and from the demons and gargoyles with which legions of anonymous Flemings decked out their Gothic churches in abhorrent adornment. But whereas the grotesque in art has an ancient tradition, on the stage it does not come into its own until the romantic period—and not even then, for the romantics, cut off from actual theatres, were mostly closet dramatists. There is, however, one splendid but neglected English poet and playwright of whom Ghelderode particularly reminds us, Thomas Lovell Beddoes, who wondered "What is the lobster's tune when he is boiled?" and who would sing "Thus, as I heard the snaky mermaids sing/ In Phlegethon, that hydrophobic river,/ One May-morning in Hell."

Most of Ghelderode's fifty odd (in both senses) plays could bear the title of Beddoes's one completed drama, *Death's Jest-Book*, but Ghelderode, unlike the romantic playwrights, was a practical man of the theatre. "There is a certain Poetic Theatre —or allegedly so—which is rarely a vehicle for poetry," he warned. "Let us beware of Poetry announced by placards." For him, "a theatrical work does not exist without the sensuousness proper to the plastic arts," yet—and this is an all-important yet— "without the verbal incantation which renders it dependent on magic, the theatre disintegrates . . . and disclaims its obsessional or possessional power, its marvels." Ghelderode's is a synaesthetic theatre of visual incantation, of magic palpable to eye and ear.

In *The Ostend Interviews*, Ghelderode tells us that even as a child he was drawn to public demonstrations: fairs, strikes, funerals, carnivals, or bloody melodramas at the theatre. To his dying day he collected "marionettes, dolls, puppets, little rag creatures that the children of today scorn—also dummies with lovely mortal faces of wax . . . adorable heads of young martyrs, severed by what executioner?" But perhaps the best evocation of the dramatis personae of a typical play by Ghelderode occurs in a description of the Ostend Carnival in a speech of his country-man, model, and most kindred spirit, the painter James Ensor: "O the animal masks . . . bloated vicuña faces, misshapen birds with the tails of birds of paradise, cranes with sky-blue bills gab-bling nonsense, clay-footed architects, obtuse sciolists with moldy skulls, heartless vivisectionists, odd insects, hard shells giving shelter to soft beasts." The off-stage action of *Hop, Signor!* is the Carnival, but the on-stage action is another carnival: nasty dwarfs, homicidal lechers, a malformed sculptor, a sadistic virgin wife with an obscene craving for death, an ascetic narcissist of an executioner, and a fanatical monk rocked with unholy desire— these enact the carnival within a carnival, the freak show of life.

But what does the mask, which every character of Ghelderode's seems to be wearing, signify? It is meant neither to embellish mankind, as the impassioned words it utters might suggest, nor to execrate it, as the deeds it performs could imply.

The mask is merely the face heightened out of its languid actuality into a potentiality truer than truth: it is the face of humanity exacerbated into becoming itself.

The American première of *Hop, Signor!*, however, was a sorry affair. Among the players, only Michael Dunn, as the dwarf Tallow, gave evidence of a full-grown talent; the rest proffered pigmy performances. It is hardly worth debating now whether this or that actor gave the worst accounting of himself, although at the time it seemed the sole possible after-theatre conversation. Since none of the performers garnered a majority vote (though every one of them was nominated), we had to content ourselves with unanimously hailing Philip Meister's staging as a vintage specimen of directorial incompetence. The two memorable moments of the evening were Jerome Guardino's reference to the dwarfs as "you Pulitzer faces!" (truth sometimes comes from the mouths of actors with abominable diction) and Jane White trying to offer her breasts to the quivering monk but having considerable difficulty locating them. Suffice it to say that the evening was fraught with horror, although of a wholly un-Ghelderodian variety.

A Thousand Clowns, like so much contemporary American theatre, resembles the Carthaginian war-elephants. They would have been a tremendous weapon indeed if they had known which ones are the enemy, or even just which way is forward. But all too often the worthy beasts would turn around and rout their own troops. For, in questions of politics, the Carthaginian elephant had no point of view. And, in questions of life, neither has the Broadway theatre. To be sure, it does not frequently raise such questions. Indeed, it is when a show is hermetically sealed against reality, like *Subways Are for Sleeping*, that the results are most satisfying—albeit on the lowest of all levels. But at least *Subways* makes no pretense of touching on life this side of Sirius; whereas *A Thousand Clowns* does purport to deal with reality, and, by talking out of both sides of its mouth, ends up telling us nothing except a few jokes.

It is, of course, possible for humor to exist at a remove from immediate reality, but then it is either satire or farce; *A Thousand Clowns*, however, is too pretentious to be farce, and too scared or superficial to be satire. The play deals with a television writer, Murray Burns, who is presented as too honest and too bright to waste his talents on writing a corny TV children's show, and so quits, to become a high-minded intellectual bum. The two questions, what does he now live on and why does he refuse to seek more intelligent employment, are barely raised and certainly not answered. Our hero has a twelve-year-old nephew living with him; the child, Murray's runaway sister's bastard, is a bit of a genius. Now the Child Welfare Board, in the persons of an incredibly stodgy and infantile social worker, and of an unbelievably flighty and childish female psychologist, threatens to remove the child from our hero's loving carelessness and the Augean stable in which they live. Murray has a perfectly respectable, though staid, brother, Arnold, who is a successful theatrical agent and a fresh-fruit fiend. Why the Board should want to assign the boy to strange foster parents, rather than to another perfectly good uncle—unless, of course, they have an inveterate hatred of fresh fruit—is not apparent.

Anyway, the ludicrous young lady psychologist has a tiff with the pompous social worker, her fiancé, over how to handle the case, and promptly ends up out of a job and in bed with our hero. Soon Murray has a gruelingly homebodyish little woman fixing up his apartment, and he resents it. ("Oh God! I've been attacked by the *Ladies' Home Journal!*" which is mildly funny, but forthwith gets buried under "Place has an unusual quality now—sort of fun Gothic," and "What in hell have we got here, goddam Sunnybrook Farm?" which are not.) Yet he must have a job or lose the boy, and the only solution, apparently, is for Brother Arnold to patch up things with the oily children's comedian "Chuckles the Chipmunk." So, for all his wit and wisdom, Murray is harnessed into writing the same ghastly TV show. But he'll keep the boy and have a nice little mother for him, too.

Since, as Mr. Howard Taubman has written, this is a comedy about people, let us glance briefly at the cardboard characters. Sandra Markowitz, the child psychologist, begins as a sniveling booby who breaks into tears, "I hate Raymond Ledbetter, and he's only nine years old!" and has no more idea of how to treat a bright twelve-year-old than of how to handle a grown man. Though she tumbles into bed with Murray, a perfect stranger, the next morning she is frightened out of her wits by him, and runs away while he's in the kitchen. But we soon see her come back, take over Murray's apartment and life, and be a model self-confident, bossy American wife in the making. And as if one transmogrification were not enough, she next harangues him with homilies worthy of the immortal Harry Emerson Fosdick.

As for her co-worker and ex-fiancé, Albert Amundson, he is shown first as a humorless boy scout, a petulant petty tyrant, an absolute square. Nevertheless, at the crucial point, this butt of Murray's cruel jokes comes back, admits that he has no sense of humor and none of Murray's brilliance, and proceeds to make so touchingly well-turned a profession of humanitarian faith, that one does not know for which to love him most: his modesty, idealism, or willingness to admire his tormentor.

Arnold Burns, Murray's agent brother, is first presented as someone ridiculously popping in and out with baskets of fresh fruit and laughed at even by his little nephew. Later, Murray pronounces Arnold "one of those people who've got that wise stare in their eyes, so nobody'll know their head's asleep." But already Arnold begins to have a delicately modulated self-irony: "We fellows have those offices high up there, so we can catch the wind and know which way it blows." In the last act, he emerges as the clever, thoughtful champion of the Establishment. Now this wise ant is scoring off his grasshopper brother, tosses off epigrams like "You mean, if I'm so clever, how come I ain't poor?" and ends up by judiciously, but by no means overbearingly, cutting Murray down to size. Even "Chuckles the Chipmunk," the loudmouth, phoney, and greasy opportunist par excellence, is revealed at last as an unhappy hypocrite more grinned at than grinning, aware of his nothingness and ready to go to Canossa.

As for Murray, he is clearly a high-minded, artistic type. His reason for quitting TV? "When Sandburg and Faulkner left, I left," which is gilding by association. And there he is now in his magpie nest cum pigsty of an apartment, charmingly, wittily, devastatingly superior to the rest of the world. He is free, he does not conform, and the author and audience are clearly with him in his bohemian one-upmanship. Of the 42nd-Street movie audiences, he says "Everybody figures that everybody else is a creep and sits by himself—and all of them are right," and you might think that the author condemns him here, because Murray, too, sits among these all-day audiences, but no! Witness him utter presently the play's most horribly poetic prose in praise of his nephew—which I feel compelled to write out as verse:

> He's got something crazy,
> Something valuable—
> He's one of the original people! . . .
> He sees street jokes;
> He has the good eye;
> He sees subway farce
> And crosstown bus humor. . . .

And there follows a long, Whitmanesque litany, every line of which contains the anaphora "I want him to know . . . I want him to know . . ." *ad infinitum*. Obviously, such arias are not given to anyone but the *Heldentenor*. And we are all meant to be with our hero when he glories in his nonconformity by upbraiding the neighbors through his open window for the inferior quality of their garbage, or when, on a Sunday morning, he yells up at the closed windows of Park Avenue: "Rich people, I want you all out in the street for volleyball." And if that does not convince you that Murray Burns is one of the original people, let me add that he talks back elaborately at the telephone weather service, and amuses himself by standing on street corners and apologizing to every passer-by, for the sheer splendid sophomoric hell of it. Through these and many similar jests, the play is solidly behind Murray, and every kick against organized society had (on a particularly bibulous second night) the spectators blissfully applauding. But now, all of a sudden, those Carthaginian elephants turn like worms—and the audience with them—and cheerfully trample on our hero. He who has had countless affairs with women will, clearly, marry the bumblingly domineering Miss Markowitz, will prostitute his Faulknerishly Sandburgian talents to Chuckles the Chipmunk, and conform like you and me. (Cheers from the audience.) True, he will not, he says, jump on the bandwagon completely—which I take to mean that he will continue to holler out of his window in censure of the neighbors' garbage.

Now, you might say, "Why not? After all, people aren't black and white, but various shades of grey." Quite so. But Herb Gardner has given us people who, precisely, are black and white: one side of them driven snow, then, turn them around, and the other, if not pitch black, certainly charcoal grey. Yet it is rather more likely that people would be all white or all black than that they should be so neatly half dark, half light, like the world at the equinox, and as easy to manipulate from light side to dark as a globe in a classroom demonstration. I think I know what Mr. Gardner—or his producers, one of whom also directed—had in mind. The idea is very simple: to please everybody.

The boring businessman turns out to be an eloquent sage, the offbeat rebel a good, safe family man (but, never fear, with many a prank in him yet), the imbecilic girl will make a redoubtable materfamilias, and the puerile little bureaucrat is really the salt of the earth—there is hope for everyone. Even the terrifying infant prodigy may look forward to growing up and becoming prodigiously infantile. But the unfortunate thing is that the war-elephants, when they turn about, do not do so for the exaltation of both sides, but for their demolition. A truth that about-faces does not become two truths for the price of one, but no truth at all.

Yet I do not wish to blame everything on the author. Herb Gardner has some funny lines and situations here and there, and, at first, the play may have even had a point of view. Thus the boy was, I have been told, in the original version, Murray's own illegitimate son; presumably, however, it was thought wiser, in production, to change him into a mere nephew—even if the central situation thus became less poignant and not quite logical. After all, a hero who begets bastards might give offense; but a hero who takes in bastards is a hero indeed. The main trouble is that Mr. Gardner fails to impress us with the things he admires, and that, though the play shows evidences of humor, it has not a trace of taste.

As Murray, Jason Robards, Jr. acts with dizzying prestidigitation all around the part, but never gets into it. The fault is only partly his—still, if a really great actor can recite the telephone book and make it art, why not Mr. Gardner's joke-book? Sandy Dennis starts out as a very funny Sandra Marko-witz, but eventually some of her tricks pall and others do not rise to the occasion. At times she pulls out a real "method" platitude, such as pronouncing "What?" as though it were at least trisyllabic, which indeed it is in the Studio patois. A. Larry Haines's Arnold is unimpeachable, as is William Daniels's Albert Amundson. No one, I think, has conveyed better than Mr. Daniels blue-eyed in-comprehension and thin-lipped disesteem and the guileless smug-ness of mediocrity in all their invulnerable impotence. But let him beware: he is on the verge of being pigeonholed. Gene Saks, one of our very best comedians, does what he can with the foolish chipmunkeyshines assigned to him.

Now for the child, if that is what Barry Gordon is. At the age of ten months, the program informs us, he rose in his crib to sing "Bye Bye Blues," and at three (years, to be sure), he defeated six hundred older contestants on the "Original Amateur Hour"—we are not told how, but I would guess with do-it-yourself head shrinking. By now, however, the only role in which I would cast him is Methuselah.

To repeat, A Thousand Clowns is not entirely bad, only, through its fundamental dishonesty, distasteful.

Great Day in the Morning, by Alice Cannon, was a first play of considerable but rowdy charm. The life of two Irish households (complete with hangers-on) in the St. Louis of 1928 was evoked with skill, vigor, and almost Rabelaisian humor. Faith and booze, Catholicism and carnality, genuine human warmth and no less genuine human meanness were brought to life with lusty innocence. But the quality I particularly liked in Mrs. Cannon's work was a kind of unsentimental sentimentality: her ability to remember her past with tenderness and yet write about it with robust objectivity. This is perfect tact: one holds one's subject matter close enough to commune with it sympathetically, but not so close as to have it slobber all over one, or vice versa. The weaknesses of the play, unquestionably, were there: the central plot was slight and a little remote from non-Irish Catholic experience, and there was absolutely no effort on the dramatist's part to get beyond, say, that middle distance and old-fashioned competence which are William Inge's province. But I seriously doubt that these things—what with the good direction and acting which were almost everywhere in evidence—can account for the failure of this modestly deserving play. What, then, caused its rapid demise, while spurious items like *A Thousand Clowns* flourish?

In the first place, there was truthfulness. In a play like *A Thousand Clowns*, we are presented, or at any rate left, with a world view which can be summed up as "No matter what, life is grand fun," and against this thickly pink backdrop move diaphanous characters whose shenanigans, whether pleasant or unpleasant, never interfere in any way with the general pinkness. In *Great Day* (which was at times far more comic than *Clowns*, and as concerned with reality as *Clowns* pretended to be), it was the people who made the color of living. They were the background as well as the foreground, and it was from their actions, and only from them, that existence took its confused but absorbing coloration. Thus the language—and some reviewers protested against it, coming from a woman playwright yet!— was often crude: "I am going to hell my way," says the heroine in disparagement of her priest, "and he can do the same. He's not getting tips from me!" Or: "Once they get you with your belly up under your chin," she tells her sister, "you're a dead duck." Or this: "If you don't watch out, we'll soon be walking behind you and saying how natural you look." But if this is crude, it is never vulgar. The difference is clear, but often overlooked: crudeness is something underdone and raw and at least still close to nature; vulgarity is something overdone, overcooked-up and artificial. Mrs. Cannon views her Irish—her *people*—not through lace curtains, but through naked panes, smudgy with the fingerprints of life. Note, therefore, that the humor, unlike that of *Clowns*, is always made up of something more than just the funny, whether it be the sad, the nasty, the clumsy, the religiously prejudiced, or whatever. For pure humor, even in its best or non-Gardner variety, is always somewhat inhuman.

Secondly (and this point follows from the first), *Great Day* did not have any dashing heroes or fetching heroines. In *Clowns*, one knew all along that anyone who had such smilingly crouching handsomeness as Jason Robards, Jr., or girlishly insinuating giddiness as Sandy Dennis, could not possibly come to a sticky end. But as one watched Colleen Dewhurst's bellicose adiposity, Frances Sternhagen's acerb angularity, and the deafness, obesity, drunkenness of the men around them, one could not feel safely out of reality. Now, of course, if it's Tennessee Williams or Eugene O'Neill, we know what to expect (moreover, we have the critics' unconditional guarantee that what we are seeing is Art, and, therefore, necessary though annoying); but why should a little, harmless, Hibernian comedy by a lady-playwright take us by such unwelcome surprise?

And so, down the drain went one of the rare examples of ensemble playing on the American stage: Colleen Dewhurst's at times somewhat technique-ridden but otherwise imposingly incontrovertible performance; Frances Sternhagen's slightly haggard but racy dryness which would spring to jollity with touching eagerness; J. D. Cannon's hard-won taciturnity, cloaking, though only in part, his wildness and affectionateness; and Clifton James's obtuse, foolish, fallible but unfailing humanity. Down the drain, too, several minor roles neatly handled, and José Quintero's unexpectedly muscular and purposive staging.

In the last analysis, *Great Day* had more texture than sense of direction, more atmosphere than construction. But it differs importantly from the average "local-color play" in that its color, through unflinching accuracy, transcends the merely local.

Fall 1962

With *Who's Afraid of Virginia Woolf?*, the Broadway season at last comes into possession of a play. By now everyone must know that Edward Albee's drama concerns an all-night drinking session in a New England college. The hosts, a jaded, middle-aged failure of a history professor and his despair-maddened wife, taunt and torment each other and their guests, an *arriviste* of a young biology instructor and his vapid little bride, who retaliate as best they can but end up, in turn, lacerating each other and revealing their own insecurity or hysteria. There is also a plot device about an imaginary son of the elder couple who has to be painfully exorcised from their fantasies by the end of the third act, though one wishes that he could have been exorcised from the author's fantasy before the beginning of the first. The most obvious achievement of the play is that by a generally efficacious mixture of wit, cuttingly or touchingly true dialogue, and often staggering savagery, it gives one's emotional and intellectual apparatus a well-sustained, extensive, and meaningful workout.

Mr. Albee's play assumes, artistically speaking, its rightful place in the tradition which Rilke, in a letter to his wife, correctly traced to Baudelaire's "Une Charogne." It was necessary, wrote Rilke, for artistic contemplation to be able to see "even in the horrible and the seemingly wholly repellent, the Existing, which, along with all else that exists, is valid. . . . A single turning away ever, thrusts [the artist] from the state of grace, makes him altogether sinful." Following in the footsteps of O'Neill and Williams, Albee looks unflinchingly at the putrescent cadaver, or near-cadaver, of our collective decency. But, with Albee, there is a catch. There is an old anecdote about a husband who, tied up, has to watch his wife being raped. When the assailant has fled, she unties her husband who promptly slaps her face. When she cries out in protest that she was overpowered, and could not help being raped, the husband retorts, "Yes, but you could have helped enjoying it." The trouble with Mr. Albee's play is that, instead of being motivated by stern impartiality or a fierce muckraking fervor, it seems mostly to be getting nasty little kicks from kicking society in the groin.

What is seriously wrong here is not that the structure of the play resembles too closely that of *Long Day's Journey into Night*, or that the equivocating little flicker of hope at the end smacks strongly of Tennessee Williams, or that there is a little too much transposing—whether it be Albertine strategy or simply grafting hip talk, beatnikism, and the more fearfully flamboyant aspects of Fire Island on a college community which, however corrupt and sterile, would not boast of a decay that lights up like neon signs. No, the main deficiency here is that, though Albee has splendidly mastered Baudelaire's, or Rilke's, lesson, he has not drawn the corollary conclusion: that for the artist to avert his gaze deliberately from what good persists in the world is equally delinquent and debilitating. Not that Mr. Albee does this continually; but he does it a little too often, and a little too gleefully. I object, not on moral, but on strategic grounds: the playwright is just as apt to miss his mark—the audience—by overshooting as by undershooting.

Still, Mr. Albee has made a significant and, if I may be allowed a vanishing paradox, beautiful contribution to the Poetry of the Obscene. There are times when his somberly flaming sarcasm reminds us more of the Earl of Rochester than of Baudelaire or Bosch. But even Rochester is not to be dismissed lightly. And when at its best, Albee's furibund fun produces lightnings like the definition of insanity as "Just the refuge we take when the unreality of the world weighs too heavy on our tiny heads" (note the double-edged sword), or like the richly metaphoric evocativeness of a middle-agedly professorial but youthfully cruel wife's exclaiming as she finds all her victims temporarily out of range, "Abandonèd!" How gravely and acutely, with just one accent, learning is ridiculed!

The performances, except for Uta Hagen's tendency to ham, are all imposing; Arthur Hill's history professor is more than that: a major creation in the contemporary American theatre. So, too, is Alan Schneider's magnificent staging which finds patterns of movement and vocal music befitting the author's variety of invention. And not the least salute must go to producers Barr and Wilder, who have demonstrated that for hardly more money than was needed for some of Off-Broadway's more pretentious undertakings, it is possible to bring an important play to Broadway, and, while the handsome profits are being counted, make it count as art.

∎

An Actor and an Actress

∎

High above everything else in *A Funny Thing Happened on the Way to the Forum* is the mighty Zero Mostel, towering like a monument hewn out of the whitest Parian—cheese. Pungent, fatty, succulent, infinitely malleable, he is the memorial of (at least) twelve Caesars rolled into one, carved out of goat cheese, and lecherous like the goats it came from. No—it is, to paraphrase Pater on the Mona Lisa, a grotesquerie wrought out from within upon the flesh, the deposit, large cell by cell, of strange thoughts, fantastic reveries and exquisitely gross passions. No—it is a sacred white elephant desecrated by his bestial cravings and trying to compress himself into a harmless mother goose. No—it is Zero Mostel, for whom Plautus already wrote his *Mostellaria*, and who will multiply even unto infinity like the zeroes in the defense budget. As Pseudolus, the wily slave, he manipulates the outraged pawns of the outrageous plot with the *savoir faire* of a cloudful of *dei ex machina*. When Mostel dances, he trips up the light fantastic; when he sings, it is like a choir of angels weeping; and when he mugs, we recognize the face that launched a thousand hardships on spectators averse to cluttering up the aisles with their rolling bodies. And his lines? If it is a line that has to be hit, he smacks it smartly with the back of his hand in the solar plexus, so that it never recovers. And if it is a line to be thrown away, he tosses it off with princely casualness, only to pull it short in mid-flight by an invisible rubber band. If ballet has its prima ballerina assoluta, Latin its ablative absolute, science its absolute zero, the theatre can proudly point to its Zero Absolute.

Appearing with the Düsseldorfer Schauspielhaus in Hauptmann's *Before Sundown*, Ingrid Ernest gave a performance for the like of which one has to go back to Ingrid Bergman's in *Intermezzo* or Julie Haydon's in *The Scoundrel*, but comparisons are odious; suffice it to say that nothing quite like it has been seen on an American stage or screen in a coon's age. Miss Ernest spoke or was silent, moved or was still, looked. And she gave herself, in every form of giving: a girl's, shyly proud; a woman's, quietly eager; a tomboy's, a small child's, a spoiled princess's, an unknown somebody's—unknown even to herself: astonished, frightened, and very, very sure. We were confronted with a reality so overwhelming that life would have found a way of diluting it, just so as to get us over it and beyond. But in the theatre it was there, pure and immutable and ours.

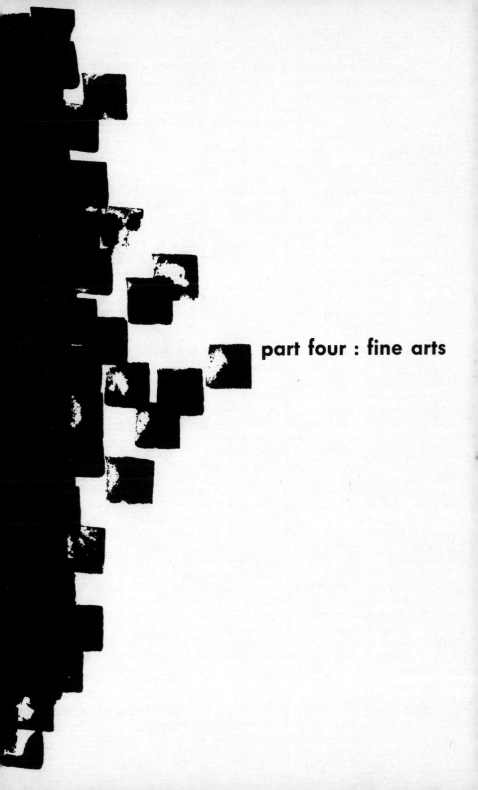

part four : fine arts

■

A Gap Filled In

■

There is a surprise coming to those doubting Thomases who like to stick their arms through a Henry Moore statue to prove that it isn't there. *Heads, Figures and Ideas* is a volume of Moore's drawings, and it is impossible to poke one's hand through its thick pages. But this remark is not made out of sheer frivolousness. Some of us have too long thought of Moore as a sculptor of overblown bagels and megalomaniac doughnuts. I must say I am still not quite reconciled to this sculpture. It is one thing to learn with alarm in school that man is over eighty per cent water, but quite another to see him sculptured as eighty per cent air. It is all very well to have recourse to cynical notions of people as vacuums with a few contours slapped onto them, or to invoke reverently the Rilkean doctrine of *Weltinnenraum,* the mysterious space that is the innermost of existence. Still, a hole is a hole, and though it may not be so unnerving in a statue as in a stocking, it is unnerving enough there too. But comes the revelation: Moore's drawings seem to me, literally and figuratively, more substantial than his sculpture.

Why should one like these drawings and lithographs so much more? Because Moore's art is an attempt to show a transition, or to reconcile opposites. In one of his many penciled notes (reproduced in this book with charm and verisimilitude—as though the artist had gone over your copy and annotated it) Moore says: "The great (continual, everlasting) problem (for me) is to combine sculptured form (POWER) with human sensitivity and meaning, i.e. to try to keep Primitive Power with humanist content." And there is that other significant superscription over a set of drawings:

"Women from Pots." These are the major phenomena we witness in Moore's work: power and grace each trying to assert itself to the fullest and yet somehow not clash with the other; and an object becoming human or a being reverting to thingness in a fluid universe that abolishes categories.

For these aims the drawing seems to me a far more suitable medium than the statue. One can see the work as a palimpsest: intention superimposed on intention. Questions confront us. Is this a woman's head regressing into that of a rooster? Or is the handle of some antique pot evolving into a human cranium? This is the kind of mystery that surrounds a number of images in the book.

But let us look more closely at this large tome which measures thirteen by nineteen inches. Art books in general tend to be solemn, portentous, even venerable. In this one, however, enchanting informality prevails: beauty is caught in her négligé. The dust jacket and cover are a delightful piece of pen and brush work by Henry Moore, and title and author's name are written out in his vigorous handwriting. The end papers are merry Moorian swirls in soft pencil. Then comes a fine color auto-lithograph on handmade paper, suitable for framing, then a title-page with haunting heads and various handwritings in facsimile, the artist's and the publishers'. Even the price, on the inside jacket flap, seems to be written in in pencil by an elegantly nonchalant hand. The preface is an enlargement of typescript: it is as if Geoffrey Grigson had beaten it out with his fists on some Gargantuan typewriter. And before I speak of the drawings, I must praise once again the notes and running commentary scribbled by the author, strictly for himself, around the drawings. Here are, modestly and straightforwardly expressed, the problems and insights of Henry Moore jotted down just as they occurred to him. And the excellent facsimile preserves them in the freshness of their penciled spontaneity.

The images of the book are exceedingly diversified: there are color lithographs, washes, and drawings in pen, pencil, and charcoal. They range from two-minute sketches to meticulously conceived and highly finished master drawings, from maquettes for large sculpture groups like "The Family" (for the Unesco Building in Paris) to studies of odd details like arthritic hands worthy of the sketchbooks of Leonardo. We go from realism to an advanced semi-abstract manner and cover all the intervening stages. The mood varies from the playful to the most disconsolate. And in the middle of it all will be, pasted in, a photograph of an Egyptian statue with Moore's humble and rapt comments underneath it. Truly we see the artist learning, thinking, planning, doing his setting-up exercises, and, finally, creating. What could be more improvisatory, immediate, and intimate, and, for all that, a permanent and immutable ship's log of a journey into uncharted waters.

I shall content myself here with examining only the initial drawing in the book, "Woman on Settee." This is a sketch for a life-size terra cotta statue, but also a beautiful and indefinably disquieting work of art. It has a distinct Pre-Raphaelite ancestry, but it is as though Rossetti's *La Pia* were revised by Leonard Baskin. The one hand absently holding a book grown useless ("La chair est triste, hélas! et j'ai lu tous les livres . . .") and the other decorously framing a head grown weary—this could be Burne-Jones or, heaven help us, even that other Moore, Albert! But there is also the head—a large expanse of blankness that might be a face, except that only such a small part of it is occupied by the paltry features. It would appear that they are striving toward the broad disk of the face from a great distance behind it—or, more likely, shriveling up, fading out of the face, and disappearing into the anonymity of non-being. "Aber der Mann in der Statue/ Zog fort," says Karl Krolow in one of his poems: the man in the statue has moved away. We see, in one form or another, life coming and going in most of these drawings. It is no small tribute to a book if we can say of it that it lets us in on the generative processes of the universe.

■

The Torments of Imagination

■

Despite certain minor aesthetic and biographical contiguities, the three artists to whom the Museum of Modern Art has been devoting its recent attention (in an exhibition* as rewarding in the answers it offers the eye as in the questions it puts to the mind) have very little in common. This is not meant as censure: three different approaches to the fantastic are far more satisfying than

* *The exhibition "Redon, Moreau and Bresdin." Winter, 1961-2.*

three versions of the same one. My only reproach is that the exhibition could have had a pedagogic and philosophical value supplementing its visual delights, had it been hung differently. The clue, after all, is there in the first alcove, where Redon, Moreau, and Bresdin are represented by one picture each.

When three artists depict, with great basic differences, similar subjects from nature, mythology, literature, dream, or the realm of decorative motifs, it behooves the exhibitors to show these kindred and yet how diverse images side by side, so that both trained and untrained eyes, both passionately concerned and pleasantly tickled minds, may be challenged to more fruitful speculation than just following chronologically an artist's development—which connoisseurs hardly need, and laymen seldom bother with. Certain parts of the show could still proceed along chronological lines—indeed, more so than they actually do—by fearless juxtaposition of graphics and oils. As things hang, the average viewer's tendency is to gorge himself on the colors of the first part of the show, and saunter heedlessly past the second as though it were something dated like, say, movies before Technicolor. Redon stands to lose a good deal by this; Bresdin, everything.

One of the difficulties, presumably, lay in the fact that the exhibition had three directors: John Rewald, director-in-chief, and in charge of the Redon paintings; Dore Ashton, responsible for Moreau; and Harold Joachim, entrusted with Bresdin and the Redon graphics. But the main problem must have been the desire of Mr. Rewald and Miss Ashton to demonstrate that these artists were forerunners of various aspects of modernism. Mr. Rewald, more cautiously, refers to elements that are "non-objective" or "abstract"; whereas Miss Ashton, under the protective covering of an "it is said," has Moreau painting very "nearly like the *tachistes* or abstract expressionists." More about this later; let us now look at the artists.

Rodolphe Bresdin (1825-85) is hardly a figure of major importance. His drawings, lithographs and, above all, etchings have a charm that is made up of archaism, extreme delicacy of line, and intense but rather repetitious imagination. What we see in his works is mostly bleak rock structures, fleecy little clouds, distant cities, an occasional solitary human being, a goodly number of beckoning or threatening skeletons, and, most of all, vegetation grown megalomaniac: trees and bushes displaying unheard-of anfractuosities, opacities, writhings, intertwining—and where a little space is left, there, to be disentangled by the eye, are little beasts: gamboling, grimacing, or gobbling up one another. Bresdin worshiped Rembrandt and, apparently, revered Dürer, and their influence on him is unmistakable; one may also be reminded of Altdorfer and other mystic masters, but here the similarity is probably coincidental.

In his best-known works, like *The Good Samaritan* and *The Holy Family Beside a Rushing Stream,* one is chiefly impressed by the enormous quantity of tiniest detail that Bresdin could marshal into a lithograph. The subject matter becomes secondary to a kind of frenzied dance of natural phenomena: polyp-like limbs of trees, burgeoning ferns and creepers, teeming leaves and clouds. Added to this muchness, and making it more so, are small animals among the proliferating roots, birds among the foliage and cirri, and, perceived through clearings, far-off cities, stunning in their almost microscopic detail. In the *Study for the Good Samaritan,* we can see such a filigree Oriental town separately, and are struck by the solidly architectural quality Bresdin could draw, as it were, on a pin's head.

But, moved perhaps by the big-heartedness of his subject, Bresdin made his *Samaritan* too large for so detailed, almost fussy, an approach. In the case of *Fishing Boats in Port,* another large lithograph, overelaboration results in smudginess. Paradoxically, the smaller the dimensions of a Bresdin etching or drawing, the more the fineness of the line and exuberant crowding of detail can convey the spaciousness of the scene and the fullness of the world; such miniatures as *The Holy Family with a Pole* and *The Knight* can move us with their microcosmic completeness. And at his best, Bresdin approaches, indeed grazes, greatness. Thus in the drawing *Nightmare,* where the technique is freer, less compulsive; or in *Aqueduct and Waterfalls,* where the aqueduct in the background is worked out in minute detail, whereas the water and rocks in the foreground are treated with a debonair sketchiness that conveys with psychological exactitude a gaze yearningly focused on the lure of the faraway. Loveliest, to me, are the etchings *The Stream* and, particularly, *The Forest of Fontainebleau,* in which the darks of foliage and lights of rocks and branches arrange themselves in such a rhythmic interplay of free forms punctuated by the more regular shapes of flowers and tree stumps as to conjure up the enchantments of *A Midsummer Night's Dream* before the elated onlooker.

It is in such works where representation and decoration are held in exquisite balance that Bresdin is most memorable; that his plants and animals here and there assume Daliesque shapes, or that some tree of his might tempt us into a Tchelitchevian game of hide and seek, is far less important. There can be little doubt that an artist who produced such impassioned filigree, who proved an inspiring teacher to Redon, and who could walk five hundred miles from Paris to Toulouse carrying a pet rabbit in his arms, deserves to be remembered.

With Gustave Moreau (1826-98) we come to an artist who is equally puzzling in quiddity and in quality. There are, first, what we would now call his salon paintings, though in their time they were shocking enough to seem to be saloon paintings. Of pictures like *Oedipus and the Sphinx,* Redon wrote that they exhilarated him in his youth—though in later years he had little enough use for them. To Huysmans, in *A Rebours,* the two big *Salomes* revealed an "art which transcended the limits of painting, borrowed from the art of writing its most subtle evocations, from the art of the ceramist its most marvelous brilliance, from the stone-cutter's and engraver's arts their most exquisite refinements." Others, however, were less impressed even at that time. Degas said of Moreau, "He wants to make us believe that the gods wore watch chains!" And Gauguin: "Of every human being he makes a piece of jewelry covered with jewelry." His brooding, epicene youths—Orpheus, Oedipus, Hercules, Narcissus—or the jewel-encrusted, alabaster-skinned seductresses—Salome, Delilah, Helen, even the all too smugly innocent Galatea—leave us as cold today as do the elaborate and carefully rendered architectural backgrounds, the anthology of overripe gems, and the whole exotic panoply. To quote Mario Praz:

> Moreau's figures are ambiguous; it is hardly possible to distinguish at the first glance which of two lovers is the man, which the woman; all his characters are linked by subtle bonds of relationship . . . lovers look as though they were related, brothers as though they were lovers, men have the faces of virgins, virgins the faces of youths; the symbols of good and evil are entwined and equivocally confused. There is no contrast between different ages, sexes, or types: the underlying meaning of this painting is incest, its most exalted figure the Androgyne, its final word sterility.

The official side of Moreau, however underplayed it may be by the current show, still gives us an idea of what his age saw in him: the pictorial equivalent of Flaubert, Baudelaire, Mallarmé in literature, and of Berlioz and Wagner in music. Now, it matters little if these men were abler in their respective fields than Moreau was in his: his heroines were just as apt to step into the popular imagination as the Salammbôs, Herodiases, Valkyries, and Rhine Maidens. We can accordingly view these works, if not with the warmth of respect, at least with the alacrity of historical interest.

We would have been helped here if Miss Ashton had seen fit to get us a few more of the representative works, such as the *Jupiter and Semele,* which both the Musée Gustave Moreau and the recent Moreau exhibition at the Louvre chose to feature. Contemplating this official side of Moreau can, at any rate, usefully remind us that works which were intoxicants to the young artists and intellectual avant-garde of their day ("sorcerer that he is," Jean Lorrain wrote of Moreau, "he has bewitched his age") can, in fairly short order, become objects of derision or, worse yet, oblivion. The lesson has particular relevance for our time.

But there is another side to Moreau which the exhibition is at great pains to demonstrate. This consists of certain oil and water-color sketches of which a prodigious number is present: they range from pieces where the subject matter is more or less discernible, such as *Circe* or *The Temptation of St. Anthony,* to others labeled merely *Sketch A* or *Sketch B,* etc., in which figures or places can, perhaps, be divined, but in which one is chiefly aware of the intrepid interplay of effervescent swirls of color. From these it is argued by the directors of the exhibition that Moreau was somewhat of an abstract painter, if not, indeed, an abstract expressionist *avant la lettre* and *sub rosa.* Writes Miss Ashton in her essay on Moreau in the exhibition catalogue: "Who, looking at the small oils, can deny that the experience of 'abstract' color and movement absorbed Moreau completely." The answer is: Anyone who then looks at the other works Moreau went on producing all his life. Also anyone who notes how in a painting like *Orpheus at the Tomb of Eurydice* interpenetrations of such sheer coloristic bravado are applied by Moreau to perfectly standard works.

Miss Ashton's arguments for viewing these sketches as finished paintings of an abstract expressionist type are that Moreau "regarded them seriously enough to frame and mount," that color is here "completely released from its signifying connotations," and that in *Sketch A* "Moreau's thumb prints are clear." Now it is evident that Moreau never threw anything away, that he took his most ephemeral productions as seriously as the need to keep his oeuvre together intact—hence his bequest of his studio and works *in toto* to the state. Hence also Degas's feeling, echoed since by many a visitor to the Rue de la Rochefoucauld, that the place was "as spooky as a family vault," or, we might add, a Narcissist temple. It is entirely consistent with this "Thesaurus," this "Gradus ad Parnassum," as Degas further called it, that even the least little preliminary color sketch should be religiously enshrined. As for color being here "released from its connotations," Miss Ashton must surely mean denotations (but then precision of language, or thought, is not her specialty), for nothing, not even the kind of contemporary painting she preconizes, is free from connotations. Actually, fiery figures between sky and earth are discernible in *Sketch A*, a monumental edifice can be guessed at in *Sketch B*, and a colonnade, or river winding between trees, can be surmised in *Sketch E*. Concerning the thumb print—well, one sees evidence of at least ten thumbs in Miss Ashton's essay, yet I for one would hesitate to call her an abstract writer.

There is, however, a middle ground between the academic paintings and the sketches: oils and water colors of a swifter, freer sort, where figures are spare or allowed to deliquesce whereas larger elements, natural or architectural, in daring compositions, preponderate. Thus the *Delilah*, where the exhaustion of the *femme fatale* is suggested by the indefinite contours; her gilded attire picks up the colors of the arid desert; her nipples and ornaments—a few small patches of red—echo the malefic red glow from the bedroom ceiling under which the monstrous deed may just have been consummated. Impressive, too, is another oil, *Thomyris and Cyrus*, in which the cruel Scythian queen and the mighty conqueror, her victim, are dwarfed by a magnificent sea of mountain snow and ice—next to which Bresdin's *Crevasse* could have provoked interesting comparisons. Moreau makes the scenery a frozen moon landscape, and with one bold flick of horizontal white upon a livid sky, he can suggest all that remains of the sun in this hyperborean world.

More impressive yet are audacious water colors like *La Toilette, Woman and Panther, Study for The Chimeras, Ganymede,* and *Hercules and the Doe.* In this context it is worth recalling Redon's criticism of the Beaux-Arts Moreau in a letter to Mme de Holstein: "il ne s'efforça pas au dedans"—so that the academic works "remain stuck in a sort of optical rhetoric." But, Redon went on, Moreau was "a great water-colorist, incontestably." In the water colors, the brush is often as dry as the forms are flowing: an uncluttered composition in rapid lines and ecstatic colors brings about something like a wedding of Guys and Vlaminck. Because of such works one may share Miss Ashton's admiration for Moreau. If Jean Lorrain assigned to him "the glory of having disturbed his entire century," we can at least grant him the skill of delighting ours with his smaller, unofficial voice.

Many who have hitherto loved Redon piecemeal can now at last make their fractured feelings whole. For John Rewald and Harold Joachim have given us an ample and diversified selection from Redon's work, which, along with occasional naïveté, reveals chiefly a many-sided mastery. Hence it is unfair to conceive of Odilon Redon (1840-1916) as a non-writing but literary adjunct to the symbolist movement of his day. One may consider Mallarmé's comment to him, "I envy you your captions," referring to the elaborate titles Redon gave his pictures (which Morris Graves, too, might envy), as an added feather in Redon's béret, but hardly as proof of "literariness" in a limiting sense. The young Cocteau made a useful distinction when he addressed Redon as "le moins littéraire et le plus poétique des génies."

The exhibition reveals a painter and graphic artist who begins as a disciple of Delacroix, Manet, and Bresdin, but soon achieves remarkably original effects. Thus in Landscape, Peyrelebade, where a flat blue sky with the tiniest admixture of green comes to spectacular life (one thinks of Mallarmé's demonic Azur), or in Trees at Peyrelebade, where the high relief of the central tree trunk contrasts strikingly with the flattening and emptying of the picture in all directions. In Street in Quimper and Near the Harbor, Brittany, iconoclastic manipulations of composition and perspective are made to pay off handsomely. An early charcoal drawing, Dante and Virgil (1865, Bonger Collection), displays the brilliantly imaginative draftsman: the two figures, made thrice remote by turning their backs on us, bending strangely backward, and by eerie backlighting, become close kindred of the weirdly slanting trees.

When Gide wrote Redon about a work in which the master had "comme dessiné un regard," he put a reverent though casual finger on one of the central points of Redon's art. For the more one examines Redon's works, the more one realizes that one is being examined by them—that, like Big Brother, they are continually watching us. The thing that looks out at us from almost every work of Redon's is The Eye; melancholy, tragic, sinister, grotesque, or merry, it is the very essence of "eyeness." It may reach out to us fondly, or fiercely stab us. If it is not nakedly an eye, then it is a face full of the eye or eyes, the whole countenance reduced to a container for the eye. And if the eye is shut, averted, or shadowed, the head itself becomes an eyeball, to nail us down as if its face were at the utmost a translucent eyelid from behind which an irrepressible gaze penetrates us—helplessly, lidlessly at its mercy. And when there are not even eye-like faces in the picture, balloons, flowers, creatures of the sea metamorphose themselves into eyes to meet and hypnotize our own.

These metamorphoses bring us to Redon's other main characteristic: he was, more than anything else, a sublime doodler. A vast majority of his works are doodles—whether playfully and gracefully slapdash, such as the pastel *Yellow Flowers,* or elaborated with supreme commitment, as, for example, *The Virgin at Dawn.* This explains why there is such a sprouting of ears, tails, spider legs, spikes, thorns, bristles all over Redon's works, and particularly the drawings: these excrescences represent the restless pencil belaboring, developing some initial doodle, extending it, feeding it to fill out the paper. "J'ai horreur d'une feuille de papier blanc," Redon reluctantly explained his mode of creation. "A sheet of paper is so shocking to me that I am forced, as soon as it is on the easel, to scrawl on it with charcoal, with a crayon or any other material, and this operation brings it to life." Similarly, Redon's friend Mallarmé was haunted by the white, taunting paper before him. Only whereas to Mallarmé it was a demon reminding him of sterility and futility, or luring him with the fascination of silence and non-being, to Redon it was a challenge to express himself, or, better, to express through himself the world of "our abstruse dreams," and illuminating "all the tragic ludicrousness of ordinary existence" with "so much intellectual fear and awesome sympathy"—as Mallarmé wrote to, and about, his friend. And again: "You ruffle in our silences the plumage of Night and Dream." Or, in Maurice Raynal's more contemporary idiom, "By the grace of the poet's vision, [Redon] tried as it were to psychoanalyze animal, vegetable, and even mineral entities, so as to make them yield their secrets."

Both the ocular obsession and compulsiveness of Redon are best seen in the many works in which staring women's faces and contemplative flowers emerge almost indiscriminately side by side, so that a picture called *Woman with Flowers* might just as well be *Flowers with Woman.* What this art conveys supremely is the interpenetration of things: a world in which, by a haunting gaze, by the merging and transmutation of objects and beings, each truly becomes part of the other, as dreaming is part of waking, and as each of us feels, or is made to feel by Redon, the universe growing right through him. And what makes this visionary world so real and indisputable is what Redon learned from sources as diverse as his early architectural training and his brief studies with Corot: that the indefinite, fantastic, obscure must be firmly juxtaposed with the concrete and logical. Many have painted their visions, but few have succeeded, like Redon, in endowing the tissue of dream with the texture, the very feel, of reality.

Lastly, Redon was a tireless experimenter. I recommend to everyone's careful scrutiny works like *The Flight into Egypt*, with its compelling use of nonsense colors; *The White Butterfly*, which out-Carrières Carrière with the range it wrests from monochrome—or, conversely, *Roger and Angelica*, where the most wildly clashing colors are brought into triumphant harmony; or such astutely allusive and echoistic use of color as in *Woman with Flowers* (1913), from which Matisse must have learned more than from all his time spent with Moreau. And always the attempt to enrich one medium with the glories of another: as in a lithograph like *Pegasus Captive*, which seems to derive from silhouette-cutting; or the so-called *Portrait of Vuillard*, where the customary lights and darks are reversed to give pen-and-ink drawing a more sculptural quality; or in the many oils which capture the intimate radiance of pastels. Even in his mistakes Redon is meaningful. Thus when he misspells the most famous Valkyrie as *Brunnehilde*, thereby unconsciously blending Teutonic severity with French delicacy—a fusion which the lithograph delightfully bears out. Or when in the signature of another lithograph, *Obsession*, he accidentally prints the N in REDON backwards—as children might do with the spendid analphabetism of innocence.

Less fortunate than these are the lapses of the exhibition catalogue. Disturbed as one may be by Mr. Rewald's vulgarisms such as "anymore," "intriguing," and "overly," these are as nothing compared to Miss Ashton's mangling of grammar, syntax, and spelling, as when she couples plural subjects with singular predicates, spells dandies as "dandys" or devotee as "devotée," turns out barbarisms like the noun "interlaces" for interlacements, jargon like "Chasseriau's painting conflict," or evidences of total insensitivity to language as in "his imagery . . . is keyed to closure." More serious are her baseless assertions such as "the traditional Romantic image of woman as the principle of evil," where she confuses romanticism with decadence, or "Not until the Fauves were non-naturalistic colors used so daringly [as by Moreau]," as if Van Gogh, Gauguin, the Nabis, and Redon himself had never existed. Her translations, too, are remarkable, as when a line of Vigny (whom she keeps referring to illiterately as "de Vigny") comes out "Fatal lovers, condemned ones of titanic shames. . . ." She is, however, at her best as a fracturer of French: the *théories de femmes* around the figure of *"Luxure"* on a lewd goat become "theories of women" around "Luxury," instead of bevies of women around Lechery (Miss Ashton's iconography keeps pace with her French), and *chantres* turn into "pagan chanters" instead of bards. At least her lack of French compensates for her even greater lack of humor.

But let it pass; the Museum of Modern Art has given us an absorbing and memorable show which illustrates three different approaches to the fantastic by artists who, each in his own way, experienced what Redon called "the torments of imagination." If we accept Novalis's definition of genius as "the ability to deal with imaginary objects as with real ones, and to treat them as such, too" (I regret not being able to translate the pun on *handeln* and *behandeln*), then, surely, Redon was a genius in the purest possible sense.

■

The Reviviscence

■

Of all the hopeless undertakings I can think of, there is none that seems to me so securely foredoomed as a history of twentieth-century painting which someone sets out to write a little after the mid-century mark. More and more brushes (where brushes are still in use) are running amok; partisanship is fanatical, and carnage is in full bloom. Movements, as well as individual painting careers, are extremely hard to follow, what with sudden turnabouts, overlappings, and basic inconsistencies. Activity proliferates in such far-flung and unpainterly cities as Zurich and

New York, or even Seattle, of whose very existence former art historians could be serenely unaware. The last eighty or ninety years, moreover, produced breaks with tradition more violent than ever seen in the history of western art; and, since the coming of various nonrepresentational forms of painting, it has become almost impossible to separate the sheep from the goats—inasmuch as the sheep are mostly squares and the goats triangles, unless, indeed, both are merely blobs. Matters are further complicated by the fact that the hundred or so years that would give one the necessary perspective have not yet elapsed, and in criticism, unlike in painting, perspective is still necessary. A further complication stems from the inadequacy of any language when faced with describing, say, a tachist painting; nor could we afford books that would reproduce in color every single picture mentioned. Over the birth of a history of contemporary painting there hover, therefore, a hundred wicked fairies, showering it with dreadful fates. What the one good fairy can do is to controvert their lulling of the author's sensibilities, perception, and integrity into sleep or death, by bestowing on him and his book the highest watchfulness: the greatest possible awakeness, alertness, and analytical acumen. This is what recommends Werner Haftmann's *Painting in the Twentieth Century*: you will not catch it sleeping where beauty of any, even the most alarming, sort can be found in modern art.

"What we do," wrote Nietzsche, "is never understood, but always only praised and blamed." Haftmann, however, wisely sets out to understand first and last, and, in between, to pass on his understanding; as for the praise and blame, let them fall where they will. And, quite correctly, to understand modern painting means something more to him than might be commonly expected. "The profoundly revolutionary developments in painting which set in about 1890," writes Haftmann, "cannot be viewed apart from modern mankind as a whole, whose situation they illustrate." Such an existential view of painting will scarcely produce a book of pretty pictures with some amiable chitchat or sleek jargon for their frames. The result, rather, is this book: more demanding, and, for that very reason, greater in scope and in rewards.

Thus the book consists of two large volumes. The first of these contains 430 pages of text, including brief biographies and bibliographies, as well as photographs, of the artists. This volume is strictly a reading book. In it, painters and painting are discussed in their proper cultural setting, which includes the other arts, science, philosophy, religion, and also politics and social conditions. The style falls short of brilliance, but is well above what passes for it in our art reviews and gallery talks. It manages to avoid both academicism and dilettantism, both jargon and "fine writing." Haftmann is able, moreover, to evoke pictures with words—not so well as a poet, perhaps, but a good deal better than that perennial effete young man or tailored and twitching spinster who is hired to do so in art columns and museum corridors. Above all, Haftmann is unlike every American art expert, in that he is not showy; unlike every French one, in that he is not chauvinistic; and unlike his German colleagues, in that he is not a rabid metaphysician. The second volume of the work contains the evidence—or some, indeed much, of it; it consists of 55 color and 340 black-and-white illustrations, along with more text: brief outlines of relevant matter from volume one, and careful commentaries on the pictures reproduced.

Now you can use this book in three ways: as a student, as an amateur, and as a man or woman of the world. As a student, you begin in the enlightened classroom of volume one, and then proceed to the field trips of volume two. As an amateur, you bask among the pictures of volume two, and whenever your curiosity is especially aroused, consult volume one for detailed information. As a man of the world, you keep these two handsome, boxed volumes within easy reach, and turn to them whenever you need some particular bit of erudition, or just some pleasurable relaxation.

At this point, however, Nietzsche and Haftmann notwithstanding, I must introduce a bit of blame. Mind you, the shortcomings of *Painting in the Twentieth Century* have a way of turning out to be blessings under their somewhat heavy disguise. It might be objected that there are too few color plates but this forces us to read Haftmann's descriptions of the pictures all the more carefully, which often proves more informative than the most sedulous picture-gazing. Again, after 1945, the author becomes a bit partial. It is not so much that he praises the abstractionists and blames the more representational painters. It is just that he dwells at length on the former and says little or nothing about the latter. Thus men like Balthus, Beaudin, Carzou, Schiele are not even mentioned, and others, like John Piper and Claude Vénard are dealt with all too laconically; among the younger Americans, for example, Michael Goldberg and Norman Bluhme are there, whereas William Thon and Robert Vickrey do not exist. If a figurative painter like Bernard Buffet gets fairly generous space, it seems to be mostly because he reminds the author, however vaguely, of non-objective painters like Hartung and Wols, whom he relishes. Even among the author's own German abstractionists, the wilder ones like Werner and Winter seem to fare better than the comparatively restrained Meistermann. However, this has the merit of alerting the more conservative ones among us to what is going on at the very forefront of the avant-garde, and places the book somewhere between abreast and ahead of its times.

There are, moreover, a few factual errors. Thus the dadaist Marcel Janco was Rumanian, not Hungarian; Maurice Prendergast's discovery of Cézanne did not come early, but only when Prendergast was forty, and then with less than felicitous consequences for his painting; in Boccioni's *Farewells,* what Haftmann takes to be "people jammed into compartments" is really a recurrent figure of someone leaning out of a train window toward another recurrent figure who stays behind. More frequent than strictly unavoidable, though, are the misspellings: the art historian René Huyghe sprouts a final "s" and the Belgian critic Haesaerts loses his second "e," and one painter's name changes from one page to the next; in such matters, however, anyone might be to blame. The translator, Ralph Manheim, is definitely not wholly innocent when he renders *Lebensgefühl* with the Teutonicism "life-feeling" or when he gives us "travelling knights" for knights-errant or when someone becomes "intrigued."

Still, *Painting in the Twentieth Century* is almost certainly the most modest, thorough, and cosmopolitan book on its subject. It encompasses more painters in more countries than other books of its kind, and its author tries valiantly—and up to 1945 successfully—to be fair to all of them. The aim throughout is to comprehend, describe, and explain without affectation or grandiloquence. If the knell of figurative painting is rung perhaps a bit prematurely and if the dishevelment of today's painting is a trifle too glibly equated with the rampage of modern physics and the *malaise* of modern psyches, these assertions have at least as much truth as most generalizations that pass unchallenged. Speaking of the painting of his day, Coleridge observed some 130 years ago: "Now in this age, we have a sort of reviviscence—not, I fear, of the power, but of a taste for the power, of the early times." Painting today is, if nothing else, reviviscent, or, in the talk of a less high table, lively. And it assuredly has a taste for power, even if not for that of the ancients. To this liveliness, to this restless surge, Herr Haftmann's book does ample justice. It is precisely the book that contemporary painting needs and deserves.

■

Macke the Knife

■

For many people expressionist painting means violence, if not downright crudity. Without being able to distinguish one expressionist from another, they tend to summon up a synthetic archetype compounded of the worst excesses of the school; they then attach to it, more or less unjustly, such names as Vasili Kandinsky, Edvard Munch, Oskar Kokoschka, George Grosz, James Ensor, and above all, Max Beckmann, and the chimera is rampant.

In reality, however, expressionism has produced some tender and graceful paintings, in which inventiveness, elegance, and passion are justly united. It subsumes the lyrical animals of Franz Marc, the incandescent flowers of Emil Nolde, Paul Klee's quizzical illuminations, Kokoschka's quintessential views of cities, and the sidewalk pastorals of August Macke, a painter who is just now beginning to receive the attention he deserves for having seen Arcadia in the sardine boxes we live in.

In April, 1914, three painter friends went off to Tunis for a fortnight. One was Louis Moilliet, who had been, and was to remain, promising. Another was Klee, the diarist of the journey, who was to become one of our foremost painters. The third was Macke, whose already excellent work started out along still more original paths in Tunis. What this might have led to we shall not know; he was killed in the war that same year at the age of twenty-seven.

Before Tunisia, Macke's work consisted chiefly of brilliant portrayals of German society in the era preceding the First World War. It is not altogether different from that of other members of the *Blaue Reiter* group, like Ernst Kirchner or Nolde, except that it is finer. For in Macke alone lyricism and wit were perfectly blended; delicately poised, like those people on bridges he liked to paint, his laughter never turned into a grimace, and his beaming colors never became glaring or merely ornamental.

In Tunisia, between April 7 and 22, 1914, Macke brought forth a welter of works, all dazzling and many beautiful; some of the best of these now appear in this handsome volume.*

* August Macke: Tunisian Watercolors and Drawings, *by Paul Klee et al.*, New York, 1960.

Not only are format, binding, choice of papers, typography, spacing unerringly good, but we are treated to a novel idea: the irreproachable reproductions, all in color, slide out from behind black or white borders and can be mounted in slip-in frames that are provided.

The book has one weakness: the critical commentaries range from pretentious to pedestrian, and there is no clear and full account of Macke's life and work. Even so major an event as his rejection of Kandinsky's abracadabra is barely mentioned; his relationships to Cézanne, Matisse, and Robert Delaunay are sketched in rather faintly; and the image of Macke himself is lopped off as much by pseudo-metaphysical verbiage as his life was by a gun.

But we are given two valuable texts. One is Macke's maxims on art and life. He writes with an engaging, naïve forthrightness that is an antidote to the cant and jargon into which many painters and art critics have leapt—not just fallen. The other text is that of Klee's journal of the trip, with which the reproductions are interfoliated, providing a brisk obbligato to the pictures.

I want to dwell on two masterpieces of this collection: "Rocky Landscape" and "Gully." "Rocky Landscape" is an ingenuous and delectable *entente cordiale* of numerous seeming irreconcilables. In the background are extremely geometric, indeed pyramidal rock formations, and their mildly cubist treatment and rich reddish browns allude to the later Cézanne. At the upper left there are some rather flat ornamental cactuses of dark, improbable brown, and on the lower right there is a rectangular area (framed by an elevated road running toward the center of the picture but turning suddenly right) furbished with aggressive patches of color, among them an intense, unlikely green embraced by fanciful violet shadows. These are the picture's *fauve* elements. The central interest is formed by two somewhat obese obelisks—the gateway to the tomb of a Moslem saint, whose cupolas, zebraed by light and shade, stretch toward the right. Slightly to the left but far above the gateway, there is a glittering Moorish castle on which sun and shadow produce dazzling contrasts of white and navy; below, on the obelisks, the contrasts are infinitely gentler—between powder blue and lemon and canary yellow. The little bit of white and the small patches of yellow seem to conduct a spirited dialogue across and above a variety of massed browns, blues, and greens.

There is something of the exquisiteness of late impressionism about this. But there is something even more remarkable in a large area of the lower left, where a series of rocks became translucent ghosts of themselves (diaphanous blues, pinks, oranges), as if they were viewed through plate glass and the play of reflections on it. We have something of Delaunay's window paintings: a glorious defenestration of the eye. What a convocation! Cézanne, Matisse, Monet, and Delaunay seem to meet around a dark green area in the middle as around a card table. But Macke the Knife fleeces them all. It is, however, less theft than borrowing for the sake of a warmly original synthesis.

"Gully," on the other hand, is pure Macke. Toward the bottom of a ravine there come—nuzzling, lapping, snakily coiling—triangles of all sorts: equilateral, isosceles, scalene, some perfect, some truncated, lopsided, dented, twisted, but all converging on that ravine bottom. You feel nothing but browns and greens: though actually there are bits of orange, pink, rose madder, and even blue interspersed, still it seems to be a vast contest of greens and browns. The whole thing has a peculiarly polypous, arachnoid life. Everything hurtles into this gully, and the pallid sky, broken up into three differently colored triangles, wanly echoes the combat. Yet the abstract forms become wholly objective, representational. Only the greatest painters can make such opposites merge.

Like Fauré in music and Hofmannsthal in poetry, Macke had daring and restraint, vitality and finesse; he was a painter who was never very far wrong and often quietly, devastatingly right.

■

Expressionism, Austrian Style

■

To the transatlantic eye the German and the Austrian may seem pretty much alike—they even talk the same language, don't they? Actually, they don't. Germans speak something more throaty, more even-keeled, more majestic. Austrians produce sounds more melodious and delightful, but less stately. Think of the difference between Hindemith and Alban Berg.

So, too, Austrian expressionism differs considerably from its better known German counterpart, as the charming and instructive show now at the Galerie St. Etienne demonstrates. The first of the four artists represented is Gustave Klimt, a bizarre, bejeweled Art-Nouveau painter, from whom, in one way or another, our three expressionists learned their lesson, only to surpass him in all respects. Still, to be an old teacher is better than being an old shoe: one shapes the mind, the other leaves no trace on the foot.

Alfred Kubin is a remarkable graphic artist as yet little known in this country, though I can foresee a time when he will have a vogue comparable to Dufy's, Chagall's, or Orozco's, for there is something in Kubin that appeals immediately and universally. The show gives us only a smattering of his later work (none of the earlier, surrealist pieces), but of this phase "Infanticide," "Dishonest Game," and "A New Robinson" are choice examples. Because they are a cross between intense social concern and childlike delight in the odd and ludicrous, they should be particularly appealing to American viewers. Thus in "A New Robinson," an ink and water-color drawing reminiscent of certain aspects of Benton and Burchfield, a dejected rustic squats before an equally godforsaken hut. It could be a very pathetic scene indeed, except for the facts that a foolish turkey comes strutting onto it, and that though the weather vane indicates a wind blowing to the left, the smoke from the chimney curls in the opposite direction, and a slender tree stands bolt upright! Funny things are going on in this sad world. "Dishonest Game" is something like Cézanne's "Card Players" as Ben Shahn might have done it, had he been illustrating an imaginary story by Gogol. How touching, above all the meanness and torpor of the various knaves and dolts, is the naïvely framed photograph of a little girl on the mantel—both the girl and the frame seem to be shrinking away from the vileness of it all, and yet it is this innocent photograph that balances in the composition the five of clubs which a particularly uncouth character is brandishing aloft. How the sweet and ugly complement each other in this life! The noble thing about Kubin's work is that, however painful the subject, as in "Infanticide," the delicate touches of water color over the heavy ink lines endow the horror with a grace that is the pictorial equivalent of Christian charity.

The Kokoschka works in the show do not seem to me, with two exceptions, distinguished. There is a rather blubber-faced goose-girl in oil; two unspectacular portraits in charcoal and sanguine, respectively; also a number of early landscapes in charcoal, which, if nothing else, attest to a sure eye for what might be called the skeleton of a landscape, and a strict frugality of line worthy of a Scotsman. None the less, even into these reductions to simplest terms, Oskar Kokoschka is able to bring a bubbling Austrian lyricism, a decorative suavity that a German expressionist's eye could not have disengaged from the landscape. But the two Kokoschkas that are wholly absorbing are the sanguine "Seated Girl," and the water color "Reclining Girl Reading." Both of them have a curious gallows humor—no, not gallows, just whipping-post humor. The seated girl has struck a pose of languid elegance, but is drawn with the sloppiest, most illiterate-seeming lines. She might almost be a drunken Silenus, indeed her nose is royally incarnadined and her right eye sleepily closed, while the left eye drifts moodily away. Kokoschka's almost schizoid draftsmanship creates an apparition of seedy elegance—a rumpled seductiveness. As for the reading girl, she is a grotesque creature, a Little Lulu out of Sacher-Masoch (one hates to think what she might be reading), but the colors have such a merry, posterish extroversion about them that one cannot help being, however maliciously, delighted.

The bulk of the show is devoted to the wonderful Egon Schiele, whose reputation is deservedly growing. In 28 short years (made shorter by war and poverty) Schiele managed to paint and draw some of the most brain-teasing, memory-haunting pictures of our times. Who else could move with such untrammeled ease from brooding, almost animalistic, sexuality to empyrean serenity (in this show, compare "Woman With Blond Hair" with "Seated Woman, the Artist's Wife"), and even cross-breed the two (as in "Standing Female Nude in Blue Robe" or "Reclining Woman With Black Stocking")? Who else could paint houses and churches—granted that here Austrian architecture helped—that seem, literally, good enough to eat? A marvelous oil, "Suburb I," shows a row of brownish houses with tiger-red chimneys against a background of modulating greys, products not of the architect's or painter's, but, rather, the inspired confectioner's art. This masterpiece is beginning to chip, and I find it hard to believe that someone didn't take a bite out of it. Even in a rapid sketch in black crayon and tempera, such as the ravishing "Church in Moedling," Schiele gives us so brilliantly yet economically deployed a set of colors, so chastely framed by unadorned black lines at the bottom and austerely blank space above and in front, that one gasps for breath before something so aromatic coming at one out of nothing, out of the empty paper, out of this painter-poet's imagination.

Paul Valéry once said of the French classic painters that "their singing vistas are to nature what opera is to daily life." The Austrian expressionists' world is that of bittersweet Viennese light opera—Strauss, if you will, but Richard, not Johann. It is a world full of a doomed sweetness, extracting sweetness out of its very doom.

■

How Pointed Are Rabbits' Ears?

■

Two specious notions have gained currency in the world of art. What makes them particularly interesting is that they tend to be accepted by professionals, connoisseurs, and laity alike. The first is that old and outlandish forms of art are not really naïve or even, heaven forbid, primitive; they are stylized, abstract, idealized and, in short, infinitely knowing. From this derives the second notion: that these aboriginal, prehistoric, or merely ancient art forms are, actually, as modern as can be.

There are many reasons for these contentions. We cannot accept the fact that people ever were different from us and saw things otherwise. It is impossible even to assume that they were in any way insensitive or ignorant, because, who knows, might not we then appear so to future ages? And, most of all, if we were forced by circumstances—in graduate schools or elsewhere—to devote years of research to Masolino or Shenstone or Quantz, then, by God, Masolino is a great painter, Shenstone a major poet, and Quantz a composer of the first rank, i.e., they are neither simple-minded nor removed from our sensibilities. Clearly the two fallacies stem from egocentricity, whether innate or thrust upon us.

Which is not to say that ancient art never shows stylization, or that there is nothing about it that can ever look modern. (Even then there is some question of precedence: the more Picasso imitates African sculpture, the more African sculpture reminds us of Picasso.) But when we turn to Byzantine or Byzantinizing mosaics, such as those in the Church of St. Mark in Venice, the salient facts are that they are primitive and unmodern. Let us, however, consider what this means. It means, for instance, that the rabbits in the Dome of the Creation have pointed ass's ears, though

206

except for a background of gold they have nothing in common with King Midas. If a modern painter, with a long tradition behind him of seeing rabbits' ears, among other things, accurately (it is amazing how many centuries it may take to see an object as it is!), were suddenly to turn them into stilettos, it would be a deliberate act of stylization, subserving a specific purpose. But your Byzantine mosaicist does not know, or care to know, better; which is why, also, his elephants looks like masquerading pigs. This is primitive. As for God, in the same mosaic, he is represented as a blonde young Christ with a somewhat Elvis Presleyish face. Doubtless the mosaicist was influenced by the *Cotton Bible,* but that does not make this image of God any less alien to us who have fashioned for ourselves a God the Father out of Michelangelo and Blake.

But why should this make the eleventh-to-fourteenth-century mosaics of St. Mark's, or the book which faithfully reproduces them, any less interesting? On the contrary, when we look at the unimpeachable color plates in *Mosaics of St. Mark's,** we are no longer merely art lovers: we are historians and, as it were, archaeologists of the human soul. For the saints and nobles, the patriarchs and plebeians in these mosaics personify an ancient world, a bygone consciousness. Even the animals and plants are old-timers: they belong in the bestiaries of the imagination, in the herbals of time. And the perspective is as ingenuous, and looks as superannuated, as a newborn babe. Here is a seriousness, angularity, plainness (in both senses), sobriety of coloring, simplicity— a world of such rough-hewn humility that we can associate it only with sanctity, nothing less.

Let it not be understood, however, that there is no aesthetic enjoyment involved. In the group "The Doge and Noblemen" from the façade of the church, for instance, who could resist the interplay of gowns? I can describe these robes only in contradictions: they are both ornate and simple, both plastic and flat, swirling in countless folds and absolutely static. Explain it at will in terms of the difficulty of getting subtle shading onto *tesserae,* or in terms of a lack of depth in the perspective, the paradox fills you with a kind of awe that brings you at least as close to godliness as the most perfumed soap.

There is even greater artistry in "The Apostles Asleep," a detail from "The Agony in the Garden." We see a tentacular, throbbing mass of garments and folds, whose colors

* Mosaics of St. Mark's, by Pietro Toesca and Ferdinando Forlati, New York, 1960.

are not so differentiated as to prevent the whole from being one billowing and seething organism—out of which, ironically, protrude flaccid faces and forsaken hands that are possessed by something more torpid, more abject than sleep. Nothing could convey more beautifully strength gone to waste.

Yet if one looks closer at some of these works, out of what rigid, unmodern conventions they are made up: regular, thick, green lines down the edges of faces for shading; perfect circles or ellipses to denote a bulging elbow or belly; schematic arrangements of folds. Still, this schematism produces its own kind of beauty. Thus in the "Rocky Landscape," another detail from "The Agony in the Garden," where the child's ingenuous oversimplification is joined to the passionate symmetry of the authoritarian. Against a background of near-parallel, diagonally ascending sinuous rock contours, their sepia nervously traversing the general beige, there spring up trees and flowers avidly vertical, in shapes with which nowadays only children could endow them, and even they only in dreams. These trees that look like intensely green parasols or kidneys on golden stems, these flowers that seem to be slightly pathetic costume jewelry, these shrubs that are the emerald paws of friendly dragons, all strive loyally, touchingly upwards. There results a marvelous counterpoint between the diagonal and the perpendicular. And when you add to this the charm of the rocky ledges which, with perfect innocence, manage to have the shape of maple leaves and echo the forms of some of the shrubbery, you get a picture so cunning and yet again so guileless that you must be, however exasperatedly, in love with it. And like love, a composition such as this is not devised. It occurs.

Consider, lastly, "Birds Taken into Noah's Ark," a detail from the Story of Noah in the narthex. I will not dwell on these enchanting storks, pelicans, herons, and one other species that I, as what would be called in German "ein ornithologisches Antitalent," cannot identify; but I will say that what makes these *rarae aves,* identified or otherwise, so endearing is that they look less like the real thing than like a toy version of it. But not like any old toys; rather like those Rolls Royces of the nursery, the Steiff woolly animals. And if the birds don't convince you of the primitiveness and antiquity of this world, glance at the "Humility" in the Dome of the Ascension, who, instead of looking like one of the staider virtues, appears to us like an egregiously foolish virgin, her brittleness further emphasized by breasts, belly, and one visible thigh looking like four eggshells.

The book contains two introductory essays: one by

Pietro Toesca on the mosaics, and another by Ferdinando Forlati on the history and architecture of St. Mark's. They are fine essays, but what delights me most about them is that Toesca has the great Andrea Dandolo rise to dogedom in 1342, whereas Forlati enthrones him in 1343. It is as though the chief patron of St. Mark's did not belong to history but to legend, just as the fascination of these mosaics cannot be explained as stylization or modernity, but only as the accurate representation of something that never was on land or sea. When you have this book in your hands, you will see with the sight of the past: you will look at beauty with the eyes of childhood—a childhood remoter than your own.

■

Classical and Semiclassical

■

The word for it is elegance. What we see before us in the Metropolitan's current* exhibition of seventeenth-century French art comes from fifty-six French churches and museums as well as from a few American sources. But wherever they may come from and whatever their orientation, these works are, above all, striving to be elegant. Let us remember the true meaning of that word: it derives not just from *legere,* to choose, but from its intensification, *legare,* and the further heightening, *elegare,* "to choose out." Not dandyism, but intense selectivity; not bedecking and bedizening, but triumphant omission.

That is what the successful works in this show accomplish. But the failures of elegance, the travesties of it, are catastrophic: the bourgeois qua bourgeois cannot possibly make as execrable an ass of himself as the bourgeois who would be *gentilhomme.* The weaver Bottom becomes almost endearing through his ass's head, but the merest ass's ears on King Midas are a monstrosity. I am afraid this show, called "The Splendid Century," has more than its share of catastrophes; still, what is good in it *is* splendid, but it is the case of a true artist here, a fine achievement

* April, 1961.

there, rather than of 115 years of unbroken magnificence before which we are asked to bow down. True, a good map must show foothills as well as peaks, but there are sections of this exhibition where a sprinkling of incomparable riches is followed by (to coin a phrase) an *embarras de pauvretés.*

What the exhibition clearly shows is the curve described by French painting in the *grand siècle*: the rise from mannerism with such crutches as Caravaggio and a few Dutchmen and Flemings whose influence dominates the earlier part of the century (Vouet and his circle), thence to a gradual achievement of originality and mastery in men like the Le Nains, La Tour, Poussin and Claude, and from there to a baroque art which, in some of the latest works shown here (La Fosse, Coypel), begins to sink into rococo.

A conspectus of these changes could be gained by following the permutations of any one subject; let me take as example the transformations in the four Dianas and two Venuses of this show. The earliest of these is Toussaint Dubreuil's drawing, *Diana and Her Nymphs.* This predates the "great century" and is essentially ornamental: the ladies are in a charming huddle, their limbs daintily elongated, the folds of their gowns dancing their own round dance around bodies on which they seem scarcely dependent. What there is of trees and greensward is similarly curved and swirling and characterless—all for love of decoration, or the world well lost. Next we come to a *Diana at the Hunt* by an unknown painter. Though placed somewhere between 1640 and 1650, this inferior work is well behind its time, and is painted in the style Vouet and Le Sueur developed two or three decades earlier. It is a large canvas, full of absurdities in the perspective and situation. Still, the effect of Diana and her nymphs is, despite some bared bosom and exposed thigh, unsensual and earnest, and the aim is chiefly, though crudely, the representation of an action. Granted, the love of the decorative persists in, say, the triangle of Diana's bent arm and head framed by the perfect circle of her billowing garment and responded to by another triangle in the arms of two nymphs extended toward the goddess. Color, too, is used showily: the royal blue of Diana's gown is a little too lush, a little too schematically balanced by the deep greens of the foliage. Yet, however clumsy it all is—as if not just the painter's models, but life itself stood still—the emphasis is on action rather than ornamentation.

Poussin's *The Death of Adonis,* for which the suggested date is 1630, is a different matter altogether. Not a masterpiece exactly, it is yet a piece by a master. The mourning for Adonis is expressed in the prevalence of horizontals in sky and earth echoing the dead youth's prostration (as does the very shape of the canvas), and by the fact that trees that might be vertical are slanting as if bent with grief. Venus herself is bending lovingly over her dead lover, pouring nectar upon him from a nearly horizontal urn. Hers is a guileless, Giorgionesque loveliness, and her nudity is not provocative. Most important here is the exquisite blend of the dramatic and the peaceful, the restraint in the coloring (except, perhaps, for the excessive greenness of the corpse), and the sadness controlled by a faint, gentle hope emanating from the beauty of the naked goddess and the charming cupids trying to revive the dead boy. Though the picture is profoundly gracious, it is not ornamental: decoration has yielded to decorum.

In *Venus at the Forge of Vulcan* by Louis and Mathieu Le Nain (1641), there is, again, a successful blend of thought and painterliness. The bare-breasted Venus, though aware of her sexuality (the left hand plays with her bosom, and the right lifts her gown rather more than needed to keep it off the floor), is still, more than anything else, an innocent spectator in her husband's workshop, the heat of which has, after all, forced the men, too, into partial disrobing. Old Vulcan contemplates his wife's charms with a mixture of longing and resignation, while his assistants, according to man's basic duality, have their eyes either on their work or on the boss's wife. There are ideas here: Vulcan recedes into chiaroscuro, whereas Venus seems to light up from within and only the minimum of shade attaches to her. We are aware of no more than two strongly colored areas: the rutilance of the flame, and the same but greater redness of Venus's gown. The workman who stares yearningly at the goddess is seen only as a head emerging between two figures of men absorbed in their labors; this would suggest that desire is only an interlude in man's toil, but then there is, to swing the balance around, Vulcan: *affaissé*, overcome by a glow beyond that of fire. It is genre painting, if you like—the Venus, though lovely, is an earthy, almost peasant, type (what ankles!)—but there is imagination in the picture to give it stature.

A very different affair is the *Diana* of Antoine Coypel, which is definitely *fin-de-grand-siècle*. Here both the pose and expression of Diana are abandoned, if not smug; her attendants are gamboling, bathing, making music, bringing flowers, or just reaching for her as if, women though they be, they were unable to keep their hands off their alluring mistress. If this Diana is a huntress at all, her quarry is surely two-footed. But however erotic the intention, there is still a certain rigorousness in the centripetality of the composition, a careful balance of elements in the way, for example, in which the vertical of Diana's left leg is continued by the perpendicularly held lute, or in the correspondence between the little bit of water in the lower right corner and the one small patch of sky in the upper left. By the time we come to the *Diana Resting* of Louis de Boullogne the Younger (1707), we have an uncohesive grouping of figures in a highly conventionalized landscape, and though there is more nudity than in any of the previous pictures, there is not even the deliberate, virile eroticism of Coypel, but a languid, bloodless sensuality that circulates, like a vague ennui, among the several figures. And though the nymph drying her feet was imitated by Watteau, *this* nymph has none of Watteau's vivacious delicacy. What Roger Fry called "the process of disinfection" is now completed: we have gone from ornamentalism through realism to a classical equipoise, then to the exaggeration of a superficial element, and, finally, to a watering down of the very exaggeration.

But what, then, are the high points of the exhibition? There are the five Georges de La Tours, to which the Metropolitan has added its own *Fortune Teller*, to show the daylight side of this painter better known for his nocturnal scenes. The earliest of these pictures, *A Woman with a Flea*, is most clearly influenced by the Dutch, and least impressive, although the grim determination of the fingers to kill the flea is nicely mirrored in the empathetically pursed lips. *St. Irene with the Wounded St. Sebastian* is a noble variant on the magnificent Berlin picture, though I must confess that I find myself most interested in the flame of the torch, painted in an unearthly silvery green—as though it were shedding moonlight —and tying itself into a knot at the top, as if to remind the onlookers of a martyrdom they must not forget. In *The Young Jesus and St. Joseph in the Carpenter's Shop*, La Tour ingeniously makes Joseph's figure swoop around three sides of the rectangular composition, while the boy Jesus gets only one. Yes, but he holds the light, and the translucency achieved in the fingers that shield the candle is about as exciting a moment in the history of painting as I know of. This is a true analogy of the *unio mystica*, the wedding of the flesh with the divine flame. In *St. Joseph and the Angel*, the chiaroscuro of the angel is rather melodramatic, but here, as everywhere in La Tour, the combination of daintiness of contour with sculptured solidity of bodies produces remarkable effects. And how nicely graduated are the flesh tones of Joseph's face as they progressively emerge from the darkness, like some humble kind of fruit ripening in mere candlelight. More affecting yet is *The Ecstasy of St. Francis,* in which the most striking results are obtained from as simple a device as making the upper half of the saint's body diagonal in a generally vertical context, and from taking liberties with the logic of light and shadow. Here the economy of the classical painter is most in evidence: nothing is present that is not absolutely essential.

What is the secret of this great artist? It is a sculptural quality, but achieved how differently from, say, Mantegna. La Tour reminds us, first of all, not of sculpture in marble or bronze, but in wax or polychromed wood. It is as if a Riemenschneider figure had been recreated in a brilliant color photograph: the lines are clearly defined, the brush work is nowhere in evidence, there are no details, it would seem, only large, sleek color surfaces seamlessly woven together. One has to think of all kinds of modern artists—Chirico, Balthus, Dali, Barlach, Gerhard Marcks—to define in contemporary terms the polish and glossiness, the convexity and geometrical boldness of these figures. And almost always there is the intense chiaroscuro to make the three-dimensionality even more obsessive. La Tour's people and things emerge a little thingier, a little more palpable, a little simpler than life. His are perhaps the only paintings around which the eye can take a walk, as our bodies can around a statue, and see the subject from all sides at once.

I doubt that we see Poussin to his best advantage in this show, but there are at least one or two examples of his purest style. The *Landscape with Diogenes,* for instance, demonstrates his uncanny ability to get us into a picture. The walk begins at a fallen tree in the left foreground (*memento mori*), then proceeds to the right along the flowing river (*panta rhei*) and reveals Diogenes discarding his cup in order to drink, like the natural man beside him, from his hands; then we meander along a path deeper into the picture, and encounter at each turning a new group of people engaged in a different pursuit. Farther back and back the picture stretches, as if successive curtains went up on inner, and innermost, stages. Nothing could better express the smallness of man compared to nature; even art at its most splendid, in this case the Vatican seen above the river, is only a modest adjunct to the natural beauties. It is of such paintings that Paul Valéry remarked, "Poussin devised noble settings for tragedy." Tragedy, however, is not quite relevant to this world; a stoic endurance rather, neither tragic nor comic, merely patient and dignified.

Happily there are only two Poussins here which are, in the words of Louis MacNeice's sonnet, full of golden tea—"and we dally and dip our spoon in the golden tea." But three lines of the sonnet are applicable to the best of Poussin:

> And the motion is still as when one walks and the
>   moon
> Walks parallel but relations remain the same
> And thus we never reach the dregs of the cup . . .

This effect of permanence within change is achieved in various ways. So in *Rebecca and Eliezer* it is the stylized, conventionalized faces that create the aura of immutability: the twelve other girls spread across the 77 ½ inches of the canvas are all minor variants of the central figure of Rebecca. How reassuring that is: *plus ça change*. . . . Everything is made from the same noble mold: mistress and servant, white girl and Moor—this is the country where Platonic ideas walk about and are called people. And how liberally the static faces are compensated for by a glorious symphony of arm and hand movements; in this orchestra, every player is a conductor. Gesticulatory brilliance distinguishes also another, poorer Poussin in the show, *The Entry of Christ into Jerusalem*, a picture I can describe only as a fugue for gestures so intricate as to inspire careful study of the score.

The exhibition catalogue is lavish in its praise of the latest Poussin shown, *Spring, or The Earthly Paradise;* it waxes similarly enthusiastic about a late Claude Lorrain, *Parnassus*. Now, both of these pictures strike me as essentially foolish; but it is also rather a mystery why two such accomplished masters of classical purity and precision should have turned in the end to primitivism: to leaves, animals, people done in the manner of, say, a less genuinely naïve Douanier Rousseau or Camille Bombois. We shall return to this problem later. There certainly are some fine pictures by Claude in the show, with enough orange, canary, and lemon-yellow light floating around in their skies to start an impressionist movement right here and now, had there not been one already. The loveliest of these pictures is *A Seaport*. Ruskin once grudgingly admitted of the man he called "filmy, futile Claude" that "he set the sun in the heaven." Well, in this one, Claude set it in the waters too, for in this extraordinarily lit scene the pale yellow light of an already set sun seems to come as much out of the sea as out of the sky.

And among its many excellent drawings, the exhibition has several stunning ones by Claude, the most notable being

Bare Branches. I suppose it is idle to say of a chalk-and-wash sketch that may have been a mere study for something bigger and more developed, that it is remarkably modern-looking, but that is exactly what one is compelled to say of it, as also of such other masterly rapid sketches as two or three by Poussin, the tantalizingly inscrutable *Landscape* of Jacques Callot, and several others. My own favorite is *A Battle* by Jacques Courtois, done in brown ink and gray wash, where these two plain colors and a minimum of pen strokes combine to render with harrowing accuracy not only the turmoil and horror of battle, but even an eerie, hallucinatory light in the sky which one's psyche fastens on to readily as the archetypal illumination for dying. Of the more finished, meticulous graphics, many of them noteworthy, I particularly admire again a few by Poussin and Claude, as well as Simon Vouet's *Nude Woman with a Lute* which foreshadows Ingres, and the superb *Man and Woman* by Antoine Coypel. Not only are the composition and draftmanship exquisite, but light is used with such expertise that it suggests a radiant welding together of the embracing bodies.

There are also a few distinguished portraits—Le Brun's of Turenne, for instance, with something like a sunburst on the great man's forehead; a charming self-portrait by Vouet, and a superlative one by Largillière. The execution of the foreshortened left hand in the latter is in itself a triumph. Mignard's *Mlle de Blois,* though rather lushly baroque, has a wistful charm that will not be gainsaid. In still lifes, too, there are one or two arresting things, but the final, and possibly most valuable, achievement of the show is that it introduces us to the extraordinary talents of Sébastien Bourdon. The portrait by him is no more than solid academic work, but *The Holy Family* (which the catalogue does not reproduce) and the *Landscape* in oil are revelations. In the former, though some of the figures are indifferently drawn, there are astonishingly daring color harmonies: the sky is a bold latticework of blue and orange, and the figures are draped in cunningly distributed pinks, oranges, and reds. And there is an area at the extreme right where walls are reflected in water: this part of the picture is almost all greyish transparencies in rectangular, often superimposed, shapes. The effect is not a little cubist. Even lovelier is the *Landscape,* surpassing by far those attractive ones by La Hyre and Gaspard Poussin (Dughet) hung close by. In it the colors are strikingly limited and modern: a brownish orange and a slate blue, against which large masses of vegetation assert themselves in greens that are close to black. Nebulous figures and water emerging from almost nowhere animate the scene with a not quite canny life. Another Bourdon landscape, this one a drawing, again shows, besides exceptional stylishness, a unique effect of compacted profusion.

But there is little to praise among the later paintings; indeed, there is a large room in which one can view only two works with pleasure, and another that can boast only one. And we come upon such monstrosities as Philippe de Champaigne's *Flight into Egypt* from the Cathedral de Senlis; aside from everything else, this is painted in the most garish blues, violets, and gold ever herded together. If there be any connoisseurship in Senlis, the church there must have a seriously dwindling flock. The sculpture, too, is generally unimpressive, though I daresay it is quite representative, and the tapestries and *objets d'art* leave me cold.

There is something cold, too, when all is said and done, about this whole splendid century. No doubt, the rise of the *bourgeoisie* and the political and economic supremacy of France contributed much to the flowering of French art in the *grand siècle*. But is an age of central despotism, however enlightened, of intellectual swagger, if not downright intolerance, going to produce a truly first-rate art? There is a regimentation, an academicism, a sycophancy about much of this work—these Le Sueurs and Le Bruns and La Hyres and Rigauds—that is not consistent with greatness. It is of this age, after all, that Molière's Alceste complains (in Richard Wilbur's translation):

> This age is vile, and I've made up my mind
> To have no further commerce with mankind . . .
> My reason bids me go, for my own good.
> My tongue won't lie and flatter as it should . . .

Is it not significant that despite the brilliance of the court at Versailles and the wealth of the Parisian *bourgeoisie,* both Poussin and Claude should have exiled themselves to Rome (Poussin's one subsequent venture into Paris for some work ended in a hasty retreat); that La Tour should have preferred to remain, despite his title of "Painter to the King," ensconced in the small Lunéville in Lorraine; and that even the good Courtois should have traipsed off to Italy at the tender age of fifteen, to live his life out in Rome after changing his name to Borgognone—more like the Romans you could not do.

So much for all that splendor. But what about the great intellectual achievement? In the catalogue to the exhibition, Theodore Rousseau, Jr., says approvingly of these painters, "Their approach was more intellectual than ours." Well, up to a point intellect does no harm to a painter. But I wonder whether Le Brun's heavily Cartesian *Méthode pour Apprendre à Dessiner les Passions* was such a blessing, enshrined as it became by the Procrustean Academy. Or whether Antoine Coypel's painting became any better because he insisted in his *Discourse to the Royal Academy* that a painter must be thoroughly acquainted with, among other things, rhetoric, versification, history, scripture, mythology, geography, geometry, architecture, physics, psychology and philosophy. (When does he paint?) And I have my doubts even about what it did for Poussin's work—besides, perhaps, worsening it—that he wished painting to model itself upon the ancient Greek musical modes? "Before a year is out," he wrote a friend, "I hope to paint a subject in this Phrygian mode." I wonder indeed whether this kind of intellection is proper to the painter, and whether it is not almost as deleterious as its opposite, total blissful ignorance of everything? Both these modes (neither of them, I think, Phrygian) have their adherents today; with what results, this is not the place to assay. Yet it seems conceivable that it is precisely this "diverse knowledge" that drove Poussin and Claude to paint pictures like *The Earthly Paradise* and *Parnassus*—reactions to their own know-how, pitiful pictorial prattle.

part five : poetry

Sleight of Foot: The New American Poetry

This is a book for everyone but two.* Parents, teachers, clergymen, psychologists, psychiatrists, sociologists, anthropologists, penologists, politicians—perhaps even tinkers and tailors—will want to read it. Only poets and poetry lovers will not.

Three years ago Donald Hall, Robert Pack, and Louis Simpson edited The New Poets of England and America. It was a passable, if by no means perfect, compilation. Now Donald M. Allen has come out with The New American Poetry 1945-1960, and he has included, by two simple criteria, poets he liked, and poets Messrs. Hall, Pack, and Simpson disliked. Not a single person made both books. Mr. Allen's anthology contains among its 44 poets quite a few who are still in their early twenties, and none who, judged by the writing, might not just as well be. Of course, when I say poets, the word is his and his blurb writer's—unless they are the same person, for who besides Mr. Allen would write that "Ginsberg's Howl . . . has already assumed the status of The Waste Land for our age"? Yet however meager fare this anthology may provide from the literary standpoint, its 450 pages of verse and prose are of paramount sociological importance. If, as Aristotle suggested, the poet is a better historian than the historian, these pseudo-poets are surely better sociologists than the sociologists. There emerges from their col-

* The New American Poetry, 1945-1960. Donald M. Allen, ed. New York, 1960.

lective work a more representative truth about our culture than is afforded us by the social historians.

When, about a year ago, a young Negro hipster who called himself "Mau-Mau" was arrested in Greenwich Village for living with, and off, an unfortunate minor girl—while more heartily carrying on with two other, prettier girls—there was discovered in the handsome apartment the minor's parents (on psychiatric advice) provided for this unsuspected experiment in communal living, a considerable arms and narcotics cache. When Mau-Mau and the three girls were questioned by the police, both he and one of the older girls gave their profession as "writing."

When, about half a year ago, police infiltrated and broke up a Harlem and Greenwich-Village narcotics ring, the supreme device by which one of the detectives convinced the gang that he was one of them was a poem he wrote. A poem against the police, and, as we saw when it was printed, a most persuasively ghastly one. For some reason or other it is not included in Mr. Allen's anthology.

When, first as a teacher and now as an editor, I was approached by young, or not so young, people who seemed to me distinguished by nothing more than their derangement, nine times out of ten they turned out to be peddling their writing, which, in the majority of cases, was putative poetry.

I shall not try to determine here why madness in America today should have for perhaps its main symptom the desire to write—though writing is clearly the most accessible form of self-expression. To be even the worst composer, sculptor, architect, or physicist some sort of training and tools are necessary; but to be a writer, all one needs is a pencil stub, the back of an envelope, and a vague acquaintance with the alphabet. (True, the professions of abstract expressionist painter and actor are almost as accessible, and we find nearly as many lunatics and charlatans there.) And of all forms of writing, poetry is the shortest and thus requires, presumably, the least endurance. Hence the prevalence of poets.

Mr. Allen's anthology divides all gall into five parts. The Black Mountain College (and Review) poets, whose mentor and model is Charles Olson; the West Coast crowd whose paraclete and publisher is Laurence Ferlinghetti and whose Mecca is San Francisco; the "Beats," such as Ginsberg, Kerouac, and Corso, who have turned the mirror in the roadway into a furor on the road; the New York group, like Ashbery, Koch, and O'Hara, who are bounded to the West by the Museum of Modern Art, to the

East by the Tibor de Nagy Gallery, to the North by Harvard, and to the South by the Cedar Bar; and, lastly, the miscellaneous ones. But, as Mr. Allen himself indicates, these categories are fluid and overlap, and there is a good deal of mingling—in every sense of the word—among their members.

The most extraordinary, and also the most damning, thing about these poets is their interchangeability. Their genealogy can be traced from Whitman through Sandburg, Fearing, and Patchen (three names almost never mentioned by our poets, lest the show be given away), with strong collateral influences from Pound, Cummings, and, above all, W. C. Williams. There may also be some kinship with Rimbaud, Robinson Jeffers, and Hart Crane. But for all this substantially acceptable ancestry, what comes out is a singularly amorphous paste, lacking in importance and, often, even meaning, and perfectly interchangeable. Take the beginning of *He* by Ferlinghetti:

> He is one of the prophets come back
> He is one of the wiggy prophets come back
> He had a beard in the Old Testament
> but shaved it off in Paterson
>
> He has a microphone around his neck . . .

and the beginning of *He* by Ashbery (not, to be sure, included in this anthology, though other, similar poems of his are):

> He cuts down the lakes so they appear straight
> He smiles at his feet in their tired mules.
> He turns up the music much louder.
> He takes down the vaseline from the pantry shelf.
> He is the capricious smile behind the colored
> bottles. . . .

A little later on, Ashbery's *He* "wears a question in his left eye," while Ferlinghetti's "has buttonhooks in his eyes."

Again, Olson writes:

> And the Indian woman and I
> enabled the blue deer
> to walk
>
> and when it got to the kitchen,
> out of our sight
> it talked
> Negro talk. . . .

> We helped walk it around the room
> because it was seeking socks
> or shoes for its hooves. . . .

In a similar vein, Robert Creeley offers us *The Three Ladies*:

> I dreamt. I saw three ladies in a tree,
> and the one that I saw most clearly
> showed her favors unto me,
> and I saw up her leg above the knee.
>
> But when the time for love was come,
> and of readiness I had made myself,
> upon my head and shoulders
> dropped the other two like an unquiet dew. . . .
>
> Oh song of wistful night! Light shows
> where it stops nobody knows, and two
> are one, and three, to me, and to look
> is not to read the book.
>
> *Oh one, two, three! Oh one, two, three!*
> *Three old ladies sat in a tree.*

And now comes Robert Duncan:

> What do you see, my little one?
> I see an owl hung in a tree
> like flesh hung on a bone.
> The thorns of the flesh run thru and thru.
> Ring out the tones of life.
> He builds the artifice of heart
> and takes his word to wife.

I am a little hesitant about continuing these collocations, for well-meaning readers are sure to suspect me of picking especial horrors from the volume. Yet I must insist that these passages are representative, and that similar ones could be gleaned from almost any part of the book. Here is a final triad. Ebbe Borregaard begins a poem:

> tonight and forever I shall be yours so says the
>   oleo king
> via dolorosa vexation of beauty soft with oil
> by the side rings of wapiti drink blood from
>   cuckoopoint stamens

tonight the wapiti wastrel move thru the lower plains
bending water fennel in vatrix streams
toward the skulls place

And Jack Kerouac begins his *230th Chorus:*

Love's multitudinous boneyard
of decay
The spilled milk of heroes,
Destruction of silk kerchiefs
by dust storm,
Caress of heroes blindfolded to posts,
Murder victims admitted to this life,
Skeletons bartering fingers and joints,
The quivering meat of the elephants of kindness
being torn apart by vultures,
Conceptions of delicate kneecaps, . . .

And one of Gary Snyder's *Myths and Texts* starts out:

A skin-bound bundle of clutchings
unborn and with no place to go
Balanced on the boundless compassion
Of diatoms, lava, and chipmunks.

Love, let it be,
Is a sacrifice
knees, the cornered eyes
Tea on a primus stove after a cold swim
Intricate doors and clocks, . . .

What connects these poets most strongly is the
vociferous variations on the theme of love. No less than fourteen
poems of the anthology, for instance, even though they have
little to do with loving, have the word "love" appear, climactically,
in their last lines. This may be either a clamorous demand for
love, or the display of one's unparalleled grip on it, or the mere
trumpeting of its magic name. These last lines run the gamut
from such elaborateness as O'Hara's "and dying in black and
white we fight for what we love, not are," or Ginsberg's "who
loves himself loves me who love myself," or Lamantia's "There
is this look of love Throne Silent look of love," through such
purer and simpler forms as Creeley's "and love her as hard as
you can," or Ray Bremser's more pregnant "and love!" or Philip
Whalen's ecstatically capitalized and italicized "LOVE *YOU*"—

all the way down to Michael McClure's basic and irreducible "love." But you cannot capture love by sprinkling salt on its tail, or even by liberally sprinkling the tails of your poems with its name. Indeed, all this dragging in of love as a *deus ex vagina* is only a sorry testimonial to the essential lovelessness of these poets: the great climax proves merely a grand climacteric.

Another common feature of Mr. Allen's poets is the wide discrepancy between their preaching and their practice. After their poetry, Mr. Allen devotes 40 pages to their "Statements on Poetics." These make fascinating reading, ranging as they do from such pseudo-learned absurdities as Olson's contention that the poem can get "immense help" from the knowledge of Hopi, "Trobriand space-Time premises," and, most important, the study of Hittite, to such simple-minded illiteracies as McClure's discovery: "There is free will I am not obviated to carry on or not carry . . . on." (In both its verse and prose, besides such malapropisms as this "obviated," the book abounds in misspellings, bad grammar, incorrect foreign quotations—in short, in every outrage that can be heaped on language.) But what I found most interesting is the discrepancy between, say, Olson's plea that a poem be "as clean as wood is," or Duncan's supposition "that a poetry will remain, cherished only by unimportant people who love or adventure" and the poetry these two write, examples of which I have quoted.

Lastly, these poets are linked by a curious blend of what Norman Podhoretz has called their "know-nothingism" and, paradoxically, a proto-academic parochialism, the dragging in of fancy references and quotations which is the intellectually *nouveau riche*'s flaunting of his letters patent. Here the last part of the book, the "Biographical Notes," is a handy aid. These 18 pages are studded with confinements—in reform schools, prisons, mental hospitals; with escapes—from families, high schools, colleges; and spectacular tergiversations such as Gary Snyder's, who got a degree from Reed College in Mythology (!), studied linguistics at Indiana, then "bummed around working at logging and forestry," then studied classical Chinese at Berkeley and went to Japan "to study the formal Zen training"; and then worked on a tanker in the Mediterranean and Pacific, hung around San Francisco, and returned to Japan. Both the ignorance and the isolated, unrelated patches of knowledge can be fathomed in terms of such lives and such schooling. In his forthcoming book *Growing Up Absurd*, Paul Goodman, himself hardly an academic square, writes: "I once taught at Black Mountain College, and to my astonishment I found that the students had never read the Bible, Milton, Dryden, Gibbon, etc., etc., nor did they feel—as a lack—that such things existed. But they knew odd facts about Mayan hieroglyphics which their teacher had been interested in." Who this teacher was, readers of my preceding paragraph will guess as easily as the consequences of such education.

Nevertheless, there are two things at which these poets can be good: rhetoric and humor. In Ginsberg's poems (as in his friend Kerouac's prose), occasionally in those of Corso, LeRoi Jones, and some others, one notices that special brand of rhetoric which consists of enumerating breathlessly, in a mad scramble, sights, sounds, thoughts, feelings, experiences. It is a kinetic, a cinematographic poetry, which depends on bodily movement. Because these poets are restlessly on the move between continents, cities, streets, dives, they have evolved a kind of linguistic photomontage, a roving retina not of cameras, which they do not own, but of eyes, which they have. And as the coffee, liquor, heroin flow in, they push out torrential flows of verbiage. *Sunflower Sutra* and the better parts of *Howl*, by Ginsberg, are good examples. As for the humor—more often than not of a gallows, bordello, or pederastic variety—it is the birthright of this absurd age, whether one thinks of it in terms of Camus and certain existentialist philosophers, or simply as the lifting of restraint, moral and artistic, from the poet. Here, again, Ginsberg, Ferlinghetti (as in the piece where the poet is compared to a high-wire artist performing "sleight-of-foot tricks"), occasionally Corso and one or another of the "New York group" are cases in point; but because the anthologist, doubtless out of pretentiousness, tends to minimize the comic side of his poets, injustice is done them by the selection.

So we see that out of their very lacks—the lack of *Sitzfleisch*, staying put, patience; and the lack of tragic, or merely serious, restraint—the main virtues of these poets take shape. There are hardly any finished, homogeneous poems, just as there are hardly any consequential ones, but there are some that are ebulliently mobile, and some that are genuinely funny. Oddly enough, there are even a few true, well-made poems in the book. Such pieces as Ginsberg's *A Supermarket in California*, Edward Field's *The Floor Is Dirty*, Corso's *Marriage*, Ashbery's *The Instruction Manual*, one or two poems by Ferlinghetti and Joel Oppenheimer are authentic and self-contained works of art. But as for the majority of Mr. Allen's poets, they are kids who took up poetry the way one takes up marijuana, Buddhism, switch-blade knives, wife-swapping, or riding in boxcars: neither more nor less seriously than other "kicks." As poets, they are neither born nor made, except possibly by one another. Happily, however, they are no threat to poetry. If one sat a thousand of them before a thousand typewriters, they would not bang out, even in a chiliad, a single line of *Hamlet*.

◼

Post Cards from Around the Corner

◼

Who among us has not wished that young poets would stop writing about half-remembered frescoes at Ferrara, the beauties of non-Euclidean geometry, or the friction of a tragic epidermis flitting by on its way from Greenwich Village to an insane asylum? Does it not behoove the poet to begin with what he knows best—his life? For this reason, the first glance at Philip Booth's *Letter from a Distant Land* (the current Lamont Poetry Selection)* is a hopeful one; here, despite the title, are post cards from around the corner: poems about fishing, sailing, mountain-climbing, gardening—about being a little boy, serving in the Air Forces, sleeping with one's wife, tossing sick in bed. Poems, in short, about the poet's life. But before we are one third of the way through this short volume, we admit we were wrong: we would give anything for a piece on the view of Florence from Fiesole (even on a foggy day) or a sonnet in praise of symbolic logic.

* Letter from a Distant Land, New York, 1957.

I do not know whether it is the probing scalpel or the life probed, but something about Mr. Booth is dull. On second thought, I would exculpate the life; to grow three young daughters in an orchard in Lincoln, Mass., to have been a varsity skier at Dartmouth and a Pfc. in World War II, to have taught at Bowdoin, Dartmouth, and Wellesley, and spent one's summers on Penobscot Bay (I am paraphrasing the jacket) is on the face of it not a whit less poetic than selling insurance in Hartford, Conn., or being an old maid in Amherst. It must be Mr. Booth's instrument, or his focus, that lacks sharpness. For one thing, he is seldom content with writing a poem once. Among the forty-two pieces of this collection there are few that do not overlap wholly or in part: *Sunday Climb, Fisherman, Heron* are almost the same poem in concept and conceits; so, too, are *This Land* and *Green Song.* The same motifs with little variation in image and vocabulary make up *The Seiners, Barred Islands, Sea Change. Raker* and *Twelfth Night* build up to the same conclusion; in the first, the raker's burning of fallen leaves is a "curbside blaze/ both funeral pyre and fire/ of his unspoken praise"; in the other, we get the burning of the Christmas tree and decorations after the holidays: "In the quick match,/ the winter watch,/ the burner is both burned and blessed." In *The Wilding,* the poet concludes by telling his beloved "This wood/ is for you"; in *Adam,* the climax is "I give you this calm morning etc." And so on and on; if Mr. Booth often ingenuously juxtaposes such poems (e.g., *Fisherman* and *Instruction in the Art*), his ingenuousness does not extend his range—it merely emphasizes the fact that he is seeing double; it is as though the Pierian spring had been mischievously spiked just before Mr. Booth drank from it. The poet is, however, aware, consciously or otherwise, that his scope must be widened, and the method he has devised for this purpose is the *mythos ex machina.* In a poem dealing with everyday matters there appears, usually towards the end, a figure like Odysseus, Adam, Icarus, Saint Peter, Theseus, or Jesus Christ, lifting the poem out of the chthonian into the sublime. This is a time-honored and perfectly respectable device if the mythic parallels can convince us of their rightness and necessity, but it seems somewhat overzealous to bring in the Crucifixion in an anodyne little piece on congressional investigations, a bit lavish to turn the insomniac into St. Peter dreading the cock's crow, or the inexperienced diver's bellyflop into the fall of Icarus. A particularly nimble tour de force introduces both Odysseus and the building of the Pyramids into a short poem about oxen, and Adam makes no fewer than four entrances in the volume, thereby winning hands down from Odysseus and Christ, tied for second place with two showings apiece. It would seem that when Mr. Booth sets out to be Icarus, he belly-flops; but when he is content, Theseus-like, to follow a string of impressions, he can do pleasant things indeed, as in *Siasconset Song, The Seiners, The Lost Boy, First Lesson,* and *Vermont: Indian Summer.*

The imagery varies in quality. Consider this stanza from *The Wilding:*

> But under woodpecker knock
> in this rabbitrun wood, in May,
> a sweet fern questionmark
> whorls green as green is today,
> and ferns ask no answer a swallow
> can't fly.

The first three and a half verses are aptly evocative, but then things become gratuitous and ultimately meaningless: "as green is today," inversion aside, is easy and uncompelling, and the attempt to force the fern and swallow into a significant relationship sheds no light on either. Images of such dubious facility are not uncommon in this poetry. Thus 'roundness' will be invoked at a moment's notice to convey joy: a sea perspective will be "calm and finally round" which is fair enough, but presently, in another poem, "the night/ is round, and we row on/ the surface of our dreams" (where "the surface of our dreams" is, by the way, as shallow as it is smooth), and in still another poem "the year is round around me now," with not even the pleonasm affording much help. But when searching for a lost boy "his awkward parents thrash/ their love against the thickets," or when the eyes of a nighthawk emerge as "unlikely jewels folded/ in an old paisley shawl," Booth's eye is in excellent understanding with his writing hand.

And what of Booth's ear? He has two fortes: enjambment and near-rhyme; he uses both effectively, albeit sometimes excessively. But whereas I appreciate his relish for homely Anglo-Saxon words (Anglo-Saxon poetry, perhaps as filtered through Hopkins and Thomas, is a strong influence here), the long sequences of monosyllables become wearying in, for example, "his flip wings prove/ the name, and his sea-/ cry dive like love/ flung down the sky"; and the disyllable of "returns" proves a veritable oasis in "and in a blind wind small forms/ are lost. At night the close cold is still,/ the tilt world returns from sun to ice." But this is nothing to such rhythmic failings as

> Eve held the twisted stem, the pulp;
> she heard the low snake hiss, and let fly
> blindly with a woman arm, careless
> where her new-won anger struck.

Or what are we to make of a piece like *Admission of Guilt* where in a welter of singsong iambics two equally singsong trochaic lines (1 and 12) wreak unaccountable and unendurable havoc, and the last line is a rhythmic and metrical chaos? Mr. Booth's ear is given to even more vagaries, perhaps, than his eye; there are many felicitous assonances and inner rhymes, but we also get jingles like "both funeral pyre and fire" or "It would have broken ten men in two, but you" or "the unmown squares of sun that man/ might seem unable, here, to clear." Still, there are times when the cadences are cogent, as in

> Wave by wave, the gray stone shore
> diminishes to sand, the known coast
> ebbs: and we stand watching, crest
> on blue and whitecap crest. . . .

There are other awkwardnesses: a sudden hypertrophic fourth line in *Schoodic Point Soliloquy* or the clumsy reaching for the rhyme in "The orchard is loud: bees/ and blossoms claim the bough;/ a meadow of frogs, a sky/ of swallows, flood the air now."

But more serious, to me, is Mr. Booth's repeated striving after grand effects, one aspect of which, the mythological, we have seen already. Another form is the inflated ending: if the poet has climbed a hill on a Sunday afternoon and identified himself with rabbit and hawk, the poem ends with him "twice alone on the last height,/ the sheer edge of human sight"; if the poet is describing *North,* he ends with a similar reduplication: "love is twice as warm in a cold place." If a tern has been depicted more or less incisively, the poem will end with the bird's "dive like love/ flung down the sky." The prestige of the vast concept "love" is, unfortunately, still unable to fill the hollowness of the image. When the poet's daughters tramp patterns into the snow, these markings, it is concluded, "will freeze, freeze/ hard: design/ within design"—it is as if some tremendous verity were being implied by that metaphysical "within" (a cousin of the just-mentioned "twice"), but what is it? *Great Farm* ends when a "big man with buckets/ sets hugely to milk a big cow," and bigness is flowing like milk. Related to this is a kind of concettistic disingenuousness, when a flashy image or insight proves, on closer inspection, factitious. Thus, in *Nightsong*, "my hand/ on your heart's breast" which suggests a causal relationship that does not exist, or "No bird/ on the wind can prove/ flight with a word," as if a bird were trying to prove it, with one word or even twenty-five. This tendency can engulf a whole poem: pieces like *The Long Night, Identification, Storm in a Formal Garden,* seem to me to consist of nothing but posturing, and at such times I would address the poet with William Morris's familiar verse (though in a new reading), "Speak but one word to me over the corn."

Yet the picture is by no means all black. I have already noted some of Mr. Booth's successful pieces; still another virtue is that Booth has already absorbed his poetic influences, and few, if any, show through in an undigested state (an exception is the Cummings of "the perhaps why/ and improbable how/ of shag flight"): both the last of the Welsh bards and the ultimate North-of-Boston prophet are grist for his mill, which, however, grinds them exceeding small. Mr. Booth has a commendable acquaintance with plants, animals, outdoor life in general, and his mellifluous catalogues of fauna and flora form not the least pleasant passages of his poetry. At times his word-pictures manage to be both convincing and personal, as in *Siasconset Song* or *Vermont: Indian Summer*. If such poems do not strike us as forcefully as they might, it is not because they lack stylistic or human authenticity, it is only that their spirit takes us rather too specifically back to the Georgian and Edwardian poets.

I cannot say whether a new Georgianism is in the making in our poetry, but green is distinctly the fashionable color this season; note the titles of recent volumes of verse: *The Greenhouse in the Garden, Green with Beasts, The Green Wall, The Green Town,* and so on. Though not actually in the title, green abounds elsewhere in Mr. Booth's collection; he has banished the unfashionable blues of past seasons and wears his green as well as anyone. On the other hand, I must return to my initial charge of a lack of keenness and scope. Even in the delightful *Siasconset Song* Mr. Booth does not get beyond the enchanting façade: he sees the girls of summer, the *jeunes filles en fleur*, but he does not perceive their *ombre* that Proust saw equally clearly. Mr. Booth can, or wishes to, see only green things: if a shadow is black, his gaze greens it over; even before his green thumb, of which he speaks somewhere, gets going, his eye, as usual quicker than the thumb, has already done the trick. Such a verdant view is not without its genuine boyish charm, and in it lies Booth's chief poetic strength. But his appetite must eventually extend beyond greens; as a steady diet, this is consistent with vegetarianism, not, I think, with truth.

■

"And, Says the Great Rilke . . ."*

■

A year or so ago in the *Times Book Review*, Richard Eberhart, the well-known polygrapher, hailed, among other West-Coast poets, those of the Northwest who, in the shadow of Mt. Rainier and Theodore Roethke and inspired by the three per cent alcoholic beer permitted by the State of Washington, produce that apple country's poetry. Alas, the best apples are wormy, and, with one noteworthy exception, Mr. Eberhart's Puget-Sound Pantheon crawled with vermiculate versifiers. But even more noteworthy was the complete omission of the most gifted of the Seattle poets, James Wright. It was nothing short of poetic justice that soon thereafter Mr. Wright's *The Green Wall* should have been picked as the fifty-third volume of the Yale Series of Younger Poets. And Mr. Wright is one of the very few Yale younger poets whose poethood can survive that epithet.

The first—and astounding—thing to be said about James Wright is that he can write beautiful poetry. It can be simple, comprehensible, traditional in form, and yet not give the

*A review of *The Green Wall*, by James Wright, New Haven, 1957.

impression that it has all been here before. Except in the sense that all has been here before: life, love, death, and even poetry. Take the graceful *To a Hostess Saying Good Night*:

> Shake out the ruffle, turn and go,
> Over the trellis blow the kiss.
> Some of the guests will never know
> Another night to shadow this.
> Some of the birds awake in vines
> Will never see another face
> So frail, so lovely anyplace
> Between the birdbath and the bines.
>
> O dark come never down to you.
> I look away and look away:
> Over the moon the shadows go,
> Over your shoulder, nebulae.
> Some of the vast, the vacant stars
> Will never see your face at all,
> Your frail, your lovely eyelids fall
> Between Andromeda and Mars.

Or take the last part of *Witches Waken the Natural World in Spring*:

> And though she made a leaflet fall
> I have forgotten what she said:
>
> Except that spring was coming on
> Or might have come already while
> We lay beside a smooth-veined stone;
> Except an owl sang half a mile
> Away; except a starling's feather
> Softened my face beside a root:
> But how should I remember whether
> She was the one who spoke, or not?

If one were petulant, one might contend that *anyplace* is a barbarism, or that instead of Andromeda and Mars it might just as well have been Betelgeuse and Altair; but such cavils can be cavalierly dismissed: if a true lyricist briefly lapses into solecism or ornamentalism, he is not therefore immediately to be viewed as a malingerer in a chain gang.

There are poems of greater scope than the two quoted; poems about a man condemned to death and a girl condemned to madness, poems about communicating with a child born deaf, or, more poignant perhaps, a child whose questions show up our own inadequate senses. But whether a little girl is on her way to school or a bigger girl is pulling down a shade before undressing, whether three good friends have died or just one friendless lady, the poet in Mr. Wright can set all these to burning with the same controlled fire. If forms and meters do not venture out onto new terrains, at least these stay-at-homes have lived among properly garnished book-shelves. And James Wright is a young poet who has not only digested his influences, but also discreetly wiped his mouth after the meal. True, there is something of E. A. Robinson and Frost (to both of whom he owns allegiance) about the longer narrative poems like *Three Speeches in a Sick Room* or *Sappho,* but these are fairly dreary pieces anyway; and there will be a touch of Yeats or Thomas or Ransom or Frost in the diction here and there, but this is as natural as perspiration after long drinking. Much more important is the quality of originality within simplicity in a stanza like this one from *Eleutheria:*

> We lay and heard the apples fall for hours,
> The stripping twilight plundered trees of boughs,
> The land dissolved beneath the rabbit's heels,
> And far away I heard a window close,
> A haying wagon heave and catch its wheels,
> Some water slide and stumble and be still.
> The dark began to climb the empty hill.

Or this, of a girl glimpsed in a window at night:

> Let us return now, my friends,
> Her love, her body to the grave
> Fancy of dreams where love depends.
> She gave, and did not know she gave.

Or this, in which the minute imperceptibly overflows into the immense:

> But lonely underneath a heap
> Of overcoat and crusted ice,
> A man goes by and looks for sleep,
> The spring of everlastingness.

There are many minor virtues in Mr. Wright's poetry, like the effective use of lines identically or near-identically repeated in different contexts throughout a poem, like enjambment achieving double meaning if the first line is perceived as end-stopped, like musically pleasing oscillation between rhyme and near-rhyme and even no rhyme. But the major virtues are a few poems which affect us immediately and lastingly, which win us over so completely that, like lovely ladies, they can be loved despite—not to say because of—their flaws. Such poems are *The Fishermen, A Girl in the Window, She Hid in the Trees from the Nurses, A Poem About George Doty in the Death House, Mutterings over the Crib of a Deaf Child, A Little Girl on Her Way to School.* A few others, like *Arrangements with Earth for Three Dead Friends,* or *A Presentation of Two Birds to My Son,* or *The Quail,* and one or two besides, may well be as good.

Minor flaws do occur, as I have said, even in the best poems. Take this admirable stanza (more so, to be sure, in context) from *The Fishermen,* in which the old men squat by the sea:

> And though the sun swayed in the sea,
> They were not moved:
> Saurian faces still as layered lime,
> The nostrils ferned in smoke behind their pipes,
> The eyes resting in whorls like shells on driftwood,
> The hands relaxing, letting out the ropes;
> And they, whispering together,
> The beaten age, the dead, the blood gone dumb.

Everything is fine until the last verse where the old men are revealed as the Beat Degeneration, and a kind of vacuous West-Coast magniloquence sets in. In *Arrangements with Earth for Three Dead Friends,* the excellent last stanza reads in part: "But she was not inclined to beg of you/ Relief from water falling or the storm"—where *storm* adds nothing except a rhyme for *warm.* Such fallings off in the diction are not infrequent; they are matched at times by faulty structure in the poems. Thus in *A Presentation of Two Birds to My Son* it is stated at one point that the swift's flight is ultimately "Stupid and meaningless. Why should it be joy/ To leave the body beaten underfoot. . . ." To parallel this, it is said of a chicken being slaughtered, "It was no joy/ To leave the body beaten underfoot . . ." But in context, we read:

> The ragged chopping block,
> The flop of wings, the jerk of the red comb
> Were a dumb agony,
> Stupid and meaningless. It was no joy
> To leave the body beaten underfoot.

What in the case of the swift's flight is a magnificent if devaluating insight, comes, in the case of the dying chicken, as an anticlimactic truism. Or, again, in that absorbing poem, *The Horse*, we find the first would-be rider "Leaped from a tree and shivered in the air./ Joy clawed inside the bones/ And flesh of the rider at the reins. . . ." Sunny enough until the reins came, and then something—in this case the reasoning rather than the construction—went amiss: next thing we'll be told the first rider got his saddle from Hermès of Paris.

Among other minor complaints would come the one against a certain repetitiousness: *tendrils, bines, fluted* (as verb or adjective), fruit and feather-dropping images are dropped all over the place; a word like *depend* in the obsolescent sense of "hang down" should not be used twice in a slim volume; some of the verbal iterations or semi-iterations do not come off— "Whorling the air of glint and shade/ . . . Whorling the glints of shade and air" is an instance where nothing is really added; and somehow, in these poems, there are altogether too many "daemons," who, for all the reconditeness of their *ae,* are apt to pall just as much as their poor relations, demons. And there is also a humorlessness about Mr. Wright which produces funny poems (like *Song for the Middle of the Night*) that are not funny, and serious ones (like *Crucifixion on Thursday*) that are.

But the *ae* brings me to a more serious problem. Mr. Wright can turn out poems like *The Ungathered Apples* or *Morning Hymn to a Dark Girl* which are rather like those blaring *fortissimo* neckties that, worse luck, light up in the dark. What are we to make of apples that are "the ruddy and the gold/ Bosoms that milked the earth/ . . . The slight lung/ Of leaves went swelling round the globes . . ."? And consider this:

> Betty, burgeoning your golden skin, you poise
> Tracing gazelles and tigers on your breasts,
> Deep in the jungle of your bed you drowse;
> Fine muscles of the rippling panthers move
> And snuggle at your calves; under your arms
> Mangoes and melons yearn; and glittering slowly,
> Quick parakeets trill in your heavy trees,
> O everywhere, Betty, between your boughs.

By the time we read, in the next stanza, the words "Soft Betty," the very name begins to sound like an obscenity. But the lack of taste need not be obscenity; when Wright addresses a fugitive from jail, "Hurry, Maguire, hammer the body down,/ Crouch to the wall again, shackle the cold/ Machine guns to the sheriff and the cars," it is not Frost and Robinson that seem his forefathers but Sandburg and Markham. Indeed, he can write a poem like *Three Husbands* that is a mere overblown version of Sara Teasdale's "Strephon kissed me in the spring" (or was it Colin, I forget?). But while Wright's critical faculty is apt to be Homerically nodding, his creativity is smiting its bloomin' lyre like anything.

And that is where the redeeming quality comes in. Granted that in the realm of taste Mr. Wright is something of a *parvenu*, ultimately it is still the *novus homo* who will save the poetical economy. It is out of such fertile zest that the revitalizing is likely to come, rather than from the most exquisite filing. In an essay on Char, Mr. Wright writes the fetching words "And, says the great Rilke . . ." What modish poet or critic would write anything so ingenuous, so medieval, so humble as those words? Mr. Wright is that elemental: a good, basic, fat, fertile poet: one of that adipose brotherhood that includes men like Chesterton, Neruda, Apollinaire. Let the precious, attenuated ones who have hailed him hysterically in their little-mag reviews beware: it may mean the slaughter of the delicate prodigals when the fatted calf comes home.

■

More Brass Than Enduring

■

In poetry, as in the other arts, it is getting harder and harder to tell the sheep from the goats. The reason for this may be that something brand new is happening, a departure so radical as to leave most of us, public and critics alike, far behind. Or it may be that there is such overproduction in the arts that, glutted by torrents of bad and mediocre work, one is too dazed and exhausted to respond freshly, enthusiastically to the good things that come along, as always, rarely. Or could it be that some of the arts have reached a Point of No Turn, from which there is not only no return, but no turning in any meaningful direction? Let us hope that it is not so, yet is it inconceivable that there should be left no further combinations of words and rhythms, lines and colors, tones and sonorities that are both sufficiently different from what has been done before and beautiful and significant enough to be valid? We have, after all, seen the ends of certain human disciplines: philosophy is no more, having been subsumed—more's the pity—by the exact sciences, psychology, sociology, and even linguistics. Geography is, for all creative purposes, extinct. Astrology has become a joke. It is merely a question of who will kill off theology: the non-believers or the theologians. Many are the crafts that have vanished from the world, and an even greater number of them is on the verge of disappearance. Though our arts have, let us say, survived until now, does that necessarily mean that they will be here forever?

But quite aside from these millenarian speculations, someone might question my initial proposition and wonder whether the good and the bad in, say, poetry are any harder to distinguish today than ever they were. For such doubters I have prepared the following test. State which of the two passages below strikes you as better poetry:

(A)   The tempering, forgotten shrines: four gardens.
        Spires and poplars—the white god—where Lilith dances
        Wild geese. Horizons.

        Wampum and old gold? The golden darkness?
        White April dreams, and a sword hidden.
        Waters. Attitudes.

(B)   And I am as greedy of her, that the black
        Horse of the literal world might come
        Directly on me. Perspective. A place

        To stand. To receive. A place to go
        Into from. The earth by language.

        Who can imagine antelope silent
        Under the night rain, the Gulf
        At Biloxi at night else?

Now that you have made your choice, let me tell you that (A) is a list, in chronological order, of the first fourteen titles in the Yale Series of Younger Poets, with only the punctuation slightly changed. (B) is the middle part of the second poem in *Views of Jeopardy* by Jack Gilbert, the fifty-eighth and current Yale Laureate, the punctuation—and everything else—exactly as Mr. Gilbert wrote it, alas.

Let us assume that you are a person of discernment and were able to tell in fairly short order which is the poem and which the imposture (I myself am not quite sure yet); the mere fact that such a question of poetic quality, indeed quiddity, could be raised is significant: can you imagine being asked to choose between Yeats's latest lyric and his shopping list? Granted that a list of book titles is not quite the same as a shopping list, neither is Mr. Gilbert quite Yeats. But it is precisely because Mr. Gilbert is a by no means untalented poet that I am so concerned: should a poem he puts into second place in his volume so closely resemble that *hasard* which threatens to abolish and supplant the poet's *coup de dés?*

In pursuit of his craft, Mr. Gilbert is sometimes cold, as in the passage quoted, sometimes getting lukewarm by ably digesting such influences as Auden ("In Perugino we have sometimes seen our country./ Incidental, beyond the Madonna, the mild hills . . .") or D. H. Lawrence ("You know I am serious about the whales./ Their moving huge through that darkness,/ Silent."); but there are times when he gets hot, as in the succinct "On Growing Old in San Francisco" (and no matter if the second verse reminds us of "In Memory of Eva Gore-Booth and Con Markiewicz"):

> Two girls barefoot walking in the rain
> Both girls lovely, one of them is sane
> Hurting me softly
> Hurting me though
> Two girls barefoot walking in the snow
> Walking in the white snow
> Walking in the black
> Two girls barefoot never coming back

It might be best now to get out of the way the various anti- and non-poets, whose tribe, regrettably, increases. Prominent here is a volume by Norman Mailer, *Deaths for the Ladies (and other disasters).* Mr. Mailer's *ars poetica* reads as follows: "Poems/ written by/ masochists/ flop like cows/ in the meadow. . . . Poems/ should be like pins/ which prick the skin/ of boredom/ and leave/ a glow/ equal in its pride/ to the gait/ of the sadist/ who stuck/ the pin/ and walked away." Clearly, in Mr. Mailer's philosophy the pin is mightier than the word—and so far as Mr. Mailer's own words are concerned, this is undoubtedly so. Again, we read "Art/ cannot/ recover/ what was lost/ to the cowardice/ of the/ knife. . . ." And "O sweet tear/ of the victim/ blind am I/ with love/ for thee." Or, fondly repeated twice, "So long/ as/ you/ use/ a knife,/ there's/ some/ love/ left." And, most concisely, a whole poem which runs: "It's me/ or/ my readers." It is a simple world, conveniently divisible into sadists, who write this sort of thing, and masochists, who read it. But at least no one can accuse Mr. Mailer of not practicing what he preaches.

If there is anything worse, however, than this, it is a kind of non-poetry made up of sheer free association, and, I suspect, not even honest free association at that, but deliberate cultivation of the meaningless, a willed collocation of the disconnected, unspontaneous, and ungrammatical: the arrogant assumption that *disjecta membra* can make you *poeta*. I am about to speak of three poets all of whom have been connected with the action painters—writing rave reviews of, catalogues for, and poem-paintings with, them—indeed, living with them in closest intimacy. These abstract expressionists in words are every bit as undistinguished and indistinguishable as their confreres of the drip, dribble, and squirt. There is, first, Barbara Guest with her volume *Poems,* a typical one of which begins, "All grey-haired my sisters/ what is it in the more enduring/ clime of Spring that waits?/ The tiger his voice once prayerful/ around the lax ochre sheen/ finally in withering sleep/ its calendar,/ Relatives/ delicious plumages your scenery/ has a black musical depth/ the cardinal flies into. . . ."

An even more expert *tachiste* is John Ashbery, whose previous volume, *Some Trees,* won the Yale Poetry Prize. Since 1956, however, Mr. Ashbery has perfected his verse to the point where it almost never deviates into—nothing so square as sense!—sensibility, sensuality, or sentences. Here is the opening of the title poem in *The Tennis Court Oath:*

> What had you been thinking about
> the face studiously bloodied

heaven blotted region
I go on loving you like water but
there is a terrible breath in the way all of this
You were not elected president, yet won the race
All the way through fog and drizzle
When you read it was sincere the coasts
stammered with unintentional villages the
horse strains fatigued I guess . . . the calls . . .
I worry

the water beetle head
why of course reflecting all
then you redid you were breathing. . . .

Bearing in mind the revolutionary title, I surmised that this was a poem in code, encoded in which lay some powerful anarchic message. Summoning up all my cryptographic skills, I proceeded to read the poem backwards; to read only every third, seventh, or tenth word; to skip every odd, or even, line; alas, every way made exactly as much sense as the one in which the thing is printed, and that, of course, is scarcely enough. In another poem, "Europe," which seems to be autobiographical, section ten reads, in its entirety, "He had mistaken his book for garbage." I do not think it is up to us to know better than the poet.

Last of this trio from the so-called "New York School" is Kenneth Koch, whose *Thank You and Other Poems* comes to us from Mr. Barney Rosset's budding Grove. A typical piece of Koch (from "Pregnancy") runs like this: "Shall any laundry be put out to dry/ With so many yellow and orange sequins falling through the air?/ Yes, the donkey has become very corpulent./ Will the blue carpet be sufficiently big to cover the tennis court?/ Down the street walked a midget. 'She's a good looker, hey?'/ He said to a passer-by. O tremulous stomach!/ We've been spending the winter in Paris . . ./ It rains on the sweater . . ./ I've a dog in my stomach!" (Ellipses the author's.) After ninety-five pages of this, what stomach would remain untremulous?

This brings us to a pair of other poets who belong to the radical left wing, viz. to those anthologized in Donald Allen's *New American Poetry*. The first of these is Robert Creeley, whose poetry 1950-1960 appears in the volume *For Love*. Mr. Creeley's poems have two main characteristics: (1) they are short;

(2) they are not short enough. In his more gnomic mode, he gives us poems like "Not Now": "I can see you,/ hairy, extended, vulnerable,/ but how did you get up there./ Where were you going all alone,/ why didn't you wait/ for the others to come home/ to go too, they would/ have gone with you." More often, however, Mr. Creeley ("One of the very few contemporaries with whom it is essential to keep current"—Hugh Kenner) provides tender lyrics like "The Way":

> My love's manners in bed
> are not to be discussed by me,
> as mine by her
> I would not credit comment upon gracefully.
>
> Yet I ride by the margin of that lake in
> the wood, the castle,
> and the excitement of strongholds;
> and have a small boy's notion of doing good.
>
> Oh well, I will say here,
> knowing each man,
> let you find a good wife too,
> and love her as hard as you can.

Besides ignorance of the English language, we find here that apotheosis of love in the last line of the poem, so characteristic of Mr. Creeley and other poets of his orientation, on which I have previously commented.

The other related poet is a particularly sad case. Denise Levertov was well on her way to becoming a pleasant, minor British neo-romantic poet when an American had to come along, marry and transport her to San Francisco, and add to her already complex Judaeo-Celtic heritage the insalubrious atmosphere of the Bay Area's beatnikism: Mishna and Mabinogion, if you will; but then on to Zen and mishmash? So now, in her *The Jacob's Ladder,* behold verse like "I hear/ the tide turning. Last/ eager wave over-/ taken and pulled back/ by moon-ache. The great knots/ of moon-awake energy/ far out." Again, ". . . who can say/ the crippled broom-vendor yesterday, who passed/ just as we needed a new broom, was not/ one of the Hidden Ones?" Or this, which reads like a parody, "The authentic! I said/ rising from the toilet seat./ The radiator in rhythmic knockings/ spoke of the rising steam./ The authentic, I said/ breaking the handle of my hairbrush as I/ brushed my hair in/ rhythmic strokes: That's it,/ that's joy, it's always/ a recognition, the known/ appearing fully itself, and/ more itself than one knew." The end here is not without merit, but can do little to mitigate the triviality and grossness of the beginning. On the whole, the poems in *The Jacob's Ladder* can be fair to middling, like the title poem, "The Rainwalkers," "Partial Resemblance," "Night on Hatchet Cove," "A Solitude," and "Illustrious Ancestors," or pretentious and lumpish, like "In Memory of Boris Pasternak," "The Well," "The Necessity," "Matins," "The Tulips," and "During the Eichmann Trial." Let it be noted also that Miss Levertov's free verse is often uncompelling in its movement, and frequently as arbitrary and ostentatious in its line breaks as William Carlos Williams's at its worst. "She is the most subtly skillful poet of her generation," Kenneth Rexroth informs us, and adds, "the most profound, the most modest, the most moving." The only way I can make sense of these four superlatives is to assume that the first ("most skillful") is used to keep the other three well hidden.

We come now to a few poets on the other side of the fence, where the grass, however, is not necessarily greener. It is customary to manhandle these poets by calling them academic; but a closer examination will show that some of them go to the most desperate lengths to avoid academicism, and are, frequently, only too successful. If Francis Golffing, in his *Selected Poems,* were content with attempting less, he could achieve a good deal more —rather like Miss Levertov on the other side of the ivy. But Mr. Golffing is at great pains to produce things like "And spray will settle in your halcyon hair,/ Deriding the barrette where white birds kiss," when he can manage such elegant though conservative felicities as this, of October leaves: "Such swarming embassies/ As fall will organize/ Moving toward flocks of snow/ From half-remembered flies." Francis Fergusson's *Poems,* on the other hand, stay well within their range: the early Pounding and Elioteering, and the later contemplative pallidness of pieces like "The Autumn God: In Time of War," which concludes, "Brief and timeless is the sheen/ Of the dry grass, seen, unseeing, while/ Unseen between the seasons the void/ Is void: unreal/ Its image of death in the bright spears of grass,/ Unreal and trivial (after/ The sombre triumphant surrender) as/ The detritus of war or pleasure." A prothalamion for his daughter elicits some pleasantly authentic touches of humanity, though not especially of poetry, but an elegy on his wife's death is marred by inveighings against his bugbear, "the City," which, except for their more anemic quality, might come out of Verhaeren or Sandburg.

As Mr. Fergusson ekes out his slender poetic output with a play in prose (made scarcely more poetic by his calling it "a theater lyric"), so Reed Whittemore publishes a volume, *The Boy from Iowa,* that is one-third sophisticated poetry and two-thirds sophisticated prose, though it takes a practiced eye to tell where the one stops and the other begins. Mr. Whittemore's poems are urbane, breezy, witty, but on subjects of such rarefied nature as Browning's ghastly drama or the otiosity of a Renaissance Man *manqué*—yet, at least, he is funny and does not take himself more seriously than his topics. When, however, he does attempt to be even mildly portentous, things go ill, as in two mock epics which only seem long, but are, actually, interminable.

John Hollander's attempts at getting away from the label "academic," which, I understand, was pasted in every copy of his first volume, consist, in his new book, *Movie-Going,* chiefly in the absence of sestinas, in picking up Gregory Corso's gauntlet about no academic poetry beginning with the words "fried shoes," in the presence of a sonnet to the Marx Brothers' female foil, and, of course, in the title poem, "Movie-Going." (It should be noted, however, that intimate knowledge of old movies and movie actors has become the paramount peak of academic snobbery.) Otherwise, here is the usual foison of the academic prestidigitator, from syllabic to shaped verse, from villanelles to Anglo-Saxonizing alliterative verse, from the usual experiments with slant rhyme to the no less usual "modern" adaptation of Catullus to prove that any shoe Fitts. There is also every type of poem, from a thirty-page piece in praise of Apthorp House (the master's residence of Adams House at Harvard), with deftly turned compliments to its current occupant, to the customary *New Yorker* poem about shells in a seascape—an item that seldom fails to sell to that publication, and, among poets to be discussed, Ruthven Todd and Sylvia Plath also have in their new collections the seascape-with-shells poem duly reprinted from *The New Yorker.* But to Mr. Hollander's misfortune, nothing stales more quickly than such a custom of infinite variety behind which there is no conviction: no need for writing poetry, only the compulsion to be a Poet. Mr. Hollander's typical tone is condescending: "Going inside the cottage was/ *sillier* even than staying/ out/ here in the first place." Or "Their light housekeeping doomed always to leave each room,/ House or garden or land *messier* than the last." Again, "the unlikely house/

Carries, stuck to its roof, a/ Lantern, just as if *any fool*/ *Knew* 'a house plus a light equals a lighthouse.' " Or, again, "imaginary *birdies*/ Sang grim songs from the lamp-posts"; also references galore to "goodies," "playing footy" (shouldn't it be "footsie"?) and so on. Mr. Hollander's characteristic strategy is inflation of the insignificant (e.g., minor movie actors magniloquently identified with planets and their mythic counterparts—a particularly seedy bit of euhemerism) or deflation of the significant ("And lay there freezing slowly in the dying light/ With which the changing world outside *peeped* in" [all italics mine]). Furthermore, there are inappropriate cutenesses like "dark night/ immanent and imminent both," or, of an old man carrying a girl piggy-back, "Bottom/ To bottom will the no-backed beast run," or Nabokovian trick-parentheses like "Down to the Zoo ('Hello, Yak') or along/ Apartment house-lined chasms," and many more. Poetry cannot be produced by such frivolity, because lack of genuine feeling for the subject cannot be compensated for by any amount of patronizing cleverness.

I dwell so long on Mr. Hollander's verse because it seems to me symptomatic of what ails much of American poetry, and because Mr. Hollander appears to me too intelligent a writer not to settle down sooner or later in the niche where he belongs: critical prose. With Ruthven Todd's selected poems *Garland for the Winter Solstice,* we come to the endemic disease of British poetry, suggested by the very title: genteel, *faisandé* amateurishness. Mr. Todd's poems are, for the most part, program notes to the work and lives of painters or poets, or elaborate catalogues of shells, mushrooms, wines, weeds—even of the modes of great men's dying—full of exotic lore. But if this, from "Trout Flies," be poetry,

> And tongue familiarly, Black Midge, and August
>   Dun,
> Blue Upright, Cinnamon Sedge, Coachman and
>   Pheasant Tail,
> Red Ant, Red Hackle, Furnace Palmer, and Yellow
>   Sally, in the sun,
> Ghost, Green Midge, Half Stone and, sometimes,
>   Never Fail,

then one of the greatest poets in the English language is Sears Roebuck. Mr. Todd also offers some hectic reminiscences of his

Edinburgh childhood, of war-crossed love, and he, too, can deliver sestinas, amphisbaenics, and pantoums. But neither cultured catalogues nor cultivated metrical rugosities can disguise the thinness of most of these poems. When, however, Mr. Todd picks certain playfully quaint topics, like "William Cowper's Hares" or "The Louse," he can be charming, as also in this sestet from a sonnet to "An Upper, Left Central, Incisor" that fell out:

> Oh, tooth, companion for thirty-five odd and curious years,
> My extra hand, clipper of ends of thread and bits of string,
> I shudder as I feel your neighbours shake; I share their fears
> Of the bright mechanics that the future now must bring.
> Suffering alone, I tongue your obvious, though healing, gap,
> Lamenting, as perpetually, unwanted changes in a private map.

Three impatiently awaited volumes have proven disappointing. In Richard Wilbur's *Advice to a Prophet*, of thirty-one pieces six are translations, three are miniatures, and one is a musical-comedy lyric. But the problem is not quantity; rather it is the quality of the remaining twenty-one poems. Of these only three seem to me to come off: "A Summer Morning," "A Hole in the Floor," and "In the Smoking-Car." For the rest, we have poems that have a nice beginning ("The Aspen and the Stream," "October Maples, Portland") or a nice end ("Next Door") or a nice this or that; others, however, fail for aiming too high ("Advice to a Prophet," "She") without matching the intentions with performance, or for not aiming high enough ("The Stop," "A Christmas Hymn"). Now a poet of Richard Wilbur's distinction need not continually surpass himself, but neither should he fall disconcertingly short of his standard. Mr. Wilbur's current problem seems to be (not unlike Robert Lowell's) one of transportation. He is trying to transport his verse from the poetic trance to ports of call of reality, but whereas in the demesne of pure poetry his excellence remains unchallenged, in the domains of contemporaneity his assurance is less than complete. Consider the qualitative differences between stanzas 2 and 5 of "Fall in Corrales":

Charms, all charms, as in stillness of plumb summer
The shut head lies down in bottomless grasses,
Willing that its thought be all heat and hum,
That it not dream the time passes.

. . .

Our desires dwelt in the weather as fine as bomb-
dust;
It was our sex that made the fountains yield;
Our flesh fought in the roots, and at last rested
Whole among cows in the risen field.

As for the translations, they are, as usual, deft and
commendably faithful: in an age of "versions," they remain, laud-
ably, translations. However, in Guillén's "Death, from a Distance,"
I feel that "pear" lacks the strict universality of "fruto," and
the final "its uncapricious law" is weaker than "su ley, no su
accidente." Again, in Quasimodo's "The Agrigentum Road," it
makes little sense to translate "carraio" as "wagon-maker," and
"moon-washed" is more conventional than "nitido di luna." (The
title Wilbur chose is misleading, too; it suggests that the poet is
on the way to Agrigentum, whereas, in fact, he meditates inside
that ruined city.) In Nerval's "Anteros," "My face, like Abel's
bloody—alas!—and white,/ Burns red by turns with Cain's un-
sated fires!" is an impoverished rendering of "Sous la pâleur
d'Abel, hélas! ensanglantée,/ J'ai parfois de Caïn l'implacable
rougeur!" And an important point is missed by translating the
final "ressème" with the non-repetitive "sow."

Our second disappointment is Thom Gunn's new
volume. This remarkable young English poet gets worse as he
becomes more sucked into America: his *Fighting Terms* was a
brilliant first book of verse, *The Sense of Movement* a fair second,
and now *My Sad Captains* a poor third. The opening piece, "In
Santa Maria del Popolo" is impressive enough, despite overtones of that kind of tourist-poem mass-produced by Miss Adri-
enne Rich; other pieces tend to be explorations of an inverted,
leather-jacketed underworld, occasionally, like "The Feel of
Hands," powerful, but more often, like "L'Epreuve" and the two
"Modes of Pleasure," dreary.

The third disappointment is *Torse 3*, a first book
by another English poet, Christopher Middleton. Individual poems

by him in magazines always gave me the feeling that a genuine sensibility was at work here, and that if only I were reading some other poem of his, it would surely satisfy me completely. Well, *Torse 3* ranges from obscurity to banality, and the two successful poems, "Amigos de Corazon" and "At Porthcothan," are both of them narrative, which I consider the least interesting form of poetry. None the less, some of "Alba After Six Years," the first stanza of "Waterloo Bridge," and parts of "Rhododendron Estranged in Twilight," for all its indebtedness to Rilke, hold out promise of better things to come.

There are also five happier events to report. There is, for instance, Sylvia Plath's first volume, *The Colossus*. Miss Plath has some of the excusable faults of youth: the attempt to blow up the tiniest personal experience into an event of vast, universal and, preferably, mythic importance; intoxication with the rare word which she displays with *nouveau riche* ostentation; and obsessive fiddling with certain forms and devices, e.g., *terza rima*. But with time—the deepening of perception and strengthening of control—these temporary improprieties can become the proper pursuits of poetry: holding nature's immensities in the poem's pocket mirror; redeeming the language; and letting the parallel rails of form lead on to a meeting point in, and with, infinity. When Miss Plath resists pretentiousness, she achieves glistening, evocative poems like "Snakecharmer," "Spinster," "Man in Black," or that endearing tribute to porcine pomp, "Sow." And consider this stanza from "Blue Moles":

> Nightly the battle-shouts start up
> In the ear of the veteran, and again
> I enter the soft pelt of the mole.
> Light's death to them: they shrivel in it.
> They move through their mute rooms while I sleep,
> Palming the earth aside, grubbers
> After the fat children of root and rock.
> By day, only the topsoil heaves.
> Down there one is alone.

Another lively first volume is X. J. Kennedy's *Nude Descending a Staircase*. Mr. Kennedy is a curious cross between the *boulevardier* and the metaphysical: he believes in the well-made, witty but significant, poem, donning its top hat and its Donne. When this blend comes off, as in "First Confession," the

second section of "Faces From a Bestiary," "Landscapes With
Set-Screws," parts of "Inscriptions After Fact," "Rondeau," "Con-
spirator My Rose," "At the Ghostwriter's Deathbed," and the
title poem, the effect is rousing. But when the wit fizzles or the
elegance gets creased, things look sorry indeed. Even a relatively
successful poem like "Solitary Confinement" can leave us ill at
ease, because so serious a subject is handled with a facetious-
ness under which one looks in vain for a deeper humanity or
profounder pessimism. And I must say I am worried to find Mr.
Kennedy's work reminding me in a dozen little ways of Mr. Donald Hall's—who but Mr. Hall could have written the line "You
wake one day to find yourself abstract"?—except that it was
written by Mr. Kennedy. It is all right for young poets to emulate
and resemble the great poets of their day—but to sound deceptively like Donald Hall is to be more deceived than deceiving.
To illustrate Kennedy at his best, here is the end of "On a Child
Who Lived One Minute":

> O let us do away with elegiac
> Drivel! Who can restore a thing so brittle,
> So new in any jingle? Still I marvel
> That, making light of mountainloads of logic,
> So much could stay a moment in so little.

Probably the most tantalizing poet of this batch is
Reuel Denney. *In Praise of Adam,* coming twenty-two years after
his first collection, contains a good deal that is dashingly or delicately irresistible, and as much or more that is murky, grandilo-
quent, and dishearteningly uncommunicative. Poems like "Fixer
of Midnight," "To the Roman Bridge on Michigan Avenue," "Lady
Who Knew a Waterfall, in Trinidad," "Love Song of the Summer
Waiter," "Tickle of Labor Day," "Recollections of the Porch,"
"A Chiffonier With Glass Flowers," and several others in part or
whole are remarkable for their freshness, ease, and strange,
slightly roundabout way of getting at the essential: to read them
is like watching a knife, in slow motion, somersaulting through
the air in sheer display, only to see it straighten out suddenly
and hit the target with uncanny accuracy. This approach is somehow very European—one thinks of Jacques Prévert or Paul Celan.
But when Mr. Denney proposes to write big, as, for instance, in
"Keepsake of Below" or "The Man in Oakenwald," the result
is dismaying. It is, unfortunately, hard to convey Denney's best

in a few lines, but here at least is some of his second best from "A Criticism of Sculpture": "Statue, go back to your rock./ There is little you mean of man/ Whose arm is a rope, whose head/ Is an egg in the frying pan./ His look is a lurk. His word/ Seems a self-hurting machine./ Back, back to your boulder, mock,/ And leave us a leaner scene."

The English poet Robert Conquest (best remembered for his anthology, *New Lines,* which gave rise to that casually fastidious poetry known as the Movement) appears with a new volume of verse, *Between Mars and Venus.* This could have been more aptly called "Between Eros and Apollo," for Mr. Conquest's *beau souci* is the relationship between love and creation, between sex and art. He is an excellent literary journalist (witness his recent book, *The Pasternak Affair,* which sheds exemplary clarity on a well-obfuscated issue) and, accordingly, his poetry tends to be more agile and provocative than original or profound. But at his finest he can give us verse like "The obsessions governing art/ Are art itself, philosophy and sex./ And in their fusion verse detects/ The process that it calls the heart." Or, again, "Life finds its way to sing/ Beyond all self, all sense:/ This mere experience,/ This chime of the most real./ Thank you. Thank everything." This may be slight; but it is not to be slighted.

Close on the heels of an extraordinary first book, *Into the Stone,* James Dickey gives us his second, *Drowning with Others,* and we can no longer doubt that we are in the presence of a major talent, a true art. It is not only that for many pages poem after poem is apt to be unabatingly good—"A Dog Sleeping at My Feet," "The Movement of Fish," "The Heaven of Animals," "A Birth"; it is not just that he can be equally impressive on a variety of themes from a scratch acquired in the woods to his father's dying, from a tree house to a lupanar at Pompeii, from a real, closely observed animal to an imagined, fabulous one; nor merely that he can make iambs and anapests—particularly anapests—ripple with the enchantment but not the monotony of streams; nor yet that he can fluently sustain a long poem. These are no mean achievements, but his supreme contribution is the creation of a Dickey cosmos: a landscape into which breathe Dickey plants and in which are ensconced Dickey objects, through which race Dickey meters and metaphors overtaking the slower-moving Dickey animals and people under the gaze of emblematic Dickey-birds. Once one has been admitted *chez* Dickey, one recognizes his fox, "A creature is burning itself/ In a smoke of hair through the bushes"; his child, "An event more miraculous yet/ Is the thing I am shining to tell you./ The child is no more than a child"; his angel of autumn who will come "And deliver the year from its thinking/ To the mindless one color of life"; his country, "When it is still, when it is as still as this,/ It could be a country where no one/ Ever has died but for love."

I am not saying that Dickey does not occasionally lapse into the facile, sometimes for the length of an entire poem: "The Dream Flood," for example, falls horribly flat. But before and after it come poems like "A Screen Porch in the Country" and "The Scratch," and, once again, the world is well found. And what is Dickey's world? A family in easeful accord; love for places as far as Africa or as near as the imagination; affection for animals, though one hunts them, and fondness for men, though they be unknown or dead. And always, whether a waterfall hurtles through the poet's eye or the dead are falling through time, everything is absorbed into a world consisting of pure fundamentals in all their plainness, intricacy, and intimate miraculousness. Dickey's poetry is cosmic; whether micro- or macrocosmic, it would be difficult—and needless—to say.

Two de luxe volumes, each containing one long poem, also make their entrances. Hayden Carruth's *Journey to a Known Place* is sheer bluster and humbug, and has probably an even higher rag content than the fancy paper on which it is printed. The only known place it could possibly journey to is the wastebasket. George P. Elliott's *Fever & Chills* is a perfectly valid short story of the kind Mr. Elliott turns out in prose with so much skill, here inexplicably couched in unrhymed, irregular iambic tetrameter. This sheepish fabliau about the dullness of marriage and scarcely lesser dullness of adultery has, along with very much that is prosaic, occasional lapses into poetic grace: "But he had no true competence/ In the uses of solitude," or "Instead, he scrutinized her face/ Like an artifact, he the numb/ Keeper of a wild museum/ Inspecting her in her sadness." On the whole, however, I would not thank James Schevill (as the author does in his dedication) for helping find the meter for this tale which would gain immeasurably by the absence of measure.

Two volumes of verse translations need occupy us only briefly. *In the Interlude* comprises Boris Pasternak's poetry 1945-1960: "The Poems of Yuri Zhivago," and the handful of other verse he wrote up to his death. Henry Kamen's renderings are rhymed, though not so fully as the Russian reprinted on facing pages; conscientious, though forced to make too many concessions to the rhyme; reasonably accurate, although substituting a fair amount of padding for the terseness of the originals; they read like the very best translatorese, but translatorese all the same. They are, in fact, no worse than other translations of Pasternak that we have seen, perhaps even better, but they are not likely to make Robert Frost withdraw his contention that if Pasternak is a great poet, nothing of his in English proves him so.

It is most commendable of James Wright and Robert Bly to offer us *Twenty Poems of Georg Trakl,* but would it not have behooved at least one of the translators to learn some German? Folks who translate "am Weiler vorbei" (past the hamlet) as "a while later," "rührt die Knabenschläfe" (touches the boy's temple) as "troubles the boy's sleep," "[it] dropped down stony precipices" as "stony waterfalls sank away," "the white grandchild prepares a dark future" as "a dark future prepared for the pale grandchild" are beyond the pale, even if in every other way the translations were most competent, which they are not. However, eight mistakes in a fifteen-line poem ("Birth") do constitute a record of sorts.

Lastly, a few words about three books by Old Masters. Hugh MacDiarmid's *Collected Poems* is a volume of nearly five hundred pages. Many of the Scots poems are unreadable because of an inadequate glossary; many of the English ones, because they are turgid propaganda. Much of this verse is naïve pseudo-folk poetry, much of it dull pamphleteering in verse. But amid the farrago there are poems worthy of the passion and anger of a Dunbar, of the canny satire of an Adam Lindsay. "In the Children's Hospital" and "If I Was Not a Soldier" are inspired poetry of protest; "The Two Parents," "Of My First Love" are lyrics imbued with wisdom and compassion; and "Coronach for the End of the World" is head and shoulders above the Lallans poetry of men like Sydney Goodsir Smith. A scrupulous thinning of the selections and fattening of the glossary could make this a highly estimable book.

William Carlos Williams's *Pictures From Brueghel and Other Poems* includes his previously published volumes, *Journey to Love* and *The Desert Music,* which contain some of his most meaningful and persuasive work. The new poems are less compelling, yet the crossing of Williams's early imagism with an old man's simplicity can be quietly affecting in poems like "The Woodpecker" or "Exercise No. 2." But a note at the end of the book in which Professor Thirlwall talks of "the triadic pattern with a short fourth line to fill out the measure," and, without explaining it, of the "variable foot," is merely the perpetuating of Dr. Williams's delusion that what he writes follows a deep-rooted, ineluctable "Measure," rather than facing the fact that it is simply a perfectly legitimate indulgence of the poet's whims.

> Robert Frosts's *In the Clearing*
>   On travelers will be lost
> Who on the least snowy evening
>   Push the button "De-Frost."
>
> Yet verse may end in fire
>   Or in thick ice be lost,
> But it will not expire—
>   Or be reborn—from Frost.

part six : critics

■

In Defense of Dirty Windows

■

In reviewing Edmund Wilson's *Apologies to the Iroquois*, W. H. Auden wrote: "In poetry language calls attention to itself as an end, in prose language is a self-effacing means. The test of good prose is that the reader does not notice it any more than a man looking through a window at a landscape notices the glass; if he does, it means that the window is dirty."

This image, which Ortega y Gasset used to illustrate much the same point of view, caught many a reader's eye—as it should—and produced more than a little comment, including this from Jacques Barzun: "It is true, as W. H. Auden reminded us . . . that good prose is unnoticeable and transparent, but this quality belongs to description and narration. In criticism and polemic we want the concise rendering of the elusive, which is bound to result in a noticeable, indeed a quotable, phrase."

My own feelings on the matter, in the simplest— not to say, the most transparent—terms, are these. If we leave aside prose style in general, and concentrate on critical prose (and, since he was talking of Edmund Wilson, I imagine that Mr. Auden had principally this in mind), I must come out in partial disagreement with Mr. Auden. True, some fine criticism has been written in the translucent style advocated by him. For an example we need go no farther than Mr. Auden's own critical writings. Still, if one notices the windowpane through which one looks, this does not necessarily mean that the glass is dirty. It may simply mean that, for some sound and useful purpose, it has been tinted.

Like Mr. Barzun, I am for the well-turned phrase. But I am also for all those devices which Mr. Auden would arrogate to poetry, and which, in toned-down form, are appropriate even to critical prose—which serves not merely to convey, but also to convince. To do this, it must play on the reader's emotions and senses as well as on his intellect: his laughter, his compassion, his scorn, and admiration must be invoked by turns, and sometimes simultaneously. There is nothing reprehensible about this (a caricature may well be truer than a photograph), provided the critic does not betray truth to pretentiousness, and beauty to partisan rhetoric. The landscape of truth is hard and glittering; to acclimatize our eyes to it, we may need sunglasses. But such is the quality of good sunglasses that we are aware of the greenness of the glass and the qualities of the landscape both at once. The parallel between this and the work of the critic should be evident.

It was the romantics who introduced a stylistically heightened form of criticism in modern times. The symbolists went even farther in this direction, and the miniature critical essays of Mallarmé or Stefan George are poems in prose. They are also good criticism. Thus George wrote of Verlaine: "Here for the first time we heard our soul of today throbbing freed from all accessories of talk: knew that no buskin and no mask was required any longer and the simple flute sufficed to divulge the deepest to mankind." What artful praise of simplicity!

Maurice Blanchot, perhaps the most remarkable contemporary French critic, spoke once of Lautréamont's "invisible manner of appearing." It is this manner, in which even the lens of a microscope makes itself felt to the sensitive eye looking through it, that critical style can achieve: it can be ingratiating and persuasive without being in the least obscurantist.

And another thing. Mr. Auden, if I understood him correctly, implied that nothing could be worse than dirty glass. Yet when we were children, it was through smoked glass that we watched our first solar eclipse. The critic can put such artificially dirtied glass to even better use: he will not only contemplate the eclipse of some dazzling though undeserved literary reputation, but actually hasten it.

■

The Theatre Critic and His Double*

■

In his previous book, *Tolstoy or Dostoevsky,* George Steiner set up straw men who raised the question "Can 'tragedy' signify anything if we use it at once of *Antigone,* of *King Lear,* and of *Phèdre?"* Ask a foolish question, and you will, if you are George Steiner, get up a bookful of foolish answers.

In *The Death of Tragedy,* Mr. Steiner's thesis is that tragedy, after its glorious heyday in Greece, and again, though in quite different trappings, in Elizabethan England, made its farewell appearance in 17th-century France. Thereupon, because science and optimism, commercialism, and the rise of the masses replaced myths, heroic individualism, and the sacramental-tragic view of life, tragedy went into an inexorable decline. The romantics tried to redeem it from its dreary neoclassical crawl by crossbreeding the prize-winning stables of Pericles and Elizabeth, but because the novel and prose had by now come into their own, the old and true verse tragedy was doomed except for a few flukes. With Ibsen and Chekhov it raises once again its lovely, though prosified, head—but only about shoulder-high: when disaster can be averted by "saner economic relations and better plumbing," tragedy is no longer the inevitable human condition and we can barely recognize the vestiges of the old dramatic flame. The same goes for the heirs of Ibsen and Chekhov, despite some exceptions, i.e., plays that Steiner is particularly fond of. Then comes a brief but quaint conclusion: tragedy is either indeed dead, or still dimly present without our being quite aware of it, or about to reappear in its full glory. With the body of Steiner's argument one can, by and large, hardly disagree, because it is, or should be, common knowledge; with his triple conclusion one can quarrel even less: no doubt about it, tragedy is either dead,

* The Death of Tragedy, by George Steiner, New York, 1961. Curtains, by Kenneth Tynan, New York, 1961.

or alive, or about to be born. Besides eating his tragedy and having it too, Steiner can feed on the dream of tragedy to come.

Disregarding the triple crown which the end bestows on this work, *The Death of Tragedy* is in its outline not much different from the average sophomore course in "World Drama." Where it does differ, however, is in its detail, in which it is worse. And I speak as one who has little enough respect for courses in world drama. Let us turn, then, to a pair of typical passages from the book which illustrate what I shall call, for lack of a worse word, Steiner's method.

We are given, first, 1782 as the date of Schiller's *Die Räuber,* which was performed in 1781 and written three or four years earlier. Presently Schiller is described as "a true romantic." Now Schiller was never a romantic, not even an untrue one, a fact which Mr. Steiner must know as well as the next Fellow of Churchill College. But he is, as always, trying to construct schemata: between Racine and Ibsen there must be only one theatre of any importance, the romantic (this simplifies matters for reader and writer alike), and so Mr. Steiner makes romantics out of Schiller, Lenz, Büchner, Alfieri, even Dostoevsky and Valéry —enough enforced conversions to do an Ottoman or Jesuit proud. Next we are told that "Schiller's treatments of Greek mythology are among the sources of that special kind of Hellenism which cast its spell over the German mind from Winckelmann to Nietzsche." Since Schiller was nine years old when Winckelmann died, I doubt that his influence on Winckelmann's Hellenism was more than marginal; but I am eager to find out what this special kind of Hellenism was, and how it differed from that of, say, Byron and Shelley, or Guérin and Nerval?

Hereupon we learn that "it is with Schiller that began the explicit search for tragic forms appropriate to the rational, optimistic, and sentimental temper of post-Pascalian man." Note the historicizing: the new drama begins with Schiller, the new world view commences with Pascal. Steiner is a great one for firsts—as well as lasts—and so we shall forthwith have Byron promoted to Schiller's first for being more daring than Schiller, and "contain[ing] the preliminaries of radical modern drama." After that, there will be Kleist, the last tragedian in the old sense, or, rather, the last last since Racine, who was also a last. After that comes Büchner who "poses in a new way the entire problem of modern tragedy," and then Ibsen with whom "the history of the drama begins anew." Steiner totally disregards the not insignificant drama of Lessing, which is every bit as "post-Pascalian" as Schiller's, and earlier to boot; but Lessing is so entrenched in the Enlightenment that even Steiner cannot hoist him into romanticism. Thus there is no discussion of Lessing, nor, for comparable reasons, of Hebbel, Zola, Becque, Hauptmann, the expressionists, Synge, O'Casey, or even of the tragic Goethe: a play like *Tasso* is said to be too autobiographical to be truly tragic, which settles that.

Now take Steiner on Byron, who, it seems, was "trying to draw . . . drama away from Shakespeare and toward the classicism of Jonson and Otway." If there is anything the history-of-ideas approach needs even more than firsts and lasts, it is movements and schools. So we have Otway joining the ranks of the classicists, even though in his best plays he was striving, counter to neoclassical trends, toward Shakespeare and even Tudor domestic tragedy. But Mr. Steiner needs a school or tradition, and since his taking-off point is *Marino Faliero*, his mind leaps, not so much by free as by enforced association, to another Venetian play, and so Otway must toe the line.

After a quotation from *Sardanapalus*, we are treated to this comment: "As in much of the finest of Byron's poetry we are near to a middle ground between verse and an intensely charged prose." We wonder, first, just what that middle ground between verse and poetic prose might be: something like the middle ground between Texas and New Mexico or between water and steam? But even granted the existence of such a middle ground, how could something standing *between* poetry and prose *be* poetry? From this we must conclude that Byron's poetry is usually at its best when it is not poetry at all. The cunning Mr. Steiner, of course, says this poetry stands *near* such a middle ground, but then: to which side of it? I think the only solution would be a map.

Next, we learn that when in Byron a breeze "crisps the broad and rolling water," this is as "Horatian" as Ben Jonson's "most Latinate conceit, where the wind crisps the 'heads' of rivers." Obviously for this conceit to be a conceit, *heads* is essential; without it the statement is not even metaphoric. But if *crisps* alone suffices to make a Latinate, Horatian conceit, then instead of on cereal, I have been breakfasting on epodes. Again, in "Though they came down/ And marshall'd me the way in all their brightness,/ I would not follow," Steiner admires "the Latin sonority of 'marshall'd' which gives the romantic boast its persuasion." The most modest dictionary could have told Mr. Steiner that *marshal* comes from the Old High German *marahscalc*, a horse-servant, which is as devoid of romantic persuasion as of Latin sonority. But Mr. Steiner, evidently equating *marshal* with *martial,* has hit upon a new discipline, etymology by homonymy, a kind of equation, or equitation, which should yield no end of pleasurable horseplay. "Could any other English poet since Milton have written that verse?" Steiner asks, remembering that Milton was a Latinate poet who, therefore, skilfully marshaled such Germanic words. At present count I can name 229 poets who could have, but by the time Mr. Steiner gets in touch with me the number should have risen considerably.

"Sardanapalus," Mr. Steiner acutely observes, "resembles a Delacroix." This, since Delacroix, too, was a tormented romantic, indeed a Byronist, and did in fact paint a "Sardanapalus," is about as revealing an insight as if we were told that Blake's graphic art resembles his poetry which it illustrates. We learn also that Byron's plays are "what the Germans call *Lesedramen,*" which, for Mr. Steiner's benefit, is what we call closet drama, but that would be too plain and simple (which the Germans call *einfach*). These dramas now require fancifully formal recitation because of their sumptuousness—though one page earlier they consisted of "plain, rapid monosyllables"; they now "look resolutely to the past," though on the preceding page they carried "forward from the best of Ben Jonson." To cap this farrago, we are told that Byron is different from Shakespeare, for "Byron, on the contrary, rejoins the tradition of the medieval mystery cycle." But only a little before, Steiner was stressing Shakespeare's dependence on the medieval.

Anyone not yet convinced of the level *The Death* of *Tragedy* manages remarkably to maintain might want to consider that Mr. Steiner refers throughout to one Macauley [*sic*]; that an *army* and *unreality* become *troupe* and *irreality* [*sic, sic*]; that commensurate *with, takes place,* to be *racked* by despair, become commensurate *to, transpires,* and *wracked* [*sic, sic, sic*], and so on. Mr. Steiner is, however, not without imagination, as when, for instance, he rewrites Wagner, and has not the Pope's but Tannhäuser's staff putting forth leaves. Nor is he lacking in resourcefulness, as when, ignorant of Spanish drama, he none the less manages to drop Calderón's name half a dozen times at strategic intervals, to make it appear in the index at least that he has said something on the subject. And he displays his neo-critical subtlety when, for example, he turns Woyzeck's touching babytalk addressed to his young son into the throwing away of words by someone who feels betrayed by language.

Let me summarize: Steiner's book is made up of commonplaces, absurd generalizations, distortions of fact to suit the absurd generalizations, and a style which is either the endless parataxis of the Hymarx Outlines, or a bizarre attempt at "fine writing." The outstanding feature is the impartiality with which Steiner can uphold both sides of any argument. Modern drama falls from grace, we learn, when it is forced into prose, the language of our times; yet Lear's madness, it seems, finds its most tragic expression in prose, and had Goethe stuck to prose, *Faust* would have been a real tragedy. There is Christian tragedy (p. 194); there can be no Christian tragedy (p. 332). *Caligula* (1938) and *No Exit* (1944) are too recent for discussion; *Mother Courage* (1941) and Anouilh's *Antigone* (1944) are not. And then the super-palinode of the last chapter: drama, or tragedy, may be alive, after all. The ultimate question, of course, is: do we need a book on the death of tragedy? As Dürrenmatt observed in his witty and incisive booklet *Theaterprobleme*, every type of drama makes use of the opportunities of its time; the *coups* of one sort of theatre are not those of another, but a period without dramatic opportunities would be hard to find. Similarly, Kenneth Tynan distinguishes two tragic actions, strangulation by fate and defeat by society. To be defeated by society, whether through one's own fault, like Uncle Vanya, or through society's, like Blanche DuBois, is, I think, as tragic as any tragedy. Jove's thunderbolt is as optional as iambics; only the playwright's wisdom and images are indispensable, and his sense of the anguish and hopelessness of the struggle.

In writing *The Death of Tragedy*, Mr. Steiner was plainly relishing the notion of being the priest who ministers at the burial of a grand theme, at whose baptism Nietzsche officiated: to fulfill the *Gestalt*, there ought to be, presumably, *The Death of Tragedy* after *The Birth*. But things do not proceed so logically in the history of criticism. Mr. Steiner, for example, was able to die as a critic without ever having been born. Still, there are those whom he can charm: *Time*, *The Times*, Alfred Knopf, and C. P. Snow, who just made him Fellow of Churchill College, Cambridge. But Sir Charles, who says that Steiner "belongs to the Edmund Wilsons of this world," obviously suffers from some kind of double vision. Thus he sees, apparently, two Edmund Wilsons where there is only one admittedly large one, two cultures where one wonders whether there is even one, and a whole wit in George Steiner.

There may be drama critics of greater erudition, or more potent charm, or truer professional aptitude than Kenneth Tynan. But on the evidence of *Curtains,* his collected writings on drama during the fifties, I doubt that there is anyone now writing drama criticism in English who possesses all three of those essentials to Mr. Tynan's degree. Since I am talking about someone who comes so close to what I consider perfection, I may as well set down my specifications for the ideal drama critic.

Of erudition, he needs three kinds. First, the literary, and Tynan is at home with anyone from Johannes Rhenanus to Amanda McKittrick Ros, from Jules Michelet to Zelda Fitzgerald. He can also spot the tiniest tinkering with any classical text in production. Secondly, the critical, and Tynan is steeped in the writings of such earlier English critics as G. H. Lewes, Beerbohm, Shaw, Agate, C. E. Montague, A. B. Walkley, Desmond MacCarthy; as well as Americans like George Jean Nathan, Stark Young, and Harold Clurman. Thirdly, knowledge of stage history, of which Tynan has, if anything, too much: some of his earlier reviews, such as that of the Old Vic's 1953 *Merchant of Venice,* suffer a little from excessive historical asides. But, on the whole, Tynan does not parade his erudition, and that is part of his charm.

Under charm, I would put three subheadings. First wit, of which Mr. Tynan has a superabundance. When his sallies come off (and they usually do), they are germane to the matter at hand, illuminating, and irresistible. Thus both the kittenish sexiness and histrionic limitations of Miss Leigh are captured in "As Lavinia, Vivien Leigh receives the news that she is about to be ravished on her husband's corpse with little more than the mild annoyance of one who would have preferred foam rubber." And not only a particular failure of Anouilh's, but French contentiousness too, is ribbed in "*Pauvre Bitos* . . . has split Paris into two camps—those who dislike it, and those who detest it." Even a mere slogan like "Judith Anderson's armpit rhetoric" has more pungency than meets the eye. Style comes next, and few critics have such a creative way with imagery as Mr. Tynan, when, for example, he pinpoints the basic problem of *Look Back in Anger:* "two attractive young animals engaged in competitive martyrdom, each with its teeth sunk deep in the other's neck, and each reluctant to break the clinch for fear of bleeding to death." It is delightful to watch in *Curtains* how the style gains in assurance with the passage of years, until such 1959 pieces as the review of Corwin's *The Rivalry,* or the tribute to Olivier's *Coriolanus,* or the summing-up pieces on French and German theatre are marvels of poised, judicious evocativeness. Lastly, there is likableness, and Mr. Tynan with his modesty, his willingness to learn, his remarkable kindness for one with such an arsenal of epigrams, is eminently likable.

Professional aptitude consists, first, of a working knowledge of the practical theatre, which Tynan, a former actor, assuredly possesses. He abounds also in the second subcategory, taste, which I shall concisely define as differing from my opinion no more than once or twice per every hundred judgments. Thirdly, he possesses flexibility, enabling him, at times, to transcend his own tenets. Fourthly, he enjoys his trade, and, rare among critics, often returns to a play once or even more times. Last, and most important, he has a point of view. Over the years, Mr. Tynan has moved from a position of pure aestheticism to one of intense social commitment. Thus we find him preferring by 1955 Shakespeare's histories to the tragedies. In 1958 he tells us that "to be civilised nowadays is to care about society and to feel a responsible part of it." "A serious dramatist who analyzes personal problems without analyzing the social problems that encircle and partly create them is neglecting a good half of his job," writes Tynan in 1959; and again: "No dramatist is an island." This leads Tynan to turn against Ionesco and Beckett, as not being *engagé;* and to overpraise poor plays like *Flowering Cherry, Summer of the Seventeenth Doll,* and *Death of a Salesman,* even an amateurish concoction of Pearl Buck's, because of their commitment. Finally, Tynan goes so far as to equate Strindberg's nihilism, if such it be, with brilliant lying. This strikes me as sad. It is not only from Brecht and Miller that one can learn, as Tynan says he did, that all drama is political. A play by Strindberg or, yes, even such a fragment of a dramatic monologue as Mallarmé's *Faune,* is political: a lesson in rejection of human vulgarity and stupidity —a slap in mankind's face, or mere dignified disdain. This too, in a broad sense, is political, only it happens to be opposed to Mr. Tynan's politics. But even so, I admire Tynan for having a political or philosophical stance, adhering to it, and still, as much as he can, applauding sheer style.

It may be safely claimed that Mr. Tynan is the critical representative of the Angry Young Men. He was at Oxford with Wain and Amis, is a friend and fan of John Osborne, and knows the whole movement from its Braine down to its Sillitoe. Hence the emphasis on social values, and, in particular, on a certain genteel leftism. Hence, too, a cosmopolitanism, an *unanimisme,* that lifts him happily out of British insularity. One wishes it might go so far as to improve his French when mangling, of all people, Mallarmé; or when misspelling the Lady of the Camellias—who for some reason seems to haunt him—"Marguérite" Gautier. But even in his lapses Mr. Tynan is charming; with just one super-erogatory acute accent he manages to gild three flowers: the daisy, the camellia, and the lily. Happily, though, Mr. Tynan never forgets his 1956 dictum about drama critics: "What counts is not their opinion, but the art with which it is expressed." No matter how engagé he may be, he is always engaging.

Put *Curtains* beside *The Death of Tragedy*: it is a patchwork quilt of occasional pieces compared to a single essay. Paradoxically, it is *Curtains* that offers a coherent point of view and sustained revelation. It is to Steiner's book as the living body of drama to its scattered bones.

■

The Confidential Eliot

■

An intelligent fourteen-year-old English girl, Margaret Waugh, wrote in a school essay: "One can read Mr. Eliot's poetry, but not the man on the other side." I should not be surprised if many older and more experienced heads came away from a reading of Eliot's verse with much the same feeling: that this poetry is not, as so much lyric poetry has been, a turning of the poet's epidermis and flesh into glass, so that the reader may see into the sensitive mechanism, after the fashion of those "Visible men" which are now sold in drugstores and are meant to acquaint children with the functioning of the human organism; rather, this poetry is a construct, an opacity, indeed a wall, placed between the reader and the poet, who, as Margaret has quite correctly noted, is "on the other side." But that, we may be sure, is where Mr. Eliot wants to stay; the work is to represent the highest thought, sensibility, diction of which the age is capable, while the poet remains behind the wall, an invisible man.

But Margaret, as the paragraph from which my quotation is taken clearly indicates (you can find it in *T. S. Eliot:*

A Symposium for His 70th Birthday), is not happy about this state of affairs. And in this too she is joined by many, if not most, of us who would like to get to know Eliot better. It is not that we want to know what his favorite newspaper is, how he spends his evenings, or whether he really thought much of Lady Ottoline Morrell; but our understanding bounces back. uncomfortably from a mysteriously permanent smile that leaves the Mona Lisa, in Pater's as well as Leonardo's version, far behind, from a kind of mammoth modesty which, even if it should prove genuine, is bloated well beyond life size, and from a blanket refusal to reveal anything about one's work.

It is here that Eliot's essays become of particular importance and interest, and especially those of his most recent collection, *On Poetry and Poets.* The pieces gathered here, though for the greater part less significant contributions to criticism than the earlier *Selected Essays,* shed a good deal more light on Eliot the human being with feelings and idiosyncrasies. The most perspicuous reasons for this are that the sixteen pieces of the book cover a full thirty years of Eliot's activity, and that, being mostly talks delivered to fellow human beings, they could not avoid a somewhat personal, autobiographic note. Indeed, in "The Three Voices of Poetry" and in "Poetry and Drama," Mr. Eliot discusses even some of his own plays—though about his more famous nondramatic poetry he remains silent.

But the most remarkable thing, to me, about these essays is how little they say about their avowed subjects. Thus "The Music of Poetry" tells almost nothing about what you or I might expect to learn about the musical aspects of verse, though it contains such priceless formulations as "the poet is occupied with frontiers of consciousness beyond which words fail, though meanings still exist." The essay on "Goethe as the Sage" tells little about Goethe and less about what constitutes true sagacity, but it does produce gems like "the poet is the least abstract of men, because he is the most bound by his own language." "What Is a Classic?" argues that the only true classic our culture has produced is Virgil, but proves this not in terms of influence, permanence, universality, but in terms of certain rules extrapolated from the circumstances of Virgil's historical environment, and, more dubious still, from Virgil's being made to square, willy-nilly, with Eliot's arbitrary prerequisites for a classic. All the same, it is in such an unsatisfactory piece that we find utterances as wise as, "Maturity of mind: this needs history, and the consciousness of history."

It is clear, however, that for *On Poets and Poetry* to be the important book it is, it must have more to offer than such incidental felicities and insights, frequent as these may be. The momentousness of the book lies in the fact that it reveals, more readily than any other, the essential personality or, more accurately perhaps, *persona* of T. S. Eliot. The main features of this, as I see it, are four: irony, a constant need for qualification or circumscription or just egregious cautiousness, ambiguity, and an Olympian detachment and superiority.

Space permits me only a few examples. For irony, consider the two essays on Milton. The first, of 1936, though an attack, continually implies that Milton is still better than most of his detractors or, indeed, champions; the second, the so-called recantation of 1947, though a panegyric, manages to praise Milton for the very things he and most of his admirers would consider only a small and unimportant part of him, and thus implies that Milton is after all a much lesser poet than one might think. By a similar irony, in the essay on Byron, Byron's plots are praised, except that Eliot wonders "if they deserve that name," and proceeds to demonstrate that they are scarcely plots at all. As for the need to qualify, consider this: "it seems to me possible to maintain that Hölderlin was at moments more inspired than Goethe. . . ." There is, in close order, the *seems,* the *possible,* the *at moments,* and the *more inspired* of which one can't be quite sure how, if at all, it means "more meaningful" or "more valuable." For ambiguity, take this example from "Sir John Davies," where we are told that "Davies had that strange gift, so rarely bestowed, for turning thought into feeling"; but also, on the next page, that in him "thought is not exploited for the sake of feeling, it is pursued for its own sake." (Such statements can be, and often are, reconciled, but they remain at best in a labile equilibrium.) The Olympian superiority can be found, peeping through the continuous self-deprecation, in a reference like the one to World War II as "a moment, some years ago" when Eliot's picture of Goethe had to be removed, for safety's sake, from the mantelpiece; a picture which, however, "survived and ignored the incidents of that disturbed time."

There remains a yet more important reason to watch the unfurling of these four Eliotine characteristics in *On Poets and Poetry.* It familiarizes us with the main stances of today's major poets, for these characteristics make up the most enshrined persona (to use once again Pound's concept adopted by Eliot), the reigning image of The Great Modern Poet. I say *poet,* though my demonstration was made from Eliot's criticism. With slight variations, this image fits, among others, Benn in Germany, St.-John Perse in France, Montale in Italy, Seferis in Greece, Wallace Stevens in America. To translate the words of the great scholar-critic Ernst Robert Curtius: "In Eliot's attitude . . . we always feel as it were a remnant of Jansenism and Puritanism. In back of this lies the unresolved antagonism between the artistic and the religious point of view, as a possibly unavoidable . . . form of the spiritual conflicts of our time. This position would suffice to secure a berth for Eliot among the eminent manifestations of the epoch. It explains the reverberations he produces in the old and new world alike."

To this, having read *On Poets and Poetry*, I would merely like to add: Yes, Margaret, there *is* a Mr. Eliot.

■

Let Us Now Praise James Agee

■

There are only two principal kinds of female star in Hollywood: the soft kind, made of three chunks of foam rubber: one for the hips, one for the bosom, one for the brain; and the hard kind, with the fiercely glittering eye of the Ancient Mariner, no doubt acquired by delaying so many male wedding guests at her own weddings. Movie critics fall, in the main, into the same two categories. There is the soft type that likes half the motion pictures he sees—a pernicious position because its seeming closeness to the law of averages disguises its very real distance from the truth. And there is the hard type that, armed with intellect, a ready (not to say ready-made) wit, and a welter of facts, forgets that he is meant to be a critic and becomes a journalistic prima donna. Even the best movie critics are prone to an occupational disease: from watching with suspicion the emotional and intellectual foul play of the films, they have turned into line-referees whose chief duty is to yell "Out of bounds!" the moment the movie falls short of reality, and who therefore cannot even contemplate its being pitched beyond reality, into art.

From reviewers and critics such as these, James Agee stood out, not only because he knew what he was talking about and wrote it down so well, but also because he was at the same time beautifully and (with no light use of the word) tragically humane. In the pages of *Agee on Film* the conflict of astute judgment and deep-rooted humanity is constantly before us: *In Which We Serve*, Agee tells us, may be a film correctly honoring the generous core of man, but its artistry is too calculated to be wholly satisfactory; *Open City* may, in its best moments, carry artlessness to the heights of art, but some of the most important human and political comments are false. Yet whether we see in Agee's reviews the man rejoicing and the critic wretched, or the reverse, our reward is that we are privileged to observe at all times a connoisseur confronting the art of other men, and a man struggling with the quiddity of life. But though we are moved by both these contests, they work on us as one.

For this is what Agee ceaselessly demonstrates, by example much more than by precept, that to have views on life and views on motion pictures (or, if you prefer, art) is, despite the surface difference, ultimately the same thing. Consider his closing paragraph on *The Raider:*

> It seems to me striking that in this film and in others the English have done so well in their handling of real people in films, and that we as a rule have done so badly. (One must, thank heaven, except several of our war record films.) The chief reason, so well as I can understand it, is an ugly one. Few Americans either behind or in front of our cameras give evidence of any recognition or respect for themselves or one another as human beings, or have any desire to be themselves or let others be themselves. On both ends of the camera you find very few people who are not essentially, instead, just promoters, little racketeers, interested in "the angle." I suspect it will some day be possible to deduce out of our nonfiction films alone that the supposedly strongest nation on earth collapsed with such magical speed because so few of its members honored any others, or even themselves, as human beings. (October 1946.)

Clearly this paragraph was not written about the movies and *also* about life, or about life and *also* about the movies; rather it was written about a primordial and indivisible experience which James Agee was never so esoteric as to try to sort out into life and art. Whether he saw as in a glass, darkly, or as on a screen, luminously, mattered little: the pictures made of celluloid or the *tableaux vivants* made of human existence were to him only one dimension more or less. The point of it all, like a point in geometry, is beyond dimension.

I can put it another way. If you read our movie critics from A to Z—though I doubt that you'll have the endurance to get much beyond C—you will rarely if ever find a man talking to you in his own voice. There will be the typical highbrow or the typical lowbrow or some hybrid inveighing and expostulating and extolling. But in Agee's reviews there is a man talking, telling you, among other things, that he very much dislikes going to the barber, and adores Mozart. Now I happen to prefer any number of composers to Mozart and do not consider getting a haircut an inordinately trying experience. But I respect a man who can display his personal loves and hates, and I love a man who can display them innocently, and without ostentation. Thus the fact that in the course of these often despairing movie reviews the love of Mozart comes so frequently, genuinely, and somehow appositely, to the rescue, makes Agee the man and critic real to me. What I read emerges not from the most anonymously brilliant electric brain but from a human being who loathed scissors equally in the hands of censors and barbers, and who loved precision as much in the composer of *Così fan tutte* as in the creators of *Modern Times* and *Potemkin*.

There are also many ancillary virtues in *Agee on Film*. There is, for instance, Agee's unfailing prophetic power to warn us about perils and guide us toward good things. Thus he foresaw the noisome horning in of television, the disaster of foreign films when they would start imitating Hollywood, and the sinisterness of "method" acting that was to be the Group Theatre's Pandora's Box; he hailed the rise of the "independents," of neo-realism with its reliance on amateur performers, the abandonment of musical scores in favor of the intelligent use of sounds and silences, such growing talents as that of John Huston, and great, fading achievements in danger of unjust oblivion, like those of Dovzhenko and Jean Vigo. Which brings me to another virtue: the enshrining of a fine supporting performance or less-noticed film that has to be protected against evanescence. So he will single out for praise the work of a George Macready, a Henry Daniell, an Evelyn Keyes, that must not be buried with its mortal coils of film; he will fight for the considerable good there is in even such lesser films as *The Story of G. I. Joe, Ride the Pink Horse,* and *The Clock,* as well as for the relative good that can be found even in vulgarity and in what he so frequently refers to as "intelligent trash." Indeed, there is a lesson in tolerance to be derived from this book, but it is a difficult tolerance on a high level. For a man of such Empedoclean cast as Agee, who loved and hated so wisely and so well, it was not easy merely to like. Yet he managed to like—not only the likable, but even, in just measure, the partly likable.

This matter of love and hate brings me to the quintessence of Agee which, whether you regard it as his major virtue or his supreme vice, is what makes this book, and the man who wrote it, heroic. For though it is a book full of good humor ("I would like to make *The Affairs of Susan* sound half as bad as it is, but I know when I'm licked") and wit ("All the talk here is in words of less than one syllable") and poetic perception ("As the audience watches from a hill . . . a mere crossroads imparts qualities of pity and terror which, to be sure, it always has, but which it seldom shows us except under tilted circumstances"), it is, above all, a book of love and hate. It is a book of hate for everything that is routine, humbug, cowardice, stupidity in life, and therefore in movies; and of love for whatever is bold, individual, resourceful, and illuminating in movies, and therefore in life.

Why, you may ask, should such sterling emotions be, to any reader, Agee's "supreme vice"? Because, to his bad luck and the world's, good and evil do not oblige by staying neatly separate, or at least, like oil and water, separable, but rather, like freedom and death, tread the same sword's edge. Agee, consequently, is forced into a kind of ambivalence. But it is not the pusillanimous pseudo-sophistication of the cocktail-party wit who comments on a movie "It was so lousy that I loved it!" nor is it the neurotic double-mindedness of Gide's Boris whose Yes and No are Siamese twins. Agee can write of *Voice in the Wind* that it "showed an unequivocal and reckless passion for saying the best things possible in the best way possible"; but that in nearly every other way it was poor. Again he writes: "I enjoyed *Great Expectations* more than Carol Reed's *Odd Man Out,* but I was more interested in Reed's film, and I liked it more." Of the guiding principle in *Zéro de conduite:* "I would accept this aesthetically for its enrichment of poetic perception, metaphor, and device, even if I rejected it intellectually." And one must read his painfully dichotomous accounts of movies he admired, like *Man's Hope* and *Henry V*, even movies he worshiped, like *Farrebique* and *Monsieur Verdoux*, to realize the terrifying integrity of his split.

Agee's tragic tergiversations stem from his search for the ideal. For whereas most of us are too wise to believe in, let alone seek after, perfection, Agee was foolish enough to demand it; in a few of his poetic, prose, and film writings, approximate it; in his critical insight and sensitivity, embody it. The failure of the films he reviewed, by one of those paradoxes which are the staff and stuff of life, becomes the triumph of Agee's critical imagination.

Let it be stressed that his perfectionism was never the pitifully gratuitous demand of those Oliver Twists of the intellect, asking simply and unconstructively for "More, please!" Agee always, to the best of his considerable abilities, explains, defines, demonstrates what he wants. This is why anyone involved in any sort of creation, in films or whatever other art, has something to learn from this book. To summarize Agee's tenets briefly, and therefore unfairly, he stands for the attainment and transcending of realism. For "the distinguishing faculty of the realist is his preference for the longest distance between two points—a preference which becomes virtually beatitude if the second point is never reached." The solution is to "show a livelier aesthetic and moral respect for reality—which 'realism' can as readily smother as liberate," and thus "perceive, record, and communicate, in full unaltered power, the peculiar kinds of poetic vitality which blaze in every real thing and which are in great degree, inevitably and properly, lost to every other kind of artist except the camera artist." In this way, perhaps, could be made whole again what Agee, in one of his poems, called "The wrecked demeanors of the mind/ That now is tamed, and once was wild."

There is one more thing: Agee could write. "*The Big Sleep* is a violent, smoky cocktail . . . which puts you, along with the cast, into a state of semi-amnesia through which tough action and reaction drum with something of the nonsensical solace of a hard rain on a tin roof." Note how image flows from, reinforces, and tops image, and how the whole is greater than the sum of its parts—as in the best poetry. Which means that *Agee on Film* should be for one more class of readers I have not previously listed: those who enjoy good writing. If that class does not include everyone, it ought to.

∎

Pilgrim of the Audile-Tactile

∎

If there is anything that characterizes this rather characterless age in which we live, it is its inability to make choices. In politics, it seems impossible to choose between disarmament and an arms race, and perfectly well-meaning people find themselves embracing both. Gone are the simple-minded days when one talked peace and meant war; now one talks peace and *means* peace, yet also prepares for, and prepares, war. Socially speaking, one dares not choose anything but conformity; but publicly speaking, one cannot choose to extol anything but independent thought. Emotionally, to choose a mate becomes harder and harder, but to opt openly for noncommitment is harder still. The great advocate of the supremacy and goodness of science spends most of his time writing bad novels, and the practitioners of that purest of all arts, music, expend most of their efforts on reducing it to mathematico-physical laboratory experiments. Under the sway of nuclear physics and Freud, the would-be artist paints the dance of the electrons or the hostilities of the subconscious; and the brilliant intellectual is consumed by his desperate attempts to be both a guiding light and the plainest of regular guys. We dare not choose either specialization or breadth, but dream of a magic formula combining both, and in the pursuit of this Both-in-One, our highest mathematics become an abortive poetry, and our poetry an aborted algebra.

The inability to choose is probably nowhere more evident than in the current English language, in which structural linguistics is by way of creating a new, organized "chaoticism," vastly superior in confusion to any former, merely disorganized, chaos. Before *Webster's Third New International Dictionary* arrived on the scene, it was possible only—to various degrees, to be sure—to know or not know English. Thanks to this masterpiece of noncommitment, however, it is now possible, by memorizing twenty equally endorsed pronunciations of one word, to know exactly how not to know; or, by not being able to accept twenty choices, not to know how to know. And this triumph of relativity need only be accepted absolutely, to enable us presently, by making us both relativists and absolutists, to shirk even that last remaining choice.

As might be expected, the apologists of the choiceless society were hardly likely to keep us waiting for their appearance. As might further be expected, the gigantic task of defending the choice of choicelessness was not going to be undertaken by any casual casuist, but would require the emergence of men with considerable resourcefulness, erudition, and authority. Such a one is Professor McLuhan of the University of Toronto whose press has just published his new book, *The Gutenberg Galaxy,** a study of the starring role typography played in the shaping of human thought and life. The thesis of the book is that man was once tribal and fully developed in all his senses, i.e., in the jargon of the trade, "audile-tactile"; "Touch," McLuhan suggests, "is not so much a separate sense as the very interplay of the senses." But the invention of the phonetic alphabet and, particularly, of printing, stressed man's visual-conceptual orientation and development, until everything from his politics to his art, from his science to his commerce, became lineal, sequential, organized according to a perspective and logic that were merely the hypertrophy and hegemony of the visual or conceptual. But the coming of the telegraph, films, radio, television, and other mass media, which demand the use of various senses and which reduce the world to a tribal village, creates a new revolution comparable to the typographic one but in the inverse direction. McLuhan claims that if we can understand the nature of this revolution, we can avoid being its victims. Perhaps, then, it would be more accurate to describe him, not as the apologist, but as the dupe of the new technologies.

As McLuhan summarizes his book, the typographic world "is the method of the fixed or specialist point of view that insists on repetition as the criterion of truth and practicality. Today our science and method strive not toward a point of view but to discover how not to have a point of view, the method not of closure and perspective but of the open 'field' and suspended judgment. Such is now the only viable method under electronic conditions of simultaneous information movement and total human

* The Gutenberg Galaxy, by *Marshall McLuhan*, Toronto, 1962.

interdependence." It follows that McLuhan's hero and model should be Harold Innis who, he alleges, "was the first person to hit upon the *process* of change as implicit in the *forms* of media technology. The present book," McLuhan continues, "is a footnote of explanation to his work." Innis, we are told, "is not reporting anybody's point of view, least of all his own. He is setting up a mosaic configuration or galaxy for insight." And what sort of thing does Innis arrive at with his galactic or "field" method of no point of view? McLuhan quotes him: "The effect of the discovery of printing was evident in the savage religious wars of the 16th and 17th Centuries. Application of power to communication industries hastened the consolidation of vernaculars, the rise of nationalism, revolution, and new outbreaks of savagery in the 20th Century." (One hates to think what Mr. Innis's statements would be like if he had a point of view.) Late in the book, McLuhan announces: "The present volume to this point might be regarded as a gloss on [this] single text of Harold Innis."

Let us consider, for the sake of our survival as readers and writers in the global village of the structuralist age, how Mr. McLuhan's book without a point of view is put together. It is, as he says himself, a footnote, but a footnote made up of footnotes. I would guess that it is about three quarters quotations, with the remaining quarter chiefly a connecting text introducing and commenting on the quotations, but also slipping in some assertions startling in their boldness and, occasionally, their irreconcilability. To turn his book "audile-tactile," he divides it into short, overlapping chapters which tend to have as little beginning and end as possible, and which may consist, for example, of quotations from Dom Jean Leclercq's *The Love of Learning and the Desire of God*, W. W. Rostow's *The Stages of Economic Growth*, Frazer's *The Golden Bough,* and the Opies' *Lore and Language of Schoolchildren* cheek by jowl. Such chapters are introduced by superscriptions in twenty-point boldface italics, and may read—or roar—as follows: "*Heidegger surfboards along on the electronic wave as triumphantly as Descartes rode the mechanical wave.*" Or, yet more "audiac" (to use a term from the book): "*Pope's Dunciad indicts the printed book as the agent of a primitivistic and Romantic revival. Sheer visual quantity evokes the magical resonance of the tribal horde. The box office looms as a return to the echo chamber of bardic incantation.*" Such configurational headlines, reminiscent of Joyce's Cave of the Winds, but meant quite seriously to reach the inner ear, are further removed from the visual and sequential by sometimes having precious little to do with the chapter itself. To make the book more of a "field," page numbers appear only on the rectos, so that one must frequently swivel one's head (a tactile phenomenon) to find out on what page one is. The book, moreover, is full of the new words of the electronic tribe: analogate, auditorially, haptic, specialisms, decentralism, etc.; as well as phrases like "civil defence against media fall-out," "Greek celature as a take-off strip for medieval manuscript culture," or "the Montaigne kodak trick of snapshotting moments," and other such felicities, meant, perhaps, to activate our olfactory sense as well.

Underneath it all, McLuhan plays the history-of-ideas game, and plays it, I am afraid, none too well. Though he avers that what is bad is not print culture but only its effect on those who do not comprehend its bias, distinctions certainly become blurred when McLuhan blames "the Gutenberg galaxy" for everything from the "compartmentalizing of human potential" to the French Revolution, and speaks of "the natural victims of print" and "people reduced to things" by it. Furthermore, McLuhan does not have the encyclopedic learning with which to back up his generalizations: often we feel that a single book on a large topic holds him in thrall, and a vast historical question is supposed to be resolved by a single contemporary quotation. With medieval deference to authority, McLuhan keeps making his obeisance to this or that "major work" or "grand study"—favorite critical terms of his. One's confidence is further shaken by references to the Bavarian composer Carl Orff as a Viennese musician, or to Umberto Boccioni, whose painting was far more important, as just a sculptor. It is, then, typical for McLuhan to make a contestable generalization about Spanish culture on the basis of two books (one a collection of essays by various hands), quotations from which are used, to say the least, deviously; thus Casalduero's statement that Don Quixote and Sancho "are of the same nature with a difference in proportion" is supposed to demonstrate that print in Spain was "effecting a new ratio in the senses."

Indeed, this is McLuhan's worst failing: the wholesale reinterpretation of texts to prove his preconceived argument. He offers lengthy misreadings of King Lear, The Dunciad, and Finnegans Wake, among others; but let me cite here a few of the numerous shorter ones. Thus he quotes Dyer's well-known poem, "My Mind to me a Kingdom is;/ Such perfect joy therein I find/ That it excels all other bliss/ Which God or Nature hath assigned" as evidence of "the power of print to install the reader in a subjective universe of limitless freedom and spontaneity." Again, Shakespeare's Sonnet LX, in which our minutes "Like as the waves . . ./ Each changing place with that which goes before,/ In sequent toil all forwards do contend," is proof to McLuhan that Shakespeare was against "lineal denudation of language" and the "mechanical repetition" inaugurated by print. If Adam Smith says that in commercial societies thinking becomes the business of a few people who furnish the public with reason, to McLuhan this means that "the intellectual is to tap the collective consciousness," which two lines later becomes "the massive unconsciousness"; forthwith Adam Smith's meaning is that the Gutenberg society casts the intellectual "in the role of the primitive seer." Irresponsibility becomes absurdity when, for example, McLuhan quotes the octave of Sonnet LXXV from the *Amoretti* as alleged proof of a point, but omits the sestet, a palinode in which Spenser himself refutes what went before.

Even more remarkable are Mr. McLuhan's contradictions, as when Euclidean geometry is still so "tactile-muscular" that later scholars criticized it for its pusillanimity, but Euclidean space is "linear, flat, straight, uniform" and a product of that literacy which, in turn, produced print culture. Film, which is sometimes viewed as part of the new electronic age, at other times becomes part of the Gutenberg galaxy: "Montaigne had all the experiences and techniques of the impressionist film . . . both modes . . . are direct extrapolations of typography." It will take a few decades to understand fully the impact of TV—"today it is futile to discuss it at all"; but we learn that Professor McLuhan is already at work on *Understanding Media,* in which he addresses himself to this and similar matters. Such inconsistency is one form of abdication of choice; another one is the hiding behind an alter ego like Harold Innis.

McLuhan's conclusion is that visual orientation resulted in the fiasco of "mechanical matching, not imaginative making . . . in the arts and sciences, in politics and education until our own time." But when it comes to suggestions for dealing with the present cultural crisis which, true apologist or dupe that he is, he does not fully recognize ("Today we live on the frontier between five centuries of mechanism and the new electronics, between the homogeneous and the simultaneous. It is painful but fruitful."), he offers no more help than he did in his previous book, *The Mechanical Bride.* There we read: "Why not use the new commercial education as a means to enlightening the intended prey? Why not assist the public to observe consciously the drama which is intended to operate upon it unconsciously?" Like Poe's sailor, we are supposed to study the maelstrom, and so discover the way out. But that is a faulty analogy. Beyond Poe's maelstrom was safety; beyond the trends that engulf our world there is no terra firma, no other world. And it is not typography or the sequential view that does us in, but any multiplication and vulgarization of ideas: the fact that the masses demand mass-production—in a way which Ruskin and Morris could not foresee, and which McLuhan's "field" view avoiding choice cannot concede—spells the end of culture, typographical or otherwise. I do not know just what about television, for example, Professor McLuhan would have us understand. How the tube works? The shoddiness of sponsors, agencies, and programs? The cloddishness of the public which dooms attempts at improvement? How would that help us to anything but choiceless acquiescence? It seems preferable to hold on to the pitifully individualistic, non-audile-tactile values of print culture: for the betterment of life, it is not death that needs understanding, but life.

■

A Breath of Smoky Air

■

There exists a little-known Caedmon record called "H. L. Mencken Speaking." When we first listen to this record, we are apt to be slightly disconcerted. If we do not belong to a generation which had its Mencken *mystique* (though he himself, sanely, would have none of it), we may at first find the voice and personality a little vulgar. The repeated croaks of "yeah, yeah" with their faint echo of an Aristophanic chorus of frogs, the occasional loud snuffle that suggests the absence of even so modest a nicety as a handkerchief, "Baltimore" pronounced as though it were almost all consonants and one whopping glottal stop, such things begin by alienating us.

But soon our defenses fall before this wonderfully common-sensical, ungrand old man. There is nothing intrinsically clever in references to "psychologists and other such frauds," or descriptions of going to college as "listening to idiot lectures, cheering football games, and other such foolish things," but there is something in the tone in which this is said that is definitely arresting. Other statements are more pungent: "the American lust for the hideous—delight in ugliness for its own sake," or "there is an idea in America that no man is worth listening to unless he's had some experience in sweatshops"; but it is not even the trenchancy of such remarks that particularly impresses us. What does affect us, involve us, and finally win us over is the tone of quiet assurance, of absolute self-confidence that permeates every syllable spoken by this rather flat, coarse-grained voice. What first captured me was the way Mencken pronounces "idealism," for which he has nothing but contempt. The accent is on the first syllable, and the word sounds like some fiendish blend of "idyllicism" and "nihilism." This word, or "trash," or the adjective "idiot" can drop from Mencken's lips with such cutting calm that one cannot help feeling in the presence of the supreme common-sense being that refuses all sham and illusion.

This characteristically Menckenesque break with incautious romanticism and cautious relativism, with the twilight of sentimentalism and the bonfire of propaganda, is made possible only by complete, undaunted faith in the self. "The idea of a newspaper reporter with any self-respect playing golf is to me almost inconceivable," Mencken pontificates, having been spared at least the insult of a president of the U.S. so engaged. When told by his interlocutor that even printers nowadays (1948) play golf, Mencken exclaims, "God almighty, that's dreadful to think of. . . . It's almost obscene." Again, he will tell us, "In my time a press agent was looked on as a loathsome creature. Nobody paid any attention to him." Now the point is not whether Mencken is right or wrong, but that we have here a person perfectly willing to offend. Not *wanting* to offend, mind you, just *willing*. As he says, he believes in "every kind of free speech up to the last limits of the endurable," which means, among other things, willingness to tell the truth as one sees it on any subject when asked, but not trying to force one's unsolicited opinions on anyone. Even so, this is much more than one hears nowadays. In our day of sterilized, hermetically sealed, artificially lighted and ventilated, symmetrical, designed-for-efficiency offices, mentalities, and lives, where conformity has been bought at the price of deformity, where everyone is afraid even if he has nothing to fear but his *angst,* a Mencken is impossible.

But in the hot, filthy, disease-ridden Baltimore of his day, which Mencken so sympathetically evokes, in the smoky, hectic offices of *The Herald* and *The Sun*, where they never heard of a forty-hour week for reporters, there still existed a survival by fitness rather than by fitting in, and this gave the man who did not succumb to the cholera or the bankruptcy of his newspaper a sense of strength and importance that enabled him to think and speak for himself.

Listening to Mencken becomes more and more engrossing with every rehearing of this record. It is good to hear someone dare to say "the orthodox Christian is an amiably comic character," or "In politics I'm a complete neutral: I think they're all scoundrels . . . especially the reformers," and convey by the composure of his voice not a chip but a head on his shoulders. Yet Mencken is neither egomaniacal (ignoring his interviewer's insistence that Mencken's Monday columns had all Baltimore agog, the old man maintains that they "hardly stirred a ripple") nor coldly rationalistic (he'll say: "A man is entitled to be a little bit irrational about himself!"). This is why the record *H. L. Mencken Speaking* comes to us as such a salutary counterirritant, whether Mencken discusses his life as a journalist or the excellence of Jack Dempsey's mint juleps, Ellery Sedgwick or a prize fight, the Scopes trial or the rules of intelligent drinking, scholarship, superstition, agnosticism, music, television, and all the rest: in each case he has something free and racy to say.

The recorded interview is wholly spontaneous, the man's answers and disquisitions quite impromptu, but based on long, independent thinking and learning and being right. One finds oneself so pleased by having Mencken to visit, so much in agreement with his views, that one cannot quarrel with him even when his mind, for once, slips as he refers to "Schiller's *Don Juan*." After all, there should have been a *Don Juan* by Schiller, even if Mencken himself had had to write it. Especially then.

■

Leslie Fiedler or How to End a Dull Party

■

Why, I ask myself, is a true social critic such an extremely rare phenomenon? By "social critic" I mean, of course, a writer—who else deserves the title "critic"?—who is also a sociologist, in the true philosophical sense: a student of society, not merely someone with an advanced degree in sociology. The answer, I should think, is that a good social critic must be both a sociologist and a man of letters, and that this is a marriage impossible to achieve. Impossible not because the partners *necessarily* despise each other—which would never, in any case, stop a marriage in its tracks—but because the sociologist, as it were, works by day, and the writer by night. Now though such schedules make for the happiest of relationships, they do not make a marriage. Accordingly, in social criticism one partner always proceeds quite independently from the other, with the muscular sociologist outdoing the effete *littérateur*. This has been the case regularly, from Parrington to Philip Rahv, from Howard Mumford Jones to Irving Howe. It would seem, therefore, that the social critic has to be a creature with two heads, each demanding, and receiving, equal time. Such a critic is Leslie Fiedler—but to confound his enemies immediately, let me say that his two heads are worn not side by side, but one inside the other.

To put it more precisely, Leslie Fiedler succeeds as a social critic for three reasons. First, because he writes with the same acuity with which he observes the world; secondly, because he is fully as interested in literature as in social problems; and, above all, because to him literature is not just a reflection of social conditions (a point of view that produces journalism or footnote-mongering), any more than the world is merely an imitation of art (a point of view that makes for sterile aestheticism). Rather, he sees something that is prior to both society and literature as we have come to know them, and that something is myth, a fund on which both society and art are constantly (though not always sufficiently) drawing, either directly or through each other. Understanding is, for Fiedler, "to be sought . . . where myth and dream are made flesh. Yet an anthropological approach to literature irks the 'pure' critic, just as a literary approach to society irks the 'pure' social scientists. All the better." There could be no fairer or more compact statement of intentions than this, and the difference between Fiedler and the average social critic can best be seen in his views on Frederick J. Hoffman, a professor who sees literature through a black umbrella, darkly, and who washes his pen with soap after writing the four-letter word "life."

"The Ant on the Grasshopper," from his new book, No! in Thunder, shows Fiedler at his best, because in it he can be what he is, a social critic. Equally good are essays like "The Un-Angry Young Men," "Walt Whitman: Portrait of the Artist as a Middle-Aged Hero," and "The Search for the Thirties." Where the sociologist predominates, after all, the results can still be estimable, as in the essay on "Leopold and Loeb: A Perspective in Time," which, despite its overindulgence in what Mr. Fiedler calls "legitimate distortion," is irresistibly pungent and witty; where the literary critic holds sway, as in a piece on "Dante: Green Thoughts in a Green Shade," he discharges his obligations creditably if not with particular éclat. But where the social critic is truly given his head—or, rather, heads—in the introduction, "No! in Thunder," there is so much glittering writing that it may take a while to realize that underneath there is a solid, all-important, and all too neglected, truth.

What endears Mr. Fiedler to me particularly is the multitude of opposites he combines in himself, so that his writing is not only useful, but also something almost unheard of in the field of criticism, entertaining. For nothing is more satisfying than to see him tread between opposites that threaten to become contradictions a dance that is part tricky passe-pied, part boisterous jig, and that, seemingly making up its steps as it goes along, reveals an ultimate cohesion and integrity. There are the already mentioned opposites of literature and sociology. There are, further, the opposites of disheveled writing cheek by jowl with utterances filed down to the highest Horatian polish. On the one hand, Mr. Fiedler will speak of things "mutually different," of Hitler being "hung," of plural "protagonists" in a single work; and he will, on occasion, ride roughshod over the niceties of syntax and spelling. In his French, he will even practice a kind of grammatical "Albertine strategy," changing the gender of acte from masculine to feminine. But, on the other hand, he will come out with those devastating and often irrefutable capsule criticisms, bitter pills indeed for his chosen victims, or, simply, perfect definitions of things that other critics drearily belabor. Thus we read in Fiedler of Steinbeck's "women of the people who offer their swollen breasts to the starving unemployed"; of "a handy rule of thumb [which] says beware of Whitman when he uses the 'thou' instead of the 'you' "; of that Whitman who "after his fortieth year . . . could not even live (much less write) anything he had not already set down in the work from which he was unable to disentangle his aging self." Thus Freud is "the new Moses of a best-selling wing of the Reformed Synagogue"; and thus the twenties "had the nerve proper to their excesses and we have only the caution proper to ours."

Again, there are those unfortunate young people who "passed directly from grade school to middle age with a copy of *Partisan Review* or *Kenyon Review* as a passport"—but, at least, "each does what he can; and construing a poem by John Crowe Ransom, though it may not be as good as writing it, is considerably better than biting your fingernails." Whether these capsules score through their wittiness—as in "the old tragedy of the poet forced into manufacturing paper bags becomes the new comedy of the proto-tycoon lecturing on the imagery of Wallace Stevens," or through the sheer neatness of phrase-making—as in "the poet, who has merely to redeem from use to wonder what was in the first instance drafted from wonder to use," passionate conviction is never sacrificed to mere wit for wit's sake. And the occasional untidiness in his writing Mr. Fiedler might justify with yet another of his capsules which he himself used to vindicate the "militant middlebrowism" of Britain's Angry Young Men "as a useful weapon in the fight against a quiet, upper-class reign of terror based on a frozen high style and a rigidified good taste."

There is, again, a near-contradiction in Mr. Fiedler's construction of his book. Considering criticism an art, he is justly eager to give *No! in Thunder* shape and unity, in spite of the fact that it is made up of shorter critical pieces on a variety of subjects. He succeeds handsomely, because these essays are honest variations on their author's basic critical themes and thus hang together, and because he has, furthermore, carefully devised headings for each group of essays which tie these groups to his central concerns. So cautious is he, that he equips his book with both a preface and an introduction, thus making it wear both belt *and* suspenders; yet he will include in *No! in Thunder* such an immature piece as "Shakespeare and the Paradox of Illusion," which requires from the reader not just a suspension, but a veritable embargo on disbelief.

Before I can come, however, to the profoundest and

most fascinating of Mr. Fiedler's antinomies, I must try to evoke his main critical tools, convey his critical stance. For this I need three headings: "No! in Thunder," "Myth," and "Shock Treatment."

I may have read better books of criticism than *No! in Thunder,* but I have surely never come across a better introduction than this book has, bearing, in turn, the title "No! in Thunder." It will help to quote the passage from Melville's letter to Hawthorne that has provided this title, and a good deal more than the title. In it Melville purports to define Hawthorne's art, but reveals (as Fiedler correctly points out) the truth about his own:

> There is the grand truth about Nathaniel Hawthorne. He says No! in thunder; but the Devil himself cannot make him say *yes.* For all men who say *yes,* lie; and all men who say *no,*—why, they are in the happy condition of judicious, unincumbered travellers in Europe; they cross the frontiers into Eternity with nothing but a carpetbag,—that is to say, the Ego.

The whole Introduction is a clarification of what this "No! in thunder" is for Fiedler: a "Hard No" which is "quite different from certain lesser *no's* in which a thriving trade is always done," such as being against McCarthy, or segregation, or the current best-seller, or whatever else is "by anticipation, tomorrow's yes." The Hard No is something very different, it predicates the writer's —or critic's—"biting the hand that feeds him," without which act of rebellion "he cannot live." The idea is developed so tightly and magisterially that it is hard to excerpt any part of Fiedler's argument, but here is one, anyhow:

> The "No! in thunder" is never partisan; it infuriates Our Side as well as Theirs, reveals that all Sides are one, insofar as they are all yea-sayers and hence all liars. There is some evidence that the Hard No is being spoken when the writer seems a traitor to those whom he loves and who have conditioned his very way of responding to the world. When the writer says of precisely the cause dearest to him what is always and everywhere the truth about all causes—that it has been imperfectly conceived and inadequately represented, and that it is bound to be betrayed, consciously or unconsciously, by its lead-

ing spokesmen—we know that he is approaching an
art of real seriousness if not of actual greatness. . . .

What Fiedler describes here, and exhibits everywhere, is his need
—and that of the writers he admires—to be in perpetual opposition, loyal as well as embittered, to the human ambiance, to the social as well as the spiritual contract inasmuch as it is contracted and
contrived. This seems to me, if I reduce it to its simplest terms, the
praiseworthy inability—as wrongheaded as it is admirable—to
accept the frailty and stupidity of man. It is, on the planes of the
mind and the spirit, both Little Big Horn and Balaklava.

Now, the thing that even the man who says the Hard
No can say yes to is Myth, which to Fiedler is the supreme truth
about life and literature. Exactly what he means by "myth" I can
illustrate here with one quotation only: "Archetypes . . . preserving
for us the assurance which belongs to ritual alone: that what is
done below is done above, what is done here and now is done
forever, what is repeated in time subsists unbroken in eternity."
Myth, then, if I may be allowed to interpret, becomes the religion
emancipated from God, having for its angels and devils men, and
for its miracles men's most marvelous actions, good or evil.

Lastly, the writer, not the least when he is a critic,
needs a language of particular potency. Just as a Mallarmé invents
a hermetic syntax which forces the reader to sit up and struggle,
Fiedler creates a language whose units are not words but thrown
gauntlets, which force the reader to stand up and fight. Examples
illustrating his shock tactics can be found in almost every paragraph; to give any here would be sheer supererogation. Suffice it
to say that nothing is sacred to Fiedler, neither Jesus Christ's puns,
nor even Ike's game of golf.

This brings me to the final and basic oppositions
within Leslie Fiedler. How does a man who thunders No's in all
directions manage to write of the world that "only as we love it
can we know it"? Why does a critic who would not wish upon a
work of art either general acclaim or espousal by an elite still
feel compelled to praise Malamud's The Natural—or indeed any
other book? And having made the effort to praise and defend it,
why is he "a little pleased to note [that The Natural] remains
still unappreciated" a few years later? And how can Mr. Fiedler,
who accepts only the most archetypal, mythic, and, in the true
sense, marvelous writers continue to admire and champion his
teacher, William Ellery Leonard, the pedestrian author of The
Locomotive God, the prosaic versifier and flat-footed translator of

Lucretius? I shall give no answer to this beyond what is implicit in the foregoing because I do not want to spoil the pleasure every reader of *No! in Thunder* will take in puzzling out the enigma.

I shall content myself here with saying only that I consider Mr. Fiedler the most amusing, most challenging, most delectably readable of our critics—and I realize that in saying so I am doing what Mr. Fiedler does all the time: leading with my chin, and that without having taken his precaution of growing a cushioning beard. For here I am saying anything but a Hard No to Mr. Fiedler, and should, for my thunderous *yes*, be smitten straight on the jaw by him. Yet what else can I say to a critic who forces us, first and last, to think? At the very least, says Mr. Fiedler, his essays have been the cause of tumultuous arguments which "brought certain dull parties to bitter and long-overdue ends." American literary criticism, thriving on impotent love letters and flea-sized backbites, has surely become the dullest of parties. If anyone can put an end to it, Leslie Fiedler is the man.

■

The Pursuit of the Whole

■

One of the most fascinating and most overlooked facts about excellence in art is that its limitations are generally due neither to the running dry of that excellence, nor to something extraneous and hostile to it, but are a part and consequence of it. Flaubert is a great stylist, and Calderón a great moralist; to the extent that they fail, this is not caused by something like Flaubert's style ultimately forsaking him or Calderón's moral sense proving fallible; it is caused by the fact that so much style must be paid for by a loss of even the illusion of spontaneity, that so much rigorous morality predicates the absence of that wayward quality, charm. And it is beside the point to say, for example, that Henry James's fastidious near-periphrases are all very well, if only he could have had a foursquare robustiousness besides: the dancing master cannot move like an athlete just because he treads the barroom rather than the ballroom floor. Milton is stuffy; but without the pompousness, would there be the pomp? Only in minor artists can the flaws be divorced from the virtues: Arthur Miller's dramaturgy in *A View from the Bridge* is good, but his straining for poetic diction and the devices of Greek tragedy is something quite different and totally disastrous.

What makes Robert Warshow a major critic,* despite the incompleteness of his cruelly truncated life's work, is precisely that his strength and weakness are inseparable, indeed identical. Perhaps the first thing that we notice as we look at any page of *The Immediate Experience*, even before we begin to read, is that it bristles with quotation marks which have nothing to do with quotations. Thus the first page of the preface, really only half a page, displays—all of them sprouting their little double horns— "popular culture," "self-made men," the "right" choice, though it would have been just as possible for Warshaw to write, for example, "we are all self-made men culturally" without putting horns on "self-made men." Yet this recurrent practice of Warshow's is anything but a mannerism: rather than just a trademark, it is a hallmark. For unlike Mallarmé's Poe (so unlike, incidentally, Poe's Poe), Warshow was not concerned with "*donner un sens plus pur aux mots de la tribu.*" On the contrary, he yearned to give a more tribal meaning to what might otherwise have been purely words. In the best and worst sense of the term, Warshow was a social critic, or, if you prefer, a sociologically oriented critic of culture and the arts, which is only a pedantic, roundabout way of saying the same thing. Therefore it was important to him to write "we are all 'self-made men' culturally" with those quotation marks: he strove thereby, almost to the point of ridiculousness, to show that he was dealing with your words and mine, with our concepts, not just with those of an individual who might, at best, be an eccentric, and, at worst, a solipsist. When I spoke of these quotation marks as horns, I did so deliberately: it is as if Warshow wanted his words to wear the insignia of cuckoldry, of promiscuity, of indiscrimination. The words were to be public, even if, and particularly if, the perceptions behind them were—no, nothing so limited as *private,* but something as universal as *unique.*

The Immediate Experience is the posthumous collection of the reviews and essays on various subjects which Robert Warshow wrote during the thirty-seven years of his life. The publishers have wrongly subtitled it "Aspects of Popular Culture" in their eagerness to find a convenient counter on which to sell the

---

* The Immediate Experience, New York, 1962.

book. In this, I admit, they may be no more errant than the public, always looking for the fashionable gimmick for which to read a book—and, failing that, to ignore it. The trouble is that the publishers have neglected a much better selling point of these by no means unrelated essays: their point of view. This, as I said, is the point of view of the social critic which here encompasses everything from movies to *The New Yorker,* from comic books to communism, from theatre to the death of one's father.

The reviewers have latched onto precisely this social point of view to beat Warshow over the head with. Thus Stanley Kauffmann has attacked him for seeing everything from a sociological standpoint and being, therefore, poor at aesthetic discrimination. This is true, but it is the truth as seen by a man so nearsighted that he cannot even see he has forgotten to put on his glasses. For in our fathers' metropolis there are many intersections, and a policeman is needed at each one of them. The confluence of Culture Boulevard and Society Avenue is just as much in need of policing as the corner of Style Street and Common Place. And Warshow is a fine policeman, using the pointing white glove equally accurately as the swinging night stick. Leslie Fiedler, in turn, has carped at Warshow's parochialism, at his seeing everything from the point of view of "a cultured New Yorker." This, again, is true, but it is like blaming Hokusai for having painted Mt. Fuji only from below, rather than from its slopes or even from its summit down. The angle of vision hardly matters; what does matter is sharpness of perception and the power to reveal. So, too, it is wrongheaded of Mr. Kauffmann to contrast Warshaw's essays on Chaplin with those of James Agee to Warshow's disadvantage. Actually, though Agee's achievement is incontestably greater than Warshow's, on the subject of Chaplin Warshow is both sounder and more penetrating, refusing to become, as Agee in this instance does, the victim of a moving but misguided sentimentality. A perceptive reviewer, in fact, would *compare* Warshow and Agee, for only a fatal heart attack could prevent Warshow from becoming Agee's wholly worthy heir—even in the mode of dying, and in its untimeliness, the two men resemble each other. The difference rests in the fact that Warshow saw man as a "*political* animal," whereas Agee saw him as a "political *animal*"—using *animal,* needless to say, as anything but a pejorative.

Still other reviewers have objected to the lack of humor in Warshow's writing. There is, actually, plenty of humor in a piece like "Woofed with Dreams," a review of *Krazy Kat,* in the quietly demolishing exposé "E. B. White and *The New Yorker,*" and even in "The 'Idealism' of Julius and Ethel Rosenberg"—this last, to be sure, a somber humor, though not a gallows or electric-chair, one. What is indeed lacking, by and large, is wit, and this lack we feel all the more keenly as we have grown accustomed to theatre and movie critics that are witty. No wonder that such critics do become wits: to contemplate and describe what they have to contemplate and describe most of the time, and *not* turn it into a witticism, would require the strength and charity of a saint. Now, I am inclined to think that it is precisely from something bordering on saintliness that Warshow *refused* to be witty, for wit is, in a sense, an assertion of superiority, and that he dearly wished to avoid. In any case, to demand wit where there is so much else would be like insisting (to revert to my earlier image) that the efficient white gloves of the traffic policeman be made of kid.

But I have not come to canonize Warshow. He has his failings: in his treatment of a film like *Day of Wrath*, for instance, where the social approach, as all critical approaches some-where must, draws a blank; or in an evaluation of horror comics, where his paternal pride makes him look a little too much through the eyes of his young son. Clearly, however, these are the limita-tions of a social critic; even to allow one's paternity to obscure one's vision a bit is surely the lapse of the family, or social, man as critic. But in this consistency lies Warshow's excellence.

What makes it, moreover, an important excellence is Warshow's deep awareness that, in bad as well as in good things, the whole is often greater than the sum of its parts. And so he always looked for that in an occurrence, in a work of art or non-art, which goes beyond the analysis of components and the evaluation of immediate causes and impacts. Continually he looked for the ultimate causation, final ramifications and repercussions, and tried to leave no implication unturned. Thus, for instance, if one reads (as I suggest one should) his brilliant essays on the Rosenbergs and on Chaplin's *Limelight*, "A Feeling of Sad Dignity," one after the other, a parallel of which Warshow himself was probably unaware will be discovered: that the dupe of his own politics and the dupe of his own artistry are, despite enormous differences, stunningly alike. But it is only because Warshow's mind inquired so unre-mittingly in the direction of the whole, and of the even greater aura surrounding the whole, that such discoveries can be made in his work—proving that it, too, is greater than the sum of its parts.